BBC ACTIVE

ITALIAN

Phrase Book
&Dictionary

Philippa
Language

D0808569

Italian Phrase Book and Dictionary

Based on the *BBC Italian Phrase Book* by Carol Stanley and Philippa Goodrich, copyright © Carol Stanley and Philippa Goodrich 1990

Published by Educational Publishers LLP trading as BBC Active
Edinburgh Gate, Harlow, Essex CM20 2JE

Published 2005
Reprinted 2005 (twice), 2006

ISBN-10: 0-5635-1920-7
ISBN-13: 9-780563-51920-1

Managing Editor: Joanna Kirby
Project Editor: Josie Frame
Index Editor: Paula Peebles
Designer: Elizabeth Burns
Concept design: Pentacor Book Design
Cover design: Two Associates
Cover photo copyright © Nadia Mackenzie/GETTYIMAGES
Senior Production Controller: Man Fai Lau

Printed and bound in China
CTPSC/02
The Publisher's policy is to use paper manufactured from sustainable forests.

how to use this book

This book is divided into colour-coded sections to help you find the language you need as quickly as possible. You can also refer to the **contents** on pages 4–5, the contents lists at the start of each section or the **index** on page 221.

Along with travel and language tips, each section contains:

 YOU MAY WANT TO SAY...
language you'll need for every situation

 YOU MAY SEE...
words and phrases you'll see on signs or in print

 YOU MAY HEAR... questions, instructions or information people may ask or give you

On page 10 you'll find **essentials**, a list of basic, all-purpose phrases to help you start communicating straight away.

Many of the phrases can be adapted by simply using another word from the dictionary. For instance, take the question Dov'è l'aeroporto? (Where is the airport?), if you want to know where the *station* is, just substitute la stazione (station) for l'aeroporto to give Dov'è la stazione?.

The **pronunciation guide** is based on English sounds, and is explained on page 6. If you want some guidance on how the Italian language works, see **basic grammar** on page 147. The **dictionary** is separated into two sections: English–Italian (page 157) and Italian–English (page 195).

We welcome any comments or suggestions about this book, but in the meantime, have a good trip – buon viaggio!

contents

pronunciation guide

✳ pronunciation

Italian pronunciation is very regular – you can tell how a word is pronounced by the way it is written, once you know which sound each letter (or group of letters) represents. A pronunciation guide is given with the phrases in this book. The system is based on English sounds, as described below.

✳ vowels

Italian vowels are pronounced the same wherever they occur, except for e and o, where there are two slightly different ways of pronouncing each letter. For simplicity's sake, only one sound is represented in these phrases. The final e in a word is always pronounced.

ITALIAN VOWELS	APPROX ENGLISH EQUIVALENT	SHOWN IN BOOK AS	EXAMPLE	
a	'a' in 'car'	a	nave	**na**ve
ai	'i' in 'pile'	iy	gennaio	jen**niyo**
ao, au	'ow' in 'cow'	ow	autobus	**ow**tobus
e	'e' in 'met'	e	bello	**bello**
ei	'ay' in 'lay'	e-ee	lei	**le**-ee
i (or sometimes)	'ee' in 'meet' 'y' in 'yet'	ee y	amico possiamo	a**mee**ko pos**sya**mo
o	'o' in 'lot'	o	notte	**no**tte
oi	'oy' in 'boy'	oy	poi	**poy**
u (or sometimes)	'oo' in 'moon' 'w' in 'wobble'	oo w	una può	**oo**na **pwo**

Pronunciation guide

✳ consonants

Many Italian consonants are pronounced in a similar way to English. All doubled consonants are pronounced with an extra long sound.

ITALIAN CONSONANTS	APPROX ENGLISH EQUIVALENT	SHOWN IN BOOK AS	EXAMPLE	
b	'b' in 'but'	b	bagno	*banyo*
c (followed by e or i)	'ch' in 'church'	ch	cena	*chena*
c (otherwise)	'c' in 'can'	k	camera	*kamera*
ch	'c' in 'can'	k	che	*ke*
d	'd' in 'dog'	d	dove	*dove*
f	'f' in 'feet'	f	famiglia	*fameelya*
g (followed by e or i)	'j' in 'jet'	j	gettone	*jettone*
g (otherwise)	'g' in 'got'	g	gamba	*gamba*
gh	'g' in 'got'	g	ghiaccio	*gyacho*
gl	'lli' in 'million'	ly	moglie	*molye*
gn	'ni' in 'onion'	ny	gnocchi	*nyokkee*
h	always silent	-	hotel	*otel*
j	'y' in 'you'	y	Juventus	*yooventoos*
l	'l' in 'look'	l	libro	*leebro*
m	'm' in 'mat'	m	mano	*mano*
n	'n' in 'not'	n	nome	*nome*
p	'p' in 'pack'	p	persona	*persona*
qu	'qu' in 'quick'	kw	quanto	*kwanto*
r	rolled as in Scottish accent	r	Roma	*roma*
rr	strongly rolled	rr	birra	*beerra*

s	's' in 'set'	s	solo	*solo*
(or)	'z' in 'zoo'	z	bisogna	*beezonya*
sc (followed by e or i)	'sh' in 'shin'	sh	lasciare	*lashare*
sc (otherwise)	'sk' in 'skin'	sk	scusi	*skoozee*
t	't' in 'tin'	t	tenda	*tenda*
v	'v' in 'vain'	v	vino	*veeno*
z	'ts' in 'hits'	ts	stazione	*statsyone*
(or)	'ds' in 'roads'	dz	zio	*dzeeo*

✳ stress

In most cases the stress is on the last but one syllable: amico, pagare. In some longer words, the stress is on the last syllable but two: vengono (they come), prendono (they take). If there is a written accent, the stress is where the accent is: città. In this book, stressed syllables are printed in bold: *statsyone*, *peetsa*.

✳ the Italian alphabet

LETTER	PRONOUNCED	LETTER	PRONOUNCED
A	*a*	N	*enne*
B	*bee*	O	*o*
C	*chee*	P	*pee*
D	*dee*	Q	*koo*
E	*e*	R	*erre*
F	*effe*	S	*esse*
G	*gee*	T	*tee*
H	*akka*	U	*oo*
I	*ee*	V	*vee*
J (I lungo)	*ee loongo*	W	*vee doppya*
K	*kappa*	X (ics)	*eeks*
L	*elle*	Y (ypsilon)	*eepseelon*
M	*emme*	Z (zeta)	*tseta*

the basics

*essentials

Hello.	Ciao.	*chow*
Good morning/ Good day.	Buongiorno.	*bwonjorno*
Goodbye.	Arrivederci.	*arreevederchee*
Yes.	Sì.	*see*
No.	No.	*no*
Please.	Per favore.	*per favore*
Thank you (very much).	(Mille) grazie.	*(meelle) gratsye*
You're welcome.	Prego.	*prego*
I don't know.	Non so.	*non so*
I don't understand.	Non capisco.	*non kapeesko*
I only speak a little bit of Italian.	Parlo solo un po' d'italiano.	*parlo solo oon po d'eetalyano*
Pardon?	Scusa/Scusi?	*skooza/skoozee*
Excuse me/Sorry.	Scusa/Scusi.	*skooza/skoozee*
I'm sorry.	Mi dispiace.	*mee deespyache*
OK, fine.	Bene.	*bene*
That's all right.	Va bene.	*va bene*
That's true/right.	Esatto.	*ezatto*
It doesn't matter.	Non importa.	*non eemporta*
More slowly.	Più lentamente.	*pyoo lentamente*

Again, please.	Di nuovo, per favore.	*dee nwovo per favore*
Could you repeat that, please?	Puoi/Può ripetere, per favore?	*pwoy/pwo reepetere per favore*
Do you speak English?	Parli/Parla inglese?	*parlee/parla eengleze*
Is there anyone who speaks English?	C'è qualcuno che parla inglese?	*che kwalkoono ke parla eengleze*
I'd like...	Vorrei...	*vorre-ee...*
What's this?	Che cos'è?	*ke koze*
What's the matter?	Qual'è il problema?	*kwale eel problema*
What time... ?	A che ora...?	*a ke ora...*
Where is/are... ?	Dov'è/Dove sono... ?	*dove/dove sono...*
Is there/Are there... ?	C'è/Ci sono... ?	*che/chee sono...*
How much is it?	Quant'è?	*kwante*
Is it possible to... ?	È possibile... ?	*e posseebeele...*
Do you have... ?	Hai/Ha...?	*iy/a...*
Can I have... ?	Posso avere...?	*posso avere...*
Can you...	Puoi/Può...	*pwoy/pwo...*
give me... ?	darmi... ?	*darmee...*
tell me... ?	dirmi... ?	*deermee...*
show me... ?	mostrarmi... ?	*mostrarmee...*
help me?	aiutarmi?	*iyootarmee...*

✳ numbers

1	uno	*oono*
2	due	*doo-e*
3	tre	*tre*
4	quattro	*kwattro*
5	cinque	*cheenkwe*
6	sei	*se-ee*
7	sette	*sette*
8	otto	*otto*
9	nove	*nove*
10	dieci	*dyechee*
11	undici	*oondeechee*
12	dodici	*dodeechee*
13	tredici	*tredeechee*
14	quattordici	*kwattordeechee*
15	quindici	*kweendeechee*
16	sedici	*sedeechee*
17	diciassette	*deechassette*
18	diciotto	*deechotto*
19	diciannove	*deechannove*
20	venti	*ventee*
21	ventuno	*ventoono*
22...	ventidue...	*venteedoo-e*
30	trenta	*trenta*
31	trentuno	*trentoono*
40	quaranta	*kwaranta*
50	cinquanta	*cheenkwanta*
60	sessanta	*sessanta*
70	settanta	*settanta*
80	ottanta	*ottanta*
90	novanta	*novanta*
100	cento	*chento*
101	centouno	*chento-oono*

102...	centodue...	*centodoo-e...*
200	duecento	*doo-echento*
250	duecentocinquanta	*doo-echento cheenkwanta*
500	cinquecento	*cheenkwechento*
1000	mille	*meelle*
100,000	centomila	*chentomeela*
one million	un milione	*oon meelyone*
one and a half million	un milione e mezzo	*oon meelyone e medzo*

✳ ordinal numbers

first	primo	*preemo*
second	secondo	*sekondo*
third	terzo	*tertso*
fourth	quarto	*kwarto*
fifth	quinto	*kweento*
sixth	sesto	*sesto*
seventh	settimo	*setteemo*
eighth	ottavo	*ottavo*
ninth	nono	*nono*
tenth	decimo	*decheemo*

✳ fractions

quarter	un quarto	*oon kwarto*
half	metà	*meta*
three-quarters	tre quarti	*tre kwartee*
a third	un terzo	*oon tertso*
two-thirds	due terzi	*doo-e tertsee*

✳ days

Monday	lunedì	*loonedee*
Tuesday	martedì	*martedee*
Wednesday	mercoledì	*merkoledee*
Thursday	giovedì	*jovedee*
Friday	venerdì	*venerdee*
Saturday	sabato	*sabato*
Sunday	domenica	*domeneeka*

✳ months

January	gennaio	*jenniyo*
February	febbraio	*febbriyo*
March	marzo	*martso*
April	aprile	*apreele*
May	maggio	*majjo*
June	giugno	*joonyo*
July	luglio	*loolyo*
August	agosto	*agosto*
September	settembre	*settembre*
October	ottobre	*ottobre*
November	novembre	*novembre*
December	dicembre	*deechembre*

✳ seasons

spring	la primavera	*la preemavera*
summer	l'estate	*lestate*
autumn	l'autunno	*lowtoonno*
winter	l'inverno	*leenverno*

✳ dates

YOU MAY WANT TO SAY...

- **What day is it today?** — Che giorno è oggi? — *ke **jor**no e **o**jee*

- **What's the date today?** — Quanti ne abbiamo oggi? — ***kwan**tee ne ab**by**amo **o**jee*

- **It's (on) the 15th of April.** — È il quindici aprile. — *e eel **kween**deechee a**pree**le*

- **Since/From 1999.** — Dal millenovecento novantanove. — *dal **mee**lenove-**chen**tonovanta**no**ve*

- **In 2005.** — Nel duemilacinque. — *nel **doo**emeela-**cheen**kwe*

✳ telling the time

To say the time in Italian you use Sono le followed by the number, for example Sono le cinque (It's five o'clock). The only exception is 'one o'clock': è l'una.

To say 'half past' you have to add e mezza (and half) after the hour: Sono le quattro e mezza (It's half past four).

Minutes past the hour are indicated in a similar way: Sono le cinque e venti means 'It's twenty past five'. For minutes to the hour, use meno (less): Sono le otto meno dieci (It's ten to eight).

telling the time

To say 'a quarter past' you have to add e un quarto (and a quarter) after the hour: Sono le tre e un quarto (It's a quarter past three).

To say 'a quarter to' you can either add e tre quarti (and three quarters) to the hour or meno un quarto (less a quarter) to the next hour. So, Sono le sei e tre quarti and Sono le sette meno un quarto both mean 'It's a quarter to seven'.

What time is it?	Che ore sono?/Che ora è?	ke ore sono/ ke ora e
What time does it...	A che ora...	a ke ora...
open?	apre?	apre
close?	chiude?	kyoode
begin?	inizia?	eeneetsya
finish?	finisce?	feeneeshe
(It's) 10 o'clock.	Sono le dieci.	sono le dyechee
(At) half past nine.	(Al) le nove e mezza.	(al)le nove e medza
Half past ten.	Le dieci e mezza.	le dyechee e medza
A quarter past nine.	Le nove e un quarto.	le nove e oon kwarto
A quarter to ten.	Le dieci meno un quarto.	le dyechee meno oon kwarto
Twenty past ten.	Le dieci e venti.	le dyechee e ventee
Twenty-five to ten.	Le nove e trentacinque.	le nove e trentacheenkwe
Ten on the dot.	Le dieci in punto.	le dyechee een poonto

the basics

It's...	È...	e...
midday	mezzogiorno	*medzojorno*
midnight	mezzanotte	*medzanotte*

- A quarter of an hour. — Un quarto d'ora. — *oon **kwarto dora***

- Half an hour. — Mezz'ora. — *medzora*

In...	Tra...	tra...
ten minutes	dieci minuti	*dyechee meenootee*
an hour	un'ora	*oonora*

✳ time phrases

today	oggi	*ojee*
tomorrow	domani	*domanee*
the day after tomorrow	dopodomani	*dopodomanee*
yesterday	ieri	*yeeree*
the day before yesterday	l'altro ieri	*laltro yeree*
this morning	stamattina/questa mattina	*stamatteena/kwesta matteena*
this afternoon	questo pomeriggio	*kwesto pomerijo*
this evening	stasera	*stasera*
tonight	stanotte	*stanotte*
on Friday	venerdì	*venerdee*
on Fridays	il venerdì	*eel venerdee*

the basics

17

next week	la settimana prossima	*la setteemana prosseema*
next month	il mese prossimo	*eel meze prosseemo*
next year	l'anno prossimo	*lanno prosseemo*
last night	la notte scorsa	*la notte skorsa*
last week	la settimana scorsa	*la setteemana skorsa*
a week ago	una settimana fa	*oona setteemana fa*
a year ago	un anno fa	*oon anno fa*
since last week	dalla scorsa settimana	*dalla skorsa setteemana*
since last month	dal mese scorso	*dal meze skorso*
since last year	dall'anno scorso	*dallanno skorso*
● every...	ogni...	*onyee...*
Friday	venerdì	*venerdee*
week	settimana	*setteemana*
● I'm here for two weeks.	Mi fermo due settimane.	*mee fermo doo-e setteemane*
● for...	per...	*per...*
two years	due anni	*doo-e annee*
a month	un mese	*oon meze*
a week	una settimana	*oona setteemana*
two weeks	due settimane	*doo-e setteemane*
● I've been here for a month.	Sono qui da un mese.	*sono kwee da oon meze*
● It's early/late.	È presto/tardi.	*e presto/tardee*

✱ false friends

Many English words may sound similar to Italian words but are 'false friends' as they have a completely different meaning. Here is a list of some of the most common ones.

FALSE FRIEND...	NOT TO BE CONFUSED WITH...
agenda (diary)	**agenda** (ordine del giorno)
annoiare (to bore)	**annoy** (scocciare)
attualmente (currently)	**actually** (veramente)
bravo (good)	**brave** (coraggioso)
camera (room)	**camera** (macchina fotografica)
cartone (cardboard)	**carton** (scatola)
cauzione (deposit)	**caution** (attenzione)
fabbrica (factory)	**fabric** (tessuto)
incidente (accident)	**incident** (episodio)
introdurre (to insert)	**introduce** (presentare)
giusto (correct)	**just (only)** (solo)
libreria (bookshop)	**library** (biblioteca)
moda (fashion)	**mode** (modo)
nubile (single woman)	**nubile** (giovane e desiderabile)
patente (permit)	**patent** (brevetto)
preservativo (condom)	**preservative** (conservante)
rumore (noise)	**rumour** (voce)
sensibile (sensitive)	**sensible** (ragionevole)
suggestivo (charming)	**suggestive** (esplicito)
sopportare (to tolerate)	**support** (sostegno)
triviale (vulgar)	**trivial** (banale)

the basics

19

● Imperial measurements are not used in Italy – you'll need to convert distances, weights, liquid measures, etc. from imperial to metric. Speed limits and distances are always in kilometres and metres. Food is sold in grammes and kilos. Liquids are measured in litres, etc.

* measurements

YOU MAY WANT TO SAY...

centimetres	centimetri	*chenteemetree*
metres	metri	*metree*
kilometres	chilometri	*keelometree*
a litre	un litro	*oon leetro*
25 litres	venticinque litri	*venteecheenkwe leetree*
a gramme	un grammo	*oon grammo*
100 grammes	cento grammi/un etto	*chento grammee/ oon etto*
200 grammes	duecento grammi/ due etti	*doo-echento grammee/ doo-e ettee*
kilo(s)	chilo/chili	*keelo/keelee*

CONVERSIONS

10cm = *4 inches*	1 inch = *2.45cm*
50cm = *19.6 inches*	1 foot = *30cm*
1 metre = *39.37 inches*	1 yard = *0.91m*
110 metres = *100 yards*	1 mile = *1.61 km*
1km = *0.62 miles*	1 litre = *1.8 pints*

100g = *3.5oz*
200g = *7oz*
½ kilo = *1.1 lb*
1 kilo = *2.2 lb*

1oz = *28g*
¼ lb = *113g*
½ lb = *225g*
1 lb = *450g*

To convert kilometres to miles, divide by 8 and multiply by 5 e.g. 16 kilometres (16 / 8 = 2, 2 x 5 = 10) = 10 miles.

For miles to kilometres, divide by 5 and multiply by 8 e.g. 50 miles (50 / 5 = 10, 10 x 8 = 80) = 80 kilometres.

✳ clothes and shoe sizes

WOMEN'S CLOTHES

UK	8	10	12	14	16	18	20
Continent	38	40	42	44	46	48	50

MEN'S CLOTHES

UK	36	38	40	42	44	46	48
Continent	46	48	50	52	54	56	58

MEN'S SHIRTS

UK	14	14½	15	15½	16	16½	17
Continent	36	37	38	39	41	42	43

SHOES

UK	2	3	4	5	6	7	8
Continent	35	36	37	38	39	41	42
UK	9	10	11	12			
Continent	43	44	45	46			

the basics

✳ national holidays and festivals

There are a lot of bank holidays in Italy, some civic and others religious. In addition to national bank holidays, each city celebrates a day dedicated to its patron saint.

Capodanno/ Primo dell'anno	**New Year's Day**	1 January
Epifania/ la Befana	**Epiphany**	6 January
Venerdì Santo	**Good Friday**	
Pasqua	**Easter Day**	
Lunedì di Pasqua/ Pasquetta	**Easter Monday**	
Liberazione	**Liberation Day**	25 April
Festa del lavoro	**May Day**	1 May
Festa della Repubblica	**Republic Day**	2 June
Ascensione	**Ascension Day**	
Assunzione/ Ferragosto	**Feast of the Assumption**	15 August
Ognissanti/ I morti	**All Saints' Day**	1 November
Vigilia di Natale	**Christmas Eve**	24 December
Natale	**Christmas Day**	25 December
Santo Stefano	**Boxing Day**	26 December
San Silvestro/ Ultimo dell'anno	**New Year's Eve**	31 December

general conversation

● Buongiorno is the general expression for 'hello', 'good day' and is used in the morning and early afternoon. Buonasera means 'good evening' and is used from the middle of the afternoon onwards. Buonanotte is simply 'good night'. Ciao is less formal, it means 'hello' and 'goodbye' and is used between friends. Salve is a less casual alternative to ciao.

● There is more than one word for 'you' in Italian. Lei is the more formal word and is used between people who don't know each other or when talking to an older person. Tu is used between friends and among young people but it is increasingly popular among middle-aged people as well.

● The ending of the verb changes depending on whether you are addressing someone as lei or tu. Since the informal tu is so much more common than it used to be, in this book we use the tu form unless otherwise specified.

✳ greetings

YOU MAY WANT TO SAY...

● **Hello!**	Ciao!	*chow*
● **Hello/Good day!**	Salve!	*salve*
● **Hi!/'Bye!**	Ciao!	*chow*
● **Good morning.**	Buongiorno.	*bwonjorno*
● **Good afternoon.**	Buon pomeriggio.	*bwon pomereejjo*
● **Good evening.**	Buonasera.	*bwonasera*

general conversation

- **Good night.** Buonanotte. *bwonanotte*
- **Goodbye.** Arrivederci. *arreevederchee*
- **See you soon.** A presto. *a presto*
- **See you later.** Ci vediamo dopo. *chi vedyamo dopo*
- **How are you?**
  (formal) Come sta? *kome sta*
  (informal) Come stai? *kome stiy*
- **How are things?** Come va? *kome va*
- **Fine, thanks.** Bene, grazie. *bene, gratsye*
- **And you?**
  (formal) E lei? *e le-ee*
  (informal) E tu? *e too*

✱ introductions

YOU MAY WANT TO SAY...

- **My name is ...** Mi chiamo... *mee kyamo...*
- **This is...** (formal) Le presento... *le prezento...*
  (informal) Ti presento... *tee prezento...*
  Jane Clark Jane Clark *Jane Clark*
  my husband/my partner mio marito/il mio compagno *meeo mareeto/eel meeo kompanyo*
  my wife/my partner mia moglie/la mia compagna *meea molye/la meea kompanya*
- **Pleased to meet you.** Piacere. *pyachere*

✳ talking about yourself

I'm...	Sono...	*sono...*
English	inglese	*eengleze*
Irish	irlandese	*eerlandeze*
Scottish	scozzese	*skotseze*
Welsh	gallese	*galleze*
I'm...	Sono...	*sono...*
from England	dall'Inghilterra	*dalleengeelterra*
from Ireland	dall'Irlanda	*dalleerlanda*
from Scotland	dalla Scozia	*dalla skotsya*
from Wales	dal Galles	*dal galles*
I live/We live...	Abito/Abitiamo...	*abeeto/abeetyamo...*
in Newcastle	a Newcastle	*a Newcastle*
in England	in Inghilterra	*in eengeelterra*
I'm 25 years old.	Ho venticinque anni.	*o venteecheenkwe annee*
He/She's 5 years old.	Lui/Lei ha cinque anni.	*loo-i/le-ee a cheenkwe annee*
I'm a...	Sono...	*sono ...*
web designer	un grafico web	*oon grafeeko web*
nurse	un/un' infermiere/a	*oon eenfermyere/a*
student	uno/una studente/ studentessa	*oono/a stoodente/ stoodentessa*
I work in/for...	Lavoro in...	*lavoro een...*
a bank	banca	*banka*
a computer firm	una società di informatica	*oona socheta dee eenformateeka*
I'm unemployed.	Sono disoccupato/a.	*sono deezokkoopato/a*

- I'm self-employed. Lavoro in proprio. *lavoro een propryo*

- I'm... Sono... *sono...*
  married sposato/a *spozato/a*
  divorced divorziato/a *deevortsyato/a*
  separated separato/a *separato/a*
  single libero/a *leebero/a*

- I have... Ho... *o...*
  three children tre figli *tre feelyee*
  one sister una sorella *oona sorella*

- I don't have... Non ho... *non o...*
  any children figli *feelyee*
  a partner un/una *oon/oona*
  compagno/a *kompanyo/a*

- I'm on holiday Sono qui in *sono kwee een*
  here. vacanza. *vakantsa*

- I'm here on Sono qui per *sono kwee per*
  business. lavoro. *lavoro*

- I'm here with... Sono qui con... *sono kwee kon...*
  my wife mia moglie *meea molye*
  my family la mia famiglia *la meea fameelya*
  my son/ mio figlio/ *meeo feelyo/*
  daughter mia figlia *meea feelya*
  a colleague un/una collega *oon/oona kollega*

- My husband/wife Mio marito/mia *meeo mareeto/meea*
  is... moglie è... *molye e...*
  a software un/un'ingegnere *oon eenjenyere*
  engineer del software *del software*
  an estate agent un/un'agente *oon ajente*
  immobiliare *eemmobeelyare*

27

✳ asking about other people

Where are you from?	Da dove sei?	da **dove** se-ee
What's your name?	Come ti chiami?	kome tee **kya**mee
Are you married?	Sei sposato/a?	se-ee spozato/a
Do you have...	Hai...	iy...
any children?	figli?	**fee**lyee
a girlfriend?	la ragazza?	la ra**gatsa**
a boyfriend?	il ragazzo?	eel ra**gatso**
How old...	Quanti anni...	**kwantee annee**...
is he/she?	ha?	a
are you?	hai?	iy
Is this your...	È...	e...
husband?	tuo marito?	**too-o mareeto**
partner?	il tuo compagno?	eel **too-o** kompanyo
(boy)friend?	il tuo ragazzo?	eel **too-o** ragatso
Is this your...	È...	e...
wife?	tua moglie?	**tooa molye**
partner?	la tua compagna?	la **tooa** kompanya
(girl)friend?	la tua ragazza?	la **tooa** ragatsa
Where are you going?	Dove vai?	**dove** viy
Where are you staying?	Dove alloggi?	**dove** allodjee
Where do you live?	Dove abiti?	**dove** abeetee

✳ chatting

YOU MAY WANT TO SAY...

- Italy is very beautiful. — L'Italia è molto bella. — *leetalya e molto bella*

- It's the first time I've been to Italy. — È la prima volta che vengo in Italia. — *e la preema volta ke vengo een eetalya*

- Do you live here? — Abiti qui? — *abeetee kwee*

- Have you ever been to... — Sei mai stato/a a... — *se-ee miy stato/a a...*
    - London? — Londra? — *Londra*
    - Edinburgh? — Edimburgo? — *Edeemboorgo*

- Did you like it? — Ti è piaciuta? — *tee e pyachoota*

YOU MAY HEAR...

- Ti piace l'Italia? — *tee pyache leetalya* — Do you like Italy?

- Sei mai stato/a in Italia prima? — *se-ee miy stato/a een eetalya preema?* — Have you been to Italy before?

- Quanto tempo ti fermi? — *kwanto tempo tee fermee* — How long are you here for?

- Parli bene l'italiano! — *parlee bene leetalyano* — Your Italian is very good!

✳ the weather

YOU MAY WANT TO SAY...

- It's a beautiful day! — È una bellissima giornata! — *e oona belleesseema jornata*

It's (very)...	Fa (molto)...	*fa (molto)...*
hot	caldo	*kaldo*
cold	freddo	*freddo*
It's (very)...	È (molto)...	*e (molto)...*
humid	afoso	*afozo*
cloudy	nuvoloso	*noovolozo*
It's raining/snowing.	Piove./Nevica.	*pyove/neveeka*
It's windy.	C'è vento.	*che vento*
What's the forecast?	Come sono le previsioni?	*kome sono le preveezyonee*

✱ likes and dislikes

I like... (singular)	Mi piace...	*mee pyache...*
beer	la birra	*la beerra*
I like... (plural)	Mi piacciono...	*mee pyachono...*
strawberries	le fragole	*le fragole*
I love...	Adoro...	*adoro...*
playing tennis	giocare a tennis	*jokare a tennees*
skiing	lo sci	*lo shee*
I don't like him/ her	Lui/Lei non mi piace	*looee/le-ee non mee pyache*
I don't like...	Non mi piacciono...	*non mee pyachono...*
tomatoes	i pomodori	*ee pomodoree*
eggs	le uova	*le oo-ova*
I can't stand him.	Non lo sopporto.	*non lo sopporto*

● I can't stand...	Non sopporto...	*non sopporto...*
swimming	il nuoto	*il nwoto*
football	il calcio	*eel kalcho*
● Do you like...	Ti piace...	*tee pyache...*
ice cream?	il gelato?	*eel gelato*
climbing?	fare l'alpinismo?	*fare lalpeeneezmo*
● I/We quite like...	Mi/Ci piace abbastanza...	*mee/chee pyache abbastantsa...*
● I/We really like...	Mi/Ci piace proprio...	*mee/chee pyache proprio...*

✱ feelings and opinions

● Are you all right?	Stai bene?	*stiy bene*
● Are you...	Sei...	*se-ee...*
happy?	contento/a?	*contento/a*
sad?	triste?	*treeste*
● Are you (too)...	Hai (troppo)...	*iy (troppo)...*
cold?	freddo?	*freddo*
hot?	caldo?	*kaldo*
● I'm (a bit)...	Sono (un po')...	*sono (oon po)...*
tired	stanco/a	*stanko/a*
embarrassed	imbarazzato/a	*eembaratsato/a*
● I'm very/a bit annoyed.	Sono molto/un po' scocciato/a.	*sono molto/oon po skochato/a*
● What do you think of it?	Cosa ne pensi?	*koza ne pensee*

I think it's...	Penso che sia...	*penso ke seea...*
great	splendido	*splendeedo*
terrible	terribile	*terreebeele*

| Did you like it? | Ti è piaciuto/a? | *tee e pyachooto/a* |

I thought it was...	Penso che fosse...	*penso ke fosse...*
beautiful	bellissimo/a	*belleesseemo/a*
fantastic	fantastico/a	*fantasteeko/a*
rubbish	una schifezza	*oona skeefetsa*

| Don't you like it? | Non ti piace? | *non tee pyache* |

| What's your favourite (film)? | Qual è il tuo (film) preferito? | *kwal e eel too-o (feelm) prefereeto* |

| My favourite (music) is... | La mia (musica) preferita è... | *la meea (moozika) prefereeta e...* |

How do people feel about...	Cosa pensa la gente...	*koza pensa la jente...*
the government?	del governo?	*del governo*
the Brits?	degli inglesi?	*dely eenglezee*
drugs?	della droga?	*della droga*

✳ making arrangements

| What are you doing tonight? | Cosa fai stasera? | *koza fiy stasera* |

Would you like...	Vorresti...	*vorrestee...*
something to drink?	qualcosa da bere?	*kwalkoza da bere*
something to eat?	qualcosa da mangiare?	*kwalkoza da manjare*

- **Do you fancy...** — Ti piacerebbe... — *tee pyacherebbe...*
  meeting up later? — vederci più tardi? — *vedercee pyoo tardee*
  going for a drink? — andare a bere qualcosa? — *andare a bere kwalkoza*
- **Yes please.** — Sì, grazie. — *see gratsye*
- **No thank you.** — No, grazie. — *no gratsye*
- **That'd be great.** — Sarebbe fantastico. — *sarebbe fantasteeko*
- **What time shall we meet?** — A che ora ci vediamo? — *a ke ora chee vedyamo*
- **Where shall we meet?** — Dove ci vediamo? — *dove chee vedyamo*
- **See you...** — Ci vediamo... — *chee vedyamo...*
  later — più tardi — *pyoo tardee*
  at seven — alle sette — *alle sette*
- **I'm looking forward to it.** — Non vedo l'ora. — *non vedo lora*
- **Sorry, we're already doing something.** — Mi dispiace, abbiamo altro in programma. — *mee deespyache, abbyamo altro een programma*
- **I have other plans for this evening.** — Ho altri piani per stasera. — *o altree pyanee per stasera*
- **Please go away.** — Vattene, per favore. — *vattene, per favore*
- **Leave me alone!** — Lasciami in pace! — *lashamee een pache*
- **I'll email you.** — Ti mando un'email. — *tee mando ooneeme-eel*
- **What's your email address?** — Qual è il tuo indirizzo email? — *kwale eel too-o een-deereetso eeme-eel*

✳ useful expressions
(see **essentials**, pages 10–11)

Congratulations!	Congratulazioni!/ Complimenti!	*kongratoolatsyonee/ kompleementee*
Happy Birthday!	Buon compleanno!/ Tanti auguri!	*bwon kompleanno/ tantee owgooree*
Happy Christmas!	Buon Natale!	*bwon natale*
Happy New Year!	Buon anno!	*bwon anno*
Best wishes	Tanti saluti	*tantee salootee*
That's... fantastic! terrible!	È... fantastico! terribile!	*e... fantasteeko terreebeele*
I'm so sorry!	Come mi dispiace!	*kome mee deespyache*
Bother! Damn!	Accidenti!	*acheedentee*
What a pity!	Che peccato!	*ke pekkato*
It doesn't matter.	Non importa.	*non eemporta*
Thank goodness!	Meno male!	*meno male*
How nice!	Che bello!	*ke bello*
Enjoy yourself!	Divertiti!	*deeverteetee*
Safe journey!	Buon viaggio!	*bwon vyajjo*
Enjoy your meal!	Buon appetito!	*bwon appeteeto*
Thank you, same to you.	Grazie, altrettanto.	*gratsye, altrettanto*
Cheers!	Cin cin!/Salute!	*cheen cheen/saloote*

travel&transport

✳ arriving in the country

● If you are an EU citizen, you can enter and stay in Italy as long as you like, provided that you can produce a valid passport. If you come from Canada, the United States, Australia, New Zealand, Israel, Japan or Switzerland, you can still enter with a valid passport, but your stay is limited to three months. All other nationals need a visa. You can contact the Italian Embassy in the UK by dialling 020 7312 2200 or by logging on to www.embitaly.org.uk.

YOU MAY SEE...

Articoli da dichiarare	Goods to declare
Cittadini UE	EU citizens
Cittadini non UE	Non-EU citizens
Controllo passaporti	Passport control
Dogana	Customs
Ritiro bagagli	Baggage reclaim
Uscita	Exit/Way out

YOU MAY WANT TO SAY...

● I am here...	Sono qui...	*sono kwee...*
on holiday	in vacanza	*een va**kan**tsa*
on business	per affari	*per af**fa**ree*
● It's for my own personal use.	È per uso personale.	*e per **oo**zo personale*

YOU MAY HEAR...

Il suo passaporto per favore.	*eel soo-o passaporto per favore*	Your passport please.
Documenti per favore.	*dokoomentee per favore*	Your documents please.
Qual è il motivo della sua visita?	*kwal e eel moteevo della sooa veezeeta*	What is the purpose of your visit?
Quanto tempo si ferma?	*kwanto tempo see ferma*	How long are you going to stay?
Per favore apra questa borsa.	*per favore apra kwesta borsa*	Please open this bag.
Ha altro bagaglio?	*a altro bagalyo*	Do you have any other luggage?
Prego, venga con me.	*prego venga kon me*	Please come with me.

✳ directions

● When you need to ask the way, the easiest method is just to name the place you're looking for and add 'please', e.g. Frascati, per favore? *(fraskatee per favore)*. Or you can start with 'Where is ...?': Dov'è ...? *(dove)*.

● To ask 'Where is the nearest (petrol station)?' you can simply say 'Is there a petrol station near here?': C'è una stazione di servizio qui vicino? *(che oona statsyone dee serveetsyo kwee veecheeno)*.

37

directions

YOU MAY SEE...

Castello, palazzo	Castle, palace
Cattedrale	Cathedral
Chiesa	Church
Corsia riservata ai cicli	Cycle track
Corso	Avenue
Fermata autobus	Bus stop
Fermata tram	Tram stop
Galleria d'arte	Art gallery
Mercato	Market place
Metropolitana	Underground, metro
Museo	Museum
Pedoni	Pedestrians
Piazza	Square
Pinacoteca	Art gallery
Privato	Private
Stazione	Station
Strada/ Via	Street
Viale	Avenue
Vietato l'accesso – i trasgressori verranno puniti	Keep out – trespassers will be prosecuted
Zona pedonale	Pedestrian precinct

YOU MAY WANT TO SAY...

- **Excuse me, please.**
  Mi scusi, per favore.
  mee skoozee per favore

- **Where is...**
  Dov'è...
  dove...
  - **the town centre?**
    il centro (città)?
    il chentro (cheetta)

the station?	la stazione?	*la statsyone*
the cashpoint?	il Bancomat?	*il bankomat*

- How do we get... | Per andare... | *per andare...*
  to the airport? | all'aeroporto? | *allaeroporto*
  to the beach? | alla spiaggia? | *alla spyajja*

- I'm lost. | Mi sono perso/a. | *mee sono perso/a*

- Is this the right way to...? | È la strada giusta per...? | *e la strada joosta per...*

- How long does it take? | Quanto tempo ci vuole? | *kwanto tempo chee vwole*

- Can I/we get there on foot? | Ci si può andare a piedi? | *chee see pwo andare a pyedee*

- Can you show me on the map, please? | Può farmelo vedere sulla cartina, per favore? | *pwo farmelo vedere soolla karteena per favore*

- Is it far? | È lontano? | *e lontano*

- Is there ... near here? | C'è ... qui vicino? | *che ... kwee veecheeno*
  a bank | una banca | *oona banka*
  a supermarket | un supermercato | *oon soopermerkato*
  an internet café | un internet café | *oon eenternet kafe*

- Where is the nearest restaurant/bar? | Dov'è il ristorante/ il bar più vicino? | *dove eel reestorante/ eel bar pyoo veecheeno*

YOU MAY HEAR...

Siamo qui.	*syamo kwee*	We are here.
Di qua/Di là.	*dee kwa/dee la*	This way/That way.
Sempre dritto.	*sempre dreetto*	Straight on.

travel and transport

39

Continua...	*conteenwa...*	Go on...
fino alla fine della strada	*feeno alla feene della strada*	to the end of the street
fino al semaforo	*feeno al semaforo*	to the traffic lights
Gira...	*jeera...*	Turn...
a destra	*a destra*	(to the) right
a sinistra	*a seeneestra*	(to the) left
Prendi la prima a sinistra	*prendee la preema a seeneestra*	Take the first on the left
È...	*e...*	It's...
davanti (a...)	*davantee (a...)*	in front (of...)
di fronte (a...)	*dee fronte (a...)*	opposite
dietro	*dyetro*	behind
vicino (a...)	*veecheeno (a...)*	close (to...)
(Non) è lontano.	*(non) e lontano*	It's (not) far away.
È qui vicino.	*e kwee veecheeno*	It's very near here.
È...	*e...*	It's...
a cinque minuti a piedi	*a cheenkwe meenootee a pyedee*	five minutes on foot
a dieci chilometri	*a dyechee keelometree*	ten kilometres away
Devi prendere l'autobus (numero...).	*devee prendere lowtoboos (noomero...)*	You have to take bus (number...).

✳ information and tickets
(see **telling the time**, page 15)

Is there a train/ bus/boat to ... today?	C'è un treno/ autobus/battello per ... oggi?	*che oon treno/ owtoboos/battello per ... ojee*

What time is...	A che ora è...	*a ke ora e...*
the next train?	il prossimo treno?	*eel **prosseemo tre**no*
the last train?	l'ultimo treno?	*loolteemo **tre**no*
the first bus?	il primo autobus?	*eel **preemo** owtoboos*
Do they go often?	Partono spesso?	*partono **spes**so*
What time does it arrive in...?	A che ora arriva a...?	*a ke ora arreeva a...*
Which platform/ bus stop for...?	Quale binario/ fermata per...?	*kwale beenaryo/ fermata per...*
Do I have to change?	Devo cambiare?	*devo kambyare*
Can I get a ticket...	Posso fare il biglietto...	*posso fare eel beelyetto...*
on the bus?	sull'autobus?	*soolowtoboos*
on the train	sul treno?	*sool **tre**no*
on the boat?	sul battello?	*sool bat**tel**lo*
Where can I buy a ticket?	Dove posso comprare un biglietto?	*dove posso comprare oon beelyetto*
One/Two tickets to ... please.	Un biglietto/Due biglietti per ... per favore.	*oon beelyetto/doo-e beelyettee per ... per favore*
Single.	Solo andata.	*solo andata*
Return.	Andata e ritorno.	*andata e reetorno*
For...	Per...	*per...*
two adults and	due adulti	*doo-e adooltee e*
two children	e due bambini	*doo-e bambeenee*
and a car	e una macchina	*e oona makkeena*

- **I want to reserve...** Vorrei prenotare... *vorre-ee prenotare...*
    - a seat   un posto   *oon posto*
    - a cabin   una cabina   *oona kabeena*

- **Is there...** C'è ... *che ...*
    - a supplement?   un supplemento?   *oon soopplemento*
    - a reduction   uno sconto   *oono sconto*
    - for students/   per studenti/   *per stoodentee/*
    - senior citizens?   anziani?   *antsyanee*

YOU MAY HEAR...

Parte alle...	*parte alle...*	It leaves at...
Arriva alle...	*arreeva alle...*	It arrives at...
Deve cambiare a...	*deve kambyare a...*	You have to change in...
È il binario/molo numero...	*al beenaryo/molo noomero...*	It's platform/pier number...
Può comprare un biglietto...	*pwo komprare oon beelyetto...*	You can buy a ticket...
sull'autobus	*soollowtoboos*	on the bus
sull'treno	*sool treno*	on the train
sull'battello	*sool battello*	on the boat
Quando vuole...	*kwando vwole...*	When do you want to...
partire?	*parteere*	travel?
tornare?	*tornare*	return?
Solo andata o andata e ritorno?	*solo andata o andata e reetorno*	Single or return?
Fumatori o non fumatori?	*foomatoree o non foomatoree*	Smoking or non-smoking?

✳ trains
(see **information and tickets**, page 40)

 ● Trenitalia, the partially privatised state railway company, is relatively inexpensive and well run. As the make-over is not yet complete, you will still see the old FS logo on some signs. You can log on to two different websites to check routes and prices: www.trenitalia.com and www.fs-on-line.com, but the two names are basically synonymous.

YOU MAY SEE...

Ai binari	To the platforms
Armadietti portabagagli	Luggage lockers
Arrivo	Arrival
Biglietteria	Ticket Office
Biglietti	Tickets
Binari, rotaie	Platforms, tracks
Binario	Platform
Deposito bagagli	Left luggage
Destinazione	Destination
Domeniche escluse	Except Sundays
Entrata	Entrance
Giornaliero	Daily
Informazioni	Information
Informazioni per alloggi	Accommodation information
Vietato fumare	No smoking
Orario dei treni	Train timetable
Partenza	Departure

travel and transport

43

trains

Prenotazioni	**Reservations**
Sala d'attesa	**Waiting room**
Oggetti smarriti	**Lost property**
Uscita	**Exit**
Vagone letto	**Sleeping car**

Are there lifts to the platform?	Ci sono ascensori per i binari?	*chee sono ashensoree per ee beenaree*
Does this train go to...?	Questo treno va a...?	*kwesto treno va a...*
Excuse me, I've reserved this seat.	Mi scusi, ho prenotato questo posto	*mee skoozee o prenotato kwesto posto*
Is this seat free?	È libero questo posto?	*e leebero kwesto posto*
May I...	Posso...	*posso...*
open the window?	aprire il finestrino?	apreere eel feenestreeno
smoke?	fumare?	foomare
Where are we?	Dove siamo?	*dove syamo*
How long does the train stop here?	Per quanto tempo il treno si ferma qui?	*per kwanto tempo eel treno see ferma kwee*
Can you tell me when we get to... ?	Può dirmi quando arriviamo a... ?	*pwo deermee kwando arreevyamo a...*

travel and transport

✳ buses and coaches
(see **information and tickets**, page 40)

YOU MAY SEE...

Entrata	**Entrance**
Fermata (dell'autobus)	**Bus stop**
Fermata a richiesta	**Request stop**
Salire dalla porta posteriore	**Enter by the back door**
Scendere dalla porta anteriore	**Exit by the front door**
Stazione degli autobus	**Bus station**
Uscita di emergenza	**Emergency exit**
Vietato entrare/uscire	**No entry/exit**
Vietato parlare all'autista	**Do not talk to the driver**

YOU MAY WANT TO SAY...

Where does the bus to the (town) centre leave from?	Da dove parte l'autobus per il centro (della città)?	*da **dove** parte lowtoboos per eel **chentro** (della **cheetta**)*
What number is it?	Che numero è?	*ke **numero** e*
Does this bus go to... ?	Questo autobus va... ?	*kwesto owtoboos va...*
Can you tell me where to get off, please?	Può dirmi dove devo scendere, per favore?	*pwo **deermee dove** devo **shendere** per favore*
The next stop, please	La prossima fermata, per favore	*la **prosseema** fermata per favore*

| Can you open the doors, please? | Può aprire le porte, per favore? | *pwo apreere le porte per favore* |

✳ underground
(see **information and tickets**, page 40)

(see **information and tickets**, page 40)

YOU MAY WANT TO SAY...

Do you have a map of the underground?	Ha una cartina della metropolitana?	*a oona karteena della metropoleetana*
Which line is it for...?	Che linea va a...?	*ke leenea va a...*
Which stop is it for...?	Qual è la fermata per...?	*kwale la fermata per...*
Is this the right stop for...?	È la fermata giusta per...?	*e la fermata joosta per...*
Does this train go to...?	Questo treno va a...?	*kwesto treno va a...*

✳ boats and ferries
(see **information and tickets**, page 40)

(see **information and tickets**, page 40)

YOU MAY SEE...

Aliscafo	Hovercraft
Battello a vapore	Steamer
Cabine	Cabins
Crociera	Cruise
Crociera in battello (a vapore)	Steam cruises
Gite sul fiume	River trips

travel and transport

46

boats and ferries

Molo, imbarcadero	Pier, embarkation point
Ponte auto	Car deck
Porto	Port, harbour
Salvagente	Lifebelt
Andata e ritorno	Round trip

Is there a car ferry to ... (today)?	C'è un traghetto per ... (oggi)?	*che oon tragetto per ... (ojee)*
Are there any boat trips?	Ci sono delle gite in battello?	*chee sono delle jeete een battello*
How long is the cruise?	Quanto dura la crociera?	*kwanto doora la crochyera*
Is there wheelchair access?	C'è accesso per le sedie a rotelle?	*che achesso per le sedye a rotelle*
What is the lake like today?	Com'è il lago oggi?	*kome eel lago ojee*
Can I/we go out on deck?	Posso/Possiamo andare fuori sul ponte?	*posso/possyamo andare fworee sool ponte*

I battelli vanno... martedì e venerdì ogni due giorni	*ee battellee vanno... martedee e venerdee onyee doo-e jornee*	The boats go on... Tuesdays and Fridays every other day

travel and transport

47

Il lago è...	*eel lago e...*	The lake is...
calmo	*kalmo*	calm
increspato	*eenkrespato*	choppy

✳ air travel
(see **information and tickets**, page 40)

YOU MAY SEE...

Allacciare le cinture	Fasten seatbelts
Arrivi	Arrivals
Innocuo per le pellicole	Film safe
Noleggio auto	Car hire
Non lasciare i bagagli incustoditi	Do not leave unattended luggage
Partenze	Departures
Partenze internazionali	International departures
Partenze nazionali	Domestic departures
Ritiro bagagli	Luggage reclaim
Sala d'aspetto	Departure lounge
Sicurezza	Security

YOU MAY WANT TO SAY...

I want to change/ cancel my ticket.	Vorrei cambiare/ annullare il mio biglietto.	*vorre-ee kambyare/ annoollare eel meeo beelyetto*
What time do I have to check in?	A che ora devo fare il check in?	*a ke ora devo fare eel chek in*
Is there a delay?	C'è un ritardo?	*che oon reetardo*

- **Which gate is it?** Che uscita è? *ke oosheeta e*

- **Have you got a wheelchair?** Ha una sedia a rotelle? *a oona sedya a rotelle*

- **My luggage hasn't arrived.** Il mio bagaglio non è arrivato. *eel meeo bagalyo non e arreevato*

- **Is there a bus/ train to the centre of town?** C'è un autobus/treno per il centro città? *che oon owtoboos/ treno per eel chentro cheetta*

YOU MAY HEAR...

- Vuole un posto vicino al finestrino o al corridoio? — *vwole oon posto veecheeno al feenestreeno o al korreedoyo* — **Do you want a window or an aisle seat?**

- Il volo imbarca alle... — *eel volo eembarka alle...* — **The flight will board at...**

- Uscita numero sette. — *oosheeta noomero sette* — **Gate number seven.**

- Il suo... — *eel soo-o...* — **Your...**
  - biglietto, per favore — *beelyetto per favore* — ticket, please
  - passaporto, per favore — *passaporto per favore* — passport, please

- La sua carta d'imbarco, per favore. — *la sooa karta deembarko per favore* — **Your boarding card, please.**

- Com'è il suo bagaglio? — *kome eel soo-o bagalyo* — **What does your luggage look like?**

| Ha la ricevuta (del bagaglio)? | *a la reechevoota (del bagalyo)* | **Do you have the reclaim tag?** |

WORDS TO LISTEN OUT FOR...

Chiamata	*kyamata*	**Call**
Volo	*volo*	**Flight**
Uscita	*oosheeta*	**Gate**
Ultima chiamata	*oolteema kyamata*	**Last call**
Ritardo	*reetardo*	**Delay**
Cancellato	*kanchellato*	**Cancelled**

✳ taxis
(see **directions**, page 37)

● Official taxis are white in cities and have a little Taxi sign on the roof or possibly the taxi name or number on the door. You can't hail them in the street, but you can find them by the stations or at a taxi rank, or call them through a radio taxi service. Unmarked taxis could prove extremely expensive.

YOU MAY WANT TO SAY...

● **Is there a taxi rank round here?**	C'è una stazione dei taxi da queste parti?	*che oona statsyone de-ee taksee da kweste partee*
● **Can you order me a taxi...**	Mi può chiamare un taxi...	*mee pwo kyamare oon taksee...*
immediately?	immediatamente?	*eemmedyatamente*
for tomorrow at nine o'clock?	per domani alle nove?	*per domanee alle nove*

- **To this address, please.** — A questo indirizzo, per favore. — *a **kwes**to eendee-**reet**so per fa**vore***

- **How much will it cost?** — Quanto costerà? — *kwanto koste**ra***

- **I'm in a hurry.** — Ho fretta. — *o **fretta***

- **Stop here, please.** — Si fermi qui, per favore. — *see **fermee** kwee per fa**vore***

- **Can you wait for me, please?** — Può aspettarmi, per favore? — *pwo aspet**tarmee** per fa**vore***

- **I think there's a mistake.** — Penso che ci sia un errore. — *penso ke chee **seea** oon er**rore***

- **That's all right.** (meaning you can keep the change) — A posto così. — *a **posto** co**see***

- **Can you give me a receipt?** — Può farmi la ricevuta? — *pwo **farmee** la reeche**voo**ta*

YOU MAY HEAR...

È a dieci kilometri.	*e a **dye**chee kee**lo**metree*	It's ten kilometres.
Costerà circa cinquanta euro.	*koste**ra cheer**ca cheen**kwan**ta e-ooro*	It'll cost about fifty euros.
C'è un supplemento...	*che oon soopple**men**to...*	There's a supplement...
per i bagagli	*per ee ba**ga**lyee*	for the luggage
per ogni valigia	*per **o**nyee va**lee**ja*	for each suitcase
per la corsa notturna	*per la **cor**sa not**toor**na*	for the night ride

✳ hiring cars and bicycles

I'd like to hire...	Vorrei noleggiare...	*vorre-ee nolejare...*
two bicycles	due biciclette	*doo-e beecheeklette*
a small car	una macchina piccola	*oona makkeena peekkola*
an automatic car	una macchina automatica	*oona makkeena owtomateeka*
For...	Per...	*per...*
the day	la giornata	*la jornata*
a week	una settimana	*oona setteemana*
two weeks	due settimane	*doo-e setteemane*
How much is it...	Quanto costa...	*kwanto kosta...*
per day?	al giorno?	*al jorno*
per week?	alla settimana?	*alla setteemana*
Is mileage (km) included?	È incluso il chilometraggio?	*e eenkloozo eel kilometrajo*
Is insurance included?	È inclusa l'assicurazione?	*e eenklooza lassikooratsyone*
My partner wants to drive too	Anche il mio compagno/la mia compagna vorrebbe guidare	*anke eel meeo kompanyo/la meea kompanya vorrebbe gweedare*
Is there a deposit?	C'è un deposito?	*che oon depozeeto*
Do you take...	Accetta...	*achetta...*
credit cards?	carte di credito?	*karte dee kredeeto*
traveller's cheques?	traveller's cheques?	*travellers cheques*

Che tipo di macchina/ bicicletta vuole?	ke **tee**po dee **ma**kkeena/ beecheekletta **v**wole	What kind of car/bicycle do you want?
Per quanto tempo?	per **kwan**to **tem**po	For how long?
La sua patente, per favore.	la **soo**a pa**ten**te per fa**vor**e	Your driving licence, please.
C'è un deposito di 100 euro.	che oon de**po**zeeto dee **chen**to e-**oor**o	There's a deposit of 100 euros.
Ha una carta di credito?	a **oon**a **kar**ta dee **kre**deeto	Have you got a credit card?
Restituisca la macchina con il serbatoio pieno, per favore.	resteetoo-**ee**ska la **ma**kkeena kon eel serba**to**yo **pye**no per fa**vor**e	Please return the car with a full tank.
Per favore, restituisca la macchina/ bicicletta entro le sei.	per fa**vor**e resteetoo**ee**ska la **ma**kkeena/ beechee**kle**tta entro le **se**-ee	Please return the car/bicycle before six o'clock.

✳ driving
(see **directions**, page 37)

● You drive on the right in Italy. Traffic from the right has priority at crossroads. Wearing seatbelts is compulsory. Both drivers and passengers of motorbikes and mopeds have to wear crash helmets. A word of warning: when Italian drivers flash their lights, it means: 'Get out of my way! I'm coming', exactly the opposite to the UK.

● Speed limits are generally 50kmph in towns, 110kmph on dual carriageways and 130kmph on motorways if your car is over 1100cc.

● Main roads are labelled as follows:

A (Autostrada) Motorway

SS (Strada Statale) Trunk road

SP (Strada Provinciale) Provincial or secondary road.

YOU MAY SEE...

Accendere i fari	Use headlights
Attenzione	Caution
Autostrada	Motorway
Casello	Toll station
Centro abitato	Town/City centre
Curva pericolosa	Dangerous bend
Dare la precedenza	Give way
Deviazione	Diversion
Divieto di fermata	No stopping
In corsia	Get in lane
Lavori in corso	Road works
Limite di velocità	Speed limit
Pedaggio	Toll
Pedaggio autostradale	Motorway toll
Pedoni	Pedestrians
Pericolo	Danger
Rallentare	Slow
Spegnere il motore	Switch your engine off
Stazione di servizio	Service/Petrol station

Strada a doppio senso di marcia	Two-way traffic
Strada a senso unico	One-way street
Strada chiusa	Road closed
Strada senza uscita	No through road
Tenere la sinistra/destra	Drive on the left/right
Ultima stazione di servizio	Last petrol station
Uscita	Exit
Velocità massima	Maximum speed
Vietata la sosta	Parking prohibited
Vietato il sorpasso	No overtaking
Vietato l'accesso	No entry

YOU MAY WANT TO SAY...

● **Where's the nearest petrol station?**	Dov'è la stazione di servizio più vicina?	*dove la statsyone dee serveetsyo pyoo veecheena*
● **Fill it up with ... please**	Mi fa il pieno di ... per favore	*mee fa eel pyeno dee ... per favore*
unleaded	benzina senza piombo	*bentseena sentsa pyombo*
diesel	gasolio	*gazolyo*
● **20 litres of unleaded, please.**	Venti litri di benzina senza piombo, per favore.	*ventee leetree dee bentseena sentsa pyombo, per favore*
● **A litre/can of oil, please.**	Un litro/Una latta di olio, per favore.	*oon leetro/oona latta dee olyo, per favore*
● **Can you check the tyre pressure, please?**	Mi controlla la pressione delle gomme, per favore?	*mee kontrolla la pressyone delle gomme, per favore*

| Can you change the tyre, please? | Mi cambia la gomma per favore? | *mee **kam**bya la **gom**ma per favore* |

* mechanical problems

● If you have to tell a mechanic what's wrong with your vehicle, the easiest way is to indicate the part affected and say 'this isn't working': questo non funziona *(**kwe**sto non **foon**tsyona)*. Otherwise, look up the word for the appropriate part; see opposite.

● My car has broken down.	La macchina si è rotta.	*la **mak**keena see e **ro**tta*
● I've run out of petrol.	Sono rimasto senza benzina.	*sono ree**mas**to **sen**tsa ben**tsee**na*
● I have a puncture.	Ho bucato.	*o boo**ka**to*
● Do you do repairs?	Fate riparazioni?	*fate reepara**tsyo**nee*
● I don't know what's wrong.	Non so cosa non funziona.	*non so **ko**za non **foon**tsyona*
● I think it's the...	Penso che sia...	*penso ke **see**a...*
● I need a...	Ho bisogno di un/ una...	*o bee**zo**nyo dee oon/ **oo**na...*
● The ... doesn't work.	Il/La ... non funziona.	*eel/la... non **foon**tsyona*
● Is it serious?	È grave?	*e grave*
● Can you repair it today?	Può ripararla oggi?	*pwo reepa**rar**la ojee*

When will it be ready?	Quando sarà pronta?	*kwando sara pronta*
How much will it cost?	Quanto costerà?	*kwanto kostera*

YOU MAY HEAR...

Cosa c'è che non va?	*koza che ke non va*	What's wrong with it?
Non ho i pezzi di ricambio.	*non o ee petsee dee reekambyo*	I don't have the necessary parts.
Sarà pronta... in un'ora lunedì	*sara pronta...* *een oonora* *loonedee*	It'll be ready... in an hour on Monday
Costerà un centinaio di euro.	*kostera oon chenteeniyo dee e-ooro*	It'll cost about a hundred euros.

✳ car parts

YOU MAY WANT TO SAY...

alternator	l'alternatore	*lalternatore*
battery	la batteria	*la battereea*
carburettor	il carburatore	*eel karbooratore*
distributor	il distributore	*eel deestreebootore*
engine	il motore	*eel motore*
fanbelt	la cinghia (della ventola)	*la cheengya (della ventola)*
fuel pump	la pompa della benzina	*la pompa della bentseena*

points	le puntine	*le poonteene*
spark plugs	le candele	*le kandele*
starter motor	il motorino d'avviamento	*eel motoreeno dee avveeamento*
bonnet	il cofano	*eel kofano*
accelerator	l'acceleratore	*lacheleratore*
boot	il baule	*eel bowle*
brakes	i freni	*ee frenee*
exhaust pipe	la marmitta	*la marmeetta*
gears	le marce	*le marche*
gearbox	la scatola del cambio	*la skatola del kambyo*
headlights	i fari	*ee faree*
hazard lights	le luci di emergenza	*le loochee dee emerjentsa*
ignition	l'accensione	*lachensyone*
indicators	le freccie	*le freche*
rear lights	le luci posteriori	*le loochee posteryoree*
side lights	le luci di posizione	*le loochee dee poseetsyone*
radiator	il radiatore	*eel radyatore*
reversing lights	le luci di retromarcia	*le loochee dee retromarchya*
spare wheel	la ruota di scorta	*la rwota dee skorta*
steering wheel	il volante	*eel volante*
tyres	le gomme	*le gomme*
window	il finestrino	*eel feenestreeno*
windscreen	il parabrezza	*eel parabretsa*
windscreen wipers	i tergicristalli	*ee terjeekreestallee*

accommodation

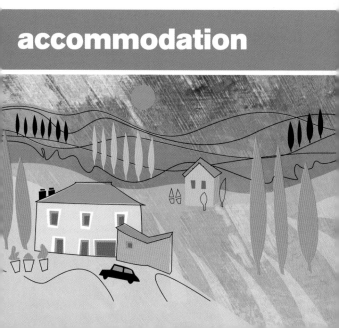

accommodation

Hotels (Alberghi) are graded from one to five stars. The rates include taxes and services, but might exclude breakfast. Locande (one-star and shared facilities) and Pensioni (one- or two-star, usually family-run with en-suite facilities) offer cheaper, more basic accommodation.

YOU MAY SEE...

Acqua potabile	Drinking water
Ascensore	Lift
Camere libere	Rooms vacant
Campeggio	Campsite
Completo	Full up
Divieto di scarico	Do not dump rubbish
Docce	Showers
Elettricità	Electricity
Hotel a cinque stelle	Five-star hotel
Lavanderia	Laundry
Mezza pensione	Half board
Ostello della gioventù	Youth Hostel
Parcheggio	Parking
Pensione	Guest house
Pensione completa	Full board
Pensione, hotel	Inn, hotel
Piano terra	Ground floor
Primo piano	First floor
Ricezione	Reception
Ristorante	Restaurant
Sala da pranzo	Dining room
Sala televisione	Television room

Salotto	Lounge
Secondo piano	Second floor
Servizio in camera	Room service
Si prega di suonare il campanello	Please ring the bell
Spazzatura	Rubbish
Toilette chimiche	Empty chemical toilets here
Toilettes	Toilets
Uscita (di emergenza)	(Emergency) exit

✳ booking in advance
(see **telephones**, page 129)

YOU MAY WANT TO SAY...

● Do you have...   Ha...   a...

a single room?	una camera singola?	*oona kamera seengola*
a double room?	una (camera) matrimoniale?	*oona (kamera) matreemonyale*
a family room?	una stanza per famiglie?	*oona stantsa per fameelye*
a twin-bedded room?	una camera doppia?	*oona kamera doppya*
space for a tent?	posto per una tenda?	*posto per oona tenda*
space for a caravan?	posto per una roulotte?	*posto per oona roolot*

● I'd like to rent... Vorrei affittare...   *vorre-ee affeettare...*

| an apartment | un appartamento | *oon appartamento* |
| your holiday home | la sua casa delle vacanze | *la sooa kaza delle vakantse* |

accommodation

61

English	Italian	Pronunciation
For...	Per...	per...
tonight	stanotte	stanotte
one night	una notte	oona notte
two nights	due notti	doo-e nottee
a week	una settimana	oona setteemana
From... to...	Da... a...	da... a...
With bath/shower	Con bagno/doccia	kon banyo/docha
It's a two-person tent.	È una tenda per due persone.	e oona tenda per doo-e persone
How much is it...	Quanto costa...	kwanto kosta...
per night?	per notte?	per notte
per week?	alla settimana?	alla setteemana
Is breakfast included?	È inclusa la colazione?	e eenklooza la kolatsyone
Is there...	C'è...	che...
a reduction for children?	uno sconto per i bambini?	oono skonto per bambeenee
a single room supplement?	un supplemento per la singola?	oon soopplemento per la seengola
wheelchair access?	accesso per le sedie a rotelle?	achesso per le sedye a rotelle
Can I pay by...	Posso pagare con...	posso pagare kon...
credit card?	la carta di credito?	la karta dee kredeeto
traveller's cheque?	traveller's cheque?	travellers chek
Can I book online?	Posso prenotare online?	posso prenotare onliyn
What's the address?	Qual è l'indirizzo?	kwale leendeereetso

Can you recommend anywhere else?	Può raccomandarmi un altro posto?	*pwo rakkomandarmee oon altro posto*

YOU MAY HEAR...

Posso aiutarla?	*posso iyootarla*	Can I help you?
Quando vuole venire?	*kwando vwole veneere*	When do you want to come?
Per quante notti?	*per kwante nottee*	For how many nights?
Per quante persone?	*per kwante persone*	For how many people?
Singola o doppia?	*seengola o doppya*	Single or double room?
Vuole un letto matrimoniale?	*vwole oon letto matreemonyale*	Do you want a double bed?
Con... bagno? doccia?	*kon... banyo docha*	With... bath? shower?
Come si chiama, per favore?	*come see kyama per favore*	What's your name, please?
Sono cento euro a notte, inclusa la colazione.	*sono chento e-ooro a notte, eenklooza la kolatsyone*	It's 100 euros per night, including breakfast.
Mi dispiace, siamo al completo.	*mee deespyache, syamo al kompleto*	I'm sorry, we're full.

accommodation

✳ checking in

I have a reservation for...	Ho prenotato per...	o prenotato per...
tonight	stanotte	stanotte
two nights	due notti	doo-e nottee
a week	una settimana	oona setteemana
two weeks	due settimane	doo-e setteemane
It's in the name of...	È a nome di...	e a nome dee...
Here's my passport.	Ecco il mio passaporto.	ekko eel meeo passaporto
I'm paying by credit card.	Pago con carta di credito.	pago kon karta dee kredeeto

Ha prenotato una camera/un posto?	a prenotato oona kamera/oon posto	Have you reserved a room/space?
Per quante notti?	per kwante nottee	For how many nights?
Come si chiama?	kome see kyama	What's your name?
Posso avere il suo passaporto, per favore?	posso avere eel soo-o passaporto, per favore	Can I have your passport, please?
Come vuole pagare?	kome vwole pagare	How do you want to pay?

REGISTRATION CARD INFORMATION

Nome	First name
Cognome	Surname
Indirizzo/Via/Numero	Home address/Street/Number
Codice di avviamento postale	Postcode
Nazionalità	Nationality
Professione	Occupation
Data di nascita	Date of birth
Luogo di nascita	Place of birth
Numero passaporto	Passport number
Proveniente da/prossima destinazione	Coming from/going to
Rilasciato a	Issued at
Data	Date
Firma	Signature

✳ hotels, B&Bs and hostels

YOU MAY WANT TO SAY...

● Where can I/we park?	Dove si può parcheggiare?	*dove see pwo parkejare*
● Can I/we see the room please?	Si può vedere la camera, per favore?	*see pwo vedere la kamera per favore*
● Do you have...	Avete...	*avete...*
a room with a view?	una camera con vista?	*oona kamera kon veesta*
a bigger room?	una camera più grande?	*oona kamera pyoo grande*
a cot for the baby?	un lettino per il bambino?	*oon letteeno per eel bambeeno*

hotels, B&Bs and hostels

● Is breakfast included?	È inclusa la colazione?	*e eenklooza la kolatsyone*
● What time...	A che ora...	*a ke ora...*
is breakfast?	è la colazione	*e la kolatsyone*
do you lock the front door?	chiudete l'ingresso principale?	*kyoodete la porta preencheepale*
● Where is...	Dov'è...	*dove...*
the dining room?	la sala ristorante?	*la sala reestorante*
the bar?	il bar?	*eel bar*
● Is there...	C'è...	*che...*
24 hour room service?	servizio in camera ventiquattr'ore su ventiquattro?	*serveetsyo een kamera venteekwattrore soo venteekwattro*
internet connection here?	un collegamento internet?	*oon kollegamento eenternet*

YOU MAY HEAR...

● Il parcheggio è... dietro l'albergo sulla strada	*eel parkejo e... dyetro lalbergo soolla strada*	The car park is... behind the hotel on the street
● La colazione è/ non è inclusa.	*la kolatsyone e/non e eenklooza*	Breakfast is/isn't included.
● La colazione si serve dalle... alle...	*la kolatsyone see serve dalle... alle...*	Breakfast is from... to...
● Chiudiamo l'ingresso principale alle...	*kyoodyamo leengresso preencheepale alle...*	We shut the front door at...

C'è servizio in camera ventiquattrore su ventiquattro.	*che serveetsyo een kamera venteekwattrore soo venteekwattro*	There's 24-hour room service.

✴ camping and caravanning
(see **directions**, page 37)

YOU MAY WANT TO SAY...

Is there a campsite/caravan site round here?	C'è un campeggio qui vicino?	*che oon kampejo kwee veecheeno*
Can we camp here?	Si può campeggiare qui?	*see pwo kampejare kwee*
Can we park our caravan here?	Possiamo parcheggiare la roulotte qui?	*possyamo parkejare la roolot kwee*
It's a two/four person tent.	È una tenda da due/ da quattro.	*e oona tenda da doo-e/da kwattro*
Where are... the toilets? the showers? the dustbins?	Dove sono... i gabinetti? le docce? le pattumiere?	*dove sono... ee gabeenettee le doche le pattoomyere*
Do we pay extra for the showers?	Si paga in più per le docce?	*see paga een pyoo per le doche*
Is the water OK for drinking?	L'acqua è potabile?	*lakwa e potabeele*
Where's the electricity?	Dov'è la corrente?	*dove la korrente*

requests and queries

YOU MAY HEAR...

Il campeggio più vicino è a ... chilometri.	*eel kampejo pyoo veecheeno e a ... keelometree*	The nearest campsite/caravan site is ... kilometres away.
Avete una piantina?	*avete oona pyanteena*	Have you got a map?
Non si può campeggiare qui.	*non see pwo kampejare kwee*	You can't camp here.
Le docce sono gratuite.	*le doche sono gratooeete*	The showers are free.
La doccia costa ... euro.	*la docha kosta ... e-ooro*	It's ... euros for a shower.

✳ requests and queries

YOU MAY WANT TO SAY...

Are there any messages for me?	Ci sono messaggi per me?	*chee sono messajee per me*
I'm expecting... a phone call a fax	Sto aspettando... una telefonata un fax	*sto aspettando... oona telefonata oon fax*
Can I... leave this in the safe? put it (payment) on my room? log on anywhere?	Posso... metterlo in cassaforte? metterlo sulla mia camera? accedere a internet da qualche parte?	*posso... metterlo een kassaforte metterlo soolla meea kamera achedere a eenternet da kwalke parte*

● Can you...
  give me my things from the safe?
  wake me up at eight o'clock?
  order me a taxi?

Può...
  darmi le mie cose dalla cassaforte?
  svegliarmi alle otto?
  chiamarmi un taxi?

pwo...
  darmee le mee-e koze dalla kassaforte
  svelyarmee alle otto
  kyamarmee oon taksee

● Do you have...
  a babysitting service?
  a baby alarm?

C'è...
  un servizio babysitter?
  un allarme per il bambino?

che...
  oon serveetsyo babeeseetter
  oon allarme per eel bambeeno

● I need...
  another pillow
  an adaptor

Ho bisogno di...
  un altro cuscino
  un adattatore

o beezonyo dee...
  oon altro koosheeno
  oon adattatore

● I've lost my key.
Ho perso la chiave.
o perso la kyave

● I've left my key in the room.
Ho lasciato la mia chiave in camera.
o lashato la meea kyave een kamera

YOU MAY HEAR...

● C'è un messaggio/ un fax per lei.
che oon messajo/oon fax per le-ee
There's a message/ fax for you.

● No, non ci sono messaggi per lei.
no non chee sono messajee per le-ee
No, there are no messages for you.

● Vuole la sveglia?
vwole la svelya
Do you want a wake up call?

● A che ora?
a ke ora
(For) what time?

accommodation

69

Quando vuole la babysitter?	kwando **vwo**le la babee**seet**ter	When do you want a babysitter?
Le chiamo qualcuno per farla entrare.	le **kya**mo kwal**koo**no per farla en**tra**re	I'll get someone to let you in.
Attenda un attimo, per favore.	at**ten**da oon at**tee**mo per fa**vo**re	Just a moment, please.

✳ problems and complaints

YOU MAY WANT TO SAY...

Excuse me...	Mi scusi...	mee **skoo**zee
The room is...	La camera è...	la **ka**mera e
too hot	troppo calda	troppo **kal**da
too cold	troppo fredda	troppo **fred**da
too small	troppo piccola	troppo **peek**kola
There isn't any...	Non c'è	non **che**
toilet paper	carta igienica	**kar**ta i**jenee**ka
hot water	acqua calda	**ak**wa **kal**da
electricity	elettricità	elet**treechee**ta
There aren't any...	Non ci sono...	non chee **so**no
towels	asciugamani	ashooga**ma**nee
pillows	cuscini	koo**shee**nee
I can't open the window.	La finestra non si apre.	la fee**nes**tra non see **a**pre
I can't turn the tap off.	L'acqua non si chiude.	**lak**wa non see **kyoo**de
I can't work the TV.	La televisione non funziona.	la televee**zyo**ne non foon**tsyo**na

- **The bed is uncomfortable.** | Il letto è scomodo. | *eel **let**to e **sko**modo*
- **The bathroom is dirty.** | Il bagno è sporco. | *eel **ban**yo e **spor**ko*
- **The toilet doesn't flush.** | Il gabinetto non scarica. | *eel gabee**net**to non **ska**reeka*
- **The drain is blocked.** | Lo scarico è otturato. | *lo **ska**reeko e ottoo**ra**to*
- **It's very noisy.** | È molto rumoroso/a. | *e molto roomo**ro**zo/a*
- **The light/key/television doesn't work.** | La luce/chiave/televisione non funziona. | *la **loo**che/**kya**ve/televee**zyo**ne non foont**syo**na*
- **There's a smell of gas.** | C'è odore di gas. | *che o**do**re dee **gaz***
- **I want to see the manager!** | Voglio vedere il direttore! | *volyo ve**de**re eel deeret**to**re*

* checking out

- **The bill, please.** | Il conto, per favore. | *eel **kon**to per favore*
- **I'd like to...** | Vorrei... | *vorre-ee*
  - check out | check out | *chek owt*
  - stay another night | stare un'altra notte | *stare oonaltra notte*
- **What time is check out?** | A che ora dobbiamo lasciare la camera? | *a ke ora dob**bya**mo la**sha**re la **ka**mera*

71

self-catering/second homes

Can I have a late check out?	Posso lasciare la camera tardi?	*posso lashare la kamera tardee*
Can I leave my bags here?	Posso lasciare qui le mie borse?	*posso lashare kwee le mee-e borse*
There's a mistake in the bill.	C'è un errore nel conto.	*che oon errore nel konto*
We've had a great time here.	Siamo stati bene qui.	*syamo statee bene kwee*

YOU MAY HEAR...

Deve liberare la camera alle...	*deve leeberare la kamera alle...*	Check out is at...
Può tenere la camera fino alle...	*pwo tenere la kamera feeno alle...*	You can have the room till...
Quante valigie?	*kwante valeeje*	How many bags?
Le lasci qui.	*le lashee kwee*	Leave them here.
Mi lasci controllare.	*mee lashee kontrollare*	Let me check it.
Torni a trovarci!	*tornee a trovarchee*	Come again!

✳ self-catering/second homes
(see **problems and complaints**, page 70)

YOU MAY WANT TO SAY...

I've rented...	Ho affittato...	*o affeettato...*
a chalet	uno chalet	*oono shale*
an apartment	un appartamento	*oon appartamento*

accommodation

72

- My name is... — Mi chiamo... — *mee kyamo...*
- We're in number... — Siamo in... — *syamo een...*
- Can you give me the key, please? — Può darmi la chiave, per favore? — *pwo darmee la kyave per favore*
- Where is... — Dov'è... — *dove*
  - the fusebox? — la scatola dei fusibili? — *la skatola de-ee foozeebeelee*
  - the stopcock? — il rubinetto principale? — *eel roobeenetto preencheepale*
- How does the ... work? — Come funziona il ... ? — *kome foontsyona eel ... ?*
- Is there... — C'è... — *che...*
  - air-conditioning? — l'aria condizionata? — *larya kondeetsyonata*
  - another gas bottle? — un'altra bombola del gas? — *oonaltra bombola del gaz*
- Are there... — Ci sono... — *chee sono*
  - any more blankets? — altre coperte? — *altre koperte*
  - any shops round here? — negozi qui vicino? — *negotsee kwee veecheeno*
- Where do I/we put the rubbish? — Dove si mettono i rifiuti? — *dove see mettono ee reefyootee*
- When do they collect the rubbish? — Quando ritirano i rifiuti? — *kwando reeteerano ee reefyootee*
- When does the cleaner come? — Quando viene la donna delle pulizie? — *kwando vyene la donna delle pooleetsye*
- Can I borrow a corkscrew? — Mi presta un apribottiglie? — *mee presta oon apreebotteelye*

accommodation

73

self-catering/second homes

- We need...
  Ci serve...
  chee serve...
    - a plumber
      un idraulico
      oon eedra-ooleeko
    - an electrician
      un elettricista
      oon elettreecheesta
    - help
      aiuto
      ayooto

- How can I contact you?
  Dove la trovo?
  dove la trovo

YOU MAY HEAR...

La scatola dei fusibili è lì.	*la skatola de-ee foozeebeelee e lee*	The fusebox is there.
Il rubinetto principale è qui.	*eel roobeenetto preencheepale e kwee*	The stopcock is here.
Funziona così.	*foontsyona cozee*	It works like this.
Prema questo bottone/ interruttore.	*prema kwesto bottone/ eenterroottore*	Press this button/ switch.
Metta i rifiuti... nella pattumiera sulla strada	*metta ee reefyootee.. nella pattoomyera soolla strada*	Put the rubbish... in the dustbin on the street
I rifiuti si ritirano il...	*ee reefyootee see reeteerano eel...*	The rubbish is collected on...
La donna delle pulizie viene il...	*la donna delle pooleetsye vyene eel...*	The cleaner comes on...
Il mio numero di cellulare è...	*eel meeo noomero dee chelloolare e...*	My mobile number is...

accommodation

74

food&drink

● Meal times in Italy are similar to those in the UK: colazione (breakfast) at around 7.30-8.00am, pranzo (lunch) between 12.30 and 2pm and cena (dinner) at about 8pm. The further south you go, the later dinner is served.

● For a quick lunch, a drink or a snack, you can go to a bar. Alternatively, go into a salumeria (delicatessen) or a small alimentari (food shop) and ask for a panino (a sandwich made with fresh bread and freshly sliced ham, Parma ham or salami) together with a soft drink or a beer.

● For a more substantial meal, you can go to an osteria, pizzeria, trattoria or ristorante, according to your budget and the kind of food you prefer. A ristorante is usually more expensive and more formal than a trattoria. Some will offer a menu turistico or menu a prezzo fisso, a tourist menu at a fixed price for two or three courses, plus wine and coffee.

YOU MAY SEE...

Birreria	Beer garden/Beer cellar
Caffè	Café
Gabinetti	Toilets
Gelateria	Ice-cream parlour
Guardaroba	Cloakroom
Locanda	Inn, guest house
Menu turistico	Tourist menu
Osteria	Inn
Paninoteca	Sandwich bar
Pollo arrosto da asporto	Roast chicken to take away

Specialità pesce	Fish specialities
Ristorante	Restaurant
Rosticceria	Roast meats to take away
Si accettano carte di credito	We take credit cards
Taverna	Inn/tavern
Tavola calda	Snack bar
Trattoria	Restaurant

✳ making bookings
(see **telling the time**, page 15)

(see **telling the time**, page 15)

YOU MAY WANT TO SAY...

I'd like to reserve a table...	Vorrei riservare un tavolo...	vorre-ee reezervare oon tavolo...
for two people	per due persone	per doo-e persone
for tomorrow evening	per domani sera	per domanee sera
at half past eight	alle otto e mezza	alle otto e medza
this evening at seven	stasera alle sette	stasera alle sette
My name is...	Mi chiamo...	mee kyamo...
My telephone/ mobile number is...	Il mio numero di telefono/di cellulare è...	eel meeo noomero dee telefono/dee chelloolare e...
Could you squeeze us in earlier/later?	Potrebbe trovarci un tavolo prima/più tardi?	potrebbe trovarchee oon tavolo preema/ pyoo tardee
Are children welcome?	Possiamo portare i bambini?	possyamo portare ee bambeenee

food and drink

YOU MAY HEAR...

Per quando desidera il tavolo?	*per kwando dezeedera eel tavolo*	When would you like the table for?
Per quante persone?	*per kwante persone*	For how many people?
Il suo nome, per favore?	*eel soo-o nome per favore*	What's your name?
Mi dispiace, ma è tutto esaurito.	*mee deespyache ma e tootto ezowreeto*	I'm sorry, we're fully booked.

✳ at the restaurant

YOU MAY WANT TO SAY...

I've booked a table.	Ho riservato un tavolo.	*o reezervato oon tavolo*
My name is...	Mi chiamo...	*mee kyamo...*
We haven't booked.	Non abbiamo prenotato.	*non abbyamo prenotato*
Have you got a table for four, please?	Avete un tavolo per quattro, per favore?	*avete oon tavolo per kwattro per favore*
Outside/On the terrace, if possible.	Fuori/In terrazza, se possibile.	*fworee/een terratsa se posseebeele*
Have you got a high chair?	Avete un seggiolone?	*avete oon sejjolone*
How long do we need to wait?	Quanto bisogna aspettare?	*kwanto beezonya aspettare*

food and drink

78

| Do you take credit cards? | Accettate carte di credito? | *achettate karte dee kredeeto* |

YOU MAY HEAR...

Avete prenotato?	*avete prenotato*	Have you got a reservation?
Dove volete sedervi?	*dove volete sedervee*	Where would you like to sit?
Fumatori o non fumatori?	*foomatoree o non foomatoree*	Smoking or non-smoking?
Un attimo, per favore.	*oon atteemo per favore*	Just a moment.
Volete aspettare?	*volete aspettare*	Would you like to wait?
(Non) accettiamo carte di credito.	*(non) achettyamo karte dee kredeeto*	We (don't) accept credit cards.

* ordering your food

● To order something, all you need do is name it and say per favore (*per favore*, please), adding per me (*per me*, for me), or per lui/lei (*per loo-ee/le-ee*, for him/her).

YOU MAY WANT TO SAY...

| Excuse me! | Scusi! | *skoozee* |
| The menu, please. | Il menu, per favore. | *eel menoo per favore* |

- **Do you have...** Avete un menu... *avete oon menoo...*
  - **a children's menu?** per bambini? *per bambeenee*
  - **a tourist menu?** turistico? *tooreesteeko*
  - **an à la carte menu?** alla carta? *alla karta*

- **Is it self-service?** È self service? *e self servees*

- **We're ready to order.** Siamo pronti per ordinare. *syamo prontee per ordeenare*

- **I'd like...** Vorrei... *vorre-ee*
  - **for starter** come antipasto *kome anteepasto*
  - **for first course** per primo *per preemo*
  - **for main course** per secondo *per sekondo*
  - **for dessert** per dolce *per dolche*

- **Does that come with vegetables?** Viene servito con la verdura? *vyene serveeto kon la verdoora*

- **What's this please?** Mi scusi, cos'è questo? *mee skoozee koze kwesto*

- **What are your specials today?** Quali sono i piatti del giorno? *kwalee sono ee pyattee del jorno*

- **What's the local speciality?** Qual è la specialità locale? *kwale la spechaleeta lokale*

- **I'll have the same as him/her.** Prendo quello che ha preso lui/lei. *prendo kwello ke a prezo loo-ee/le-ee*

- **I prefer it...** Lo preferisco... *lo prefereesko...*
  - **rare** al sangue *al sangwe*
  - **medium** a puntino *a poonteeno*
  - **well done** ben cotto *ben kotto*

Excuse me, I've changed my mind.	Mi scusi, ho cambiato idea.	*mee **skoo**zee o kambyato eede-a*

YOU MAY HEAR...

Avete deciso?	*avete de**chee**zo*	Have you decided?
Cosa desiderate per...	*koza dezeederate per...*	What would you like for...
antipasto?	*anteepasto*	starter?
primo?	*preemo*	first course?
secondo?	*sekondo*	main course?
dolce?	*dolche*	dessert?
Vi consiglio...	*vee konseelyo...*	I recommend...
Altro?	*altro*	Anything else?

✳ ordering your drinks

YOU MAY WANT TO SAY...

Can I see the wine list, please?	Si può vedere la lista dei vini, per favore?	*see pwo ve**dere** la **lees**ta de-ee **vee**nee per favore*
A bottle of this please.	Una bottiglia di questo, per favore.	*oona bot**tee**lya di **kwes**to per favore*
Half a litre of this please.	Mezzo litro di questo, per favore.	*medzo **lee**tro dee **kwes**to per favore*
A glass of the ... please.	Un bicchiere di ... per favore.	*oon beek**kye**re dee ... per favore*

ordering your drinks

We'll have the house red/white, please.	Prendiamo il rosso/ bianco della casa, per favore.	*prendyamo eel rosso/ byanko della kaza per favore*
What beers do you have?	Quali birre avete?	*kwalee beerre avete*
What beer do you recommend?	Quale birra consigliate?	*kwale beerra konseelyate*
Is that bottled or draught?	È in bottiglia o alla spina?	*e een botteelya o alla speena*
Can I have... a gin and tonic? a whisky? a vodka and coke?	Posso avere... un gin and tonic? un whisky? una vodka con cola?	*posso avere... oon geen and toneek oon weeskee oona vodka kon kola*
Do you have any herb liqueurs?	Avete digestivi?	*avete deejesteevee*
A bottle of mineral water, please.	Una bottiglia di acqua minerale, per favore.	*oona botteelya dee akkwa meenerale per favore*
What soft drinks do you have?	Che bibite avete?	*ke beebeete avete*

YOU MAY HEAR...

Ghiaccio e limone?	*gyacho e leemone*	Ice and lemon?
Volete anche dell'acqua?	*volete anke dellakkwa*	Would you like water as well?
Gassata o naturale?	*gazzata o natoorale*	Fizzy or still water?

food and drink

82

Una bottiglia grande o piccola?	*oona botteelya grande o peekkola*	A large or small bottle?

✳ bars, cafés and snack bars

I'll have...	(Io) prendo...	*(eeo) prendo...*
A coffee, please.	Un caffè, per favore.	*oon kaffe per favore*
A coffee with a dash of milk, please.	Un caffè macchiato, per favore.	*oon kaffe makkyato per favore*
A cup of tea, please.	Un tè, per favore.	*oon te per favore*
With milk/lemon.	Con latte/limone.	*kon latte/leemone*
A glass of ... please.	Un bicchiere di ... per favore.	*oon beekyere dee ... per favore*
tap water	acqua del rubinetto	*akkwa del roobeenetto*
white/red/rosé wine	vino bianco/ rosso/rosato	*veeno byanco/ rosso/rozato*
fresh orange juice	spremuta d'arancia	*spremoota darancha*
No ice, thanks.	Senza ghiacco, grazie.	*senza gyacho gratsye*
A bottle of water, please.	Una bottiglia d'acqua, per favore.	*oona botteelya dakkwa per favore*
A slice of...	Una fetta di...	*oona fetta dee...*
apple cake	torta di mele	*torta dee mele*
tiramisu	tiramisù	*teerameesoo*

food and drink

83

comments and requests

- **What kind of ... do you have?** — Che tipi di ... avete? — *ke teepee dee ... avete*

- **What kind of sandwiches do you have?** — Che tipi di tramezzini avete? — *ke teepee dee tramedzeenee avete*

- **Is there any...** — C'è del... — *che del...*
  - **tomato ketchup?** — ketchup? — *kechop*
  - **salt and pepper?** — sale e pepe? — *sale e pepe*

- **Same again, please.** — Lo stesso, per favore. — *lo stesso per favore*

- **It's my round.** — Tocca a me. — *tokka a me*

- **How much is that?** — Quanto costa? — *kwanto kosta*

YOU MAY HEAR...

Cosa vi porto?	*koza vee porto*	What can I get you?
Cosa desidera/ desiderano?	*koza dezeedera/ dezeederano*	What would you like?
Grande o piccolo/a?	*grande o peekkolo/a*	Large or small?
Gassata o naturale?	*gazzata o natoorale*	Fizzy or still?
Con ghiaccio?	*kon gyacho*	With ice?
Subito.	*soobeeto*	Right away.

✻ comments and requests

YOU MAY WANT TO SAY...

- **This is delicious.** — È ottimo. — *e otteemo*

food and drink

Can I/we have...	Si può avere...	*see pwo avere...*
some more bread?	dell'altro pane?	*dellaltro pane*
some more water?	dell'altra acqua?	*dellaltra akkwa*
Can I/we have ... please?	Si può avere ... per favore	*see pwo avere ... per favore*
another bottle of wine	un'altra bottiglia di vino	*oonaltra botteelya dee veeno*
a knife	un coltello	*oon koltello*
a fork	una forchetta	*oona forketta*
a spoon	un cucchiaio	*oon kookya-yo*
another glass	un altro bicchiere	*oonaltro beekyere*
I can't eat another thing.	Sono sazio/a.	*sono satsyo/a*

✳ special requirements

I'm...	Sono...	*sono...*
diabetic.	diabetico/a	*dyabeteeko/a*
He is...	(Lui) è...	*(loo-ee) e...*
allergic to nuts	allergico alle noci	*allerjeeko alle nochee*
allergic to cow's milk	allergico al latte vaccino	*allerjeeko al latte vacheeno*
She is...	(Lei) è..	*(le-ee) e...*
allergic to shellfish	allergica ai frutti di mare	*allerjeeka iy froottee dee mare*

food and drink

85

- I am...
  - vegetarian
  - vegan

  Sono...
  - vegetariano/a
  - vegano/a

  sono...
  - *vejetaryano/a*
  - *vegano/a*

- I can't eat...
  - dairy products

  Non posso mangiare...
  - latticini

  *non **posso** manjare...*
  - *latteecheenee*

- He/She can't eat...
  - wheat products

  Non può mangiare...
  - cibi con glutine

  non pwo manjare...
  - ***cheebee** con **gloo**teene*

- Do you have...food?
  - halal
  - kosher
  - low sodium

  - low fat

  - organic

  Avete piatti...
  - alal
  - kasher
  - a basso contenuto di sodio
  - a basso contenuto di grassi
  - biologici

  *avete **pyat**tee...*
  - *alal*
  - *kasher*
  - *a **basso** konte-**noo**to dee **sod**yo*
  - *a **basso** konte**noo**to dee **grass**ee*
  - *byo**lo**jeechee*

- Do you have anything without (meat)?

  Avete qualcosa senza (carne)?

  *avete kwal**ko**za **senza** (**karne**)*

- Is that cooked with (butter)?

  È cucinato con (burro)?

  *e koochee**na**to kon (**boor**ro)*

- Does it contain (nuts)?

  Contiene (noci)?

  *kon**tye**ne **no**chee*

YOU MAY HEAR...

- Chiedo in cucina.   *kye**do** een koo**chee**na*   I'll ask in the kitchen.
- È tutto con (burro).   *e **toot**to kon (**boor**ro)*   It's all got (butter) in.

✳ problems and complaints

Excuse me...	Mi scusi...	mee **skoo**zee...
This is...	È...	e...
cold	freddo	**fred**do
burnt	bruciato	broo**cha**to
This is underdone.	Non è cotto.	non e **kot**to
I didn't order this.	Non ho ordinato questo piatto.	non o ordee**na**to **kwe**sto **pyat**to
I ordered...	Ho ordinato...	o ordee**na**to...
When is our food coming?	Quando arriva il nostro ordine?	**kwan**do ar**ree**va eel **nos**tro **or**deene

✳ paying the bill

● Tips are not very common in Italy, as a 10–12.5% charge for servizio (service) and coperto (bread and cover) is automatically added to your bill.

The bill, please.	Il conto, per favore.	eel **kon**to per fa**vore**
Is service included?	Il servizio è compreso?	eel ser**veet**syo e kom**pre**zo
There's a mistake here.	C'è un errore.	che oon er**rore**
That was fantastic, thank you.	Era ottimo, grazie.	era **ot**teemo **grat**sye

food and drink

Il servizio non è compreso.	*eel serveetsyo non e komprezo*	Service isn't included.
Mi dispiace, accettiamo solo contanti.	*mee deespyache achettyamo solo kontantee*	Sorry, we only accept cash.

* buying food
(see **shops and services**, page 113)

YOU MAY WANT TO SAY...

I'd like...	Vorrei...	*vorre-ee...*
some of	un po' di	*oon po dee*
that	quello/a	*kwello/a*
a kilo (of...)	un chilo (di...)	*oon keelo (dee...)*
half a kilo (of...)	mezzo chilo (di...)	*medzo keelo (dee...)*
200 grammes (of...)	due etti (di...)	*doo-e ettee dee...)*
a piece (of...)	un pezzo (di...)	*oon petso (dee...)*
a slice (of...)	una fetta (di...)	*oona fetta (dee...)*
How much is...	Quanto costa...	*kwanto kosta...*
that?	quello/a?	*kwello/a*
a kilo of cheese?	un chilo di formaggio?	*oon keelo dee formajo*
What's that, please?	Che cos'è quello?	*ke koze kwello*
Have you got any bread?	Ha del pane?	*a del pane*
Have you got any more?	Ne ha dell'altro?	*ne a dellaltro*

- A bit more/less, please. | Un po' di più/di meno, per favore. | *oon po dee pyoo/dee meno per favore*

- That's enough, thank you. | Basta così, grazie. | *basta kozee gratsye*

- That's all thank you. | È tutto, grazie. | *e tootto gratsye*

- I'm looking for... | Cercavo... | *cherkavo*
  - frozen food | i surgelati | *ee soorjelatee*
  - dairy products | i latticini | *ee latteecheenee*
  - the fruit and vegetable section | il banco della frutta e verdura | *eel banko della frootta e verdoora*

- Can I have a bag please? | Posso avere un sacchetto, per favore? | *posso avere oon sakketto per favore*

YOU MAY HEAR...

Posso aiutarla?	*posso iyootarla*	Can I help you?
Cosa desidera?	*koza dezeedera*	What would you like?
Quanto ne desidera?	*kwanto ne dezeedera*	How much would you like?
Quanti ne desidera?	*kwantee ne dezeedera*	How many would you like?
Mi dispiace, sono tutti esauriti.	*mee deespyache sono toottee ezowreetee*	I'm sorry, we've sold out.
Altro?	*altro*	Anything else?

food and drink

menu reader

YOU MAY SEE...

Cena	Dinner
Colazione	Breakfast
Coperto	Cover charge
Iva compresa	VAT inclusive
Menu a prezzo fisso	Set menu
Menu del giorno	Menu of the day
Menu turistico	Tourist menu
Non si accettano carte di credito	We don't accept credit cards
Pranzo	Lunch
Servizio compreso	Service included
Si accettano carte di credito	We accept credit cards
Specialità della casa	House specials

DRINKS

acqua... water...
  gassata fizzy
  minerale mineral
  naturale still
  tonica tonic
amaretto almond liqueur
Americano vermouth with bitters, brandy and lemon peel
analcolico non alcoholic
aperitivo aperitif
aranciata fizzy orange
bibite soft drinks
birra... beer...
  alla spina draught

  chiara lager
  scura ale
  estera imported
  in bottiglia bottled
  in lattina in a can
  nazionale Italian (like lager)
camomilla camomile tea
caffè... coffee...
  americano filtered
  corretto laced with brandy or grappa
  espresso strong, black
  freddo iced
  latte with milk

lungo **longer, weaker black**
macchiato **with a dash of milk**
cappuccino **frothy white coffee, with grated chocolate on top**
cioccolata calda **hot chocolate**
digestivo **strong herb liqueur**
frullato **milk-shake**
frappé **milk-shake**
granita... **crushed-ice drink...**
  all'arancia **with orange**
  al limone **with lemon**
grappa **strong grape liqueur**
latte... **milk...**
  macchiato **with a splash of coffee**
lattina **can**
limonata **lemonade**
marsala **light Sicilian dessert wine**
ramazzotti **strong herb liqueur**
sambuca **aniseed liqueur**
spremuta... **fresh fruit juice...**
  d'arancia **fresh orange juice**
  di limone **fresh lemon juice**
  di pompelmo **fresh grapefruit juice**
spumante **sparkling champagne-like wine**

strega **strong herb liqueur**
succo di frutta **fruit juice**
  d'ananas **pineapple juice**
  di pesca **peach juice**
tè... **tea....**
  al latte **with milk**
  al limone **with lemon**
  freddo **iced**
  alla menta **peppermint tea**
vino... **wine...**
  bianco **white**
  da tavola **table wine**
  della casa **house wine**
  dolce **sweet**
  in bottiglia **bottled**
  leggero **light**
  corposo **full-bodied**
  rosato **rosé**
  rosso **red**
  secco **dry**
  sfuso **in a carafe**
  spumante **sparkling champagne-like wine**

FOOD

A

abbacchio **milk-fed lamb**
acciughe **anchovies**
aceto **vinegar**
aceto balsamico **balsamic vinegar**
affogato **poached**
affogato al caffè **vanilla ice cream with hot coffee on top**
affumicato **smoked**
aglio **garlic**
agnello **lamb**

agnello rustico **roast leg of lamb with cheese and lemon**
agnolotti **pasta envelopes filled with meat or cheese**
al burro **cooked in butter**
al forno **baked**
al vapore **steamed**
alla cacciatora **served in red wine sauce with mushrooms (lit. hunter's style)**
alla casalinga **homemade**

all'agro with a dressing of lemon juice and oil

all'arrabbiata hot tomato sauce with bacon and chillies

albicocca apricot

alici anchovies

amarene wild cherries

ananas pineapple

anatra duck

anguilla eel

anguria watermelon

antipasto starter

antipasto misto selection of cold meat, usually ham and salami

aragosta lobster

arancia orange

arancini di riso deep-fried rice balls with mozzarella cheese

aringa herring

asparagi asparagus

B

baccalà dried salt cod

bagna cauda hot anchovy and garlic dip served with raw vegetables

banane bananas

barbabietola beetroot

basilico basil

bel paese mild cheese

besciamella bechamel (white sauce)

bianco: in bianco served with butter and parmesan cheese

bistecca rump steak

bollito misto mixed boiled meats

boscaiola: alla boscaiola with mushrooms and ham sauce

brace: alla brace grilled

braciola rib steak

braciola di maiale pork chop

branzino sea bass

brasato beef stew

broccoli broccoli

brodo broth

bruschetta al pomodoro garlic bread with olive oil and fresh tomatoes

burrida fish soup, fish stew

burro butter

C

calamari squid

calzone pizza rolled up and stuffed with tomato and mozzarella cheese

cannella cinnamon

cannelloni rolls of pasta

cannelloni al forno rolls of pasta stuffed with meat sauce, baked and served with white sauce and melted cheese

cannoli fried pastries filled with ricotta, dark chocolate and candied fruit

capesante scallops

cappelletti little 'hats' of stuffed pasta

caprese tomato and mozzarella salad with basil

carbonara: alla carbonara cooked with smoked bacon, egg, parmesan and black pepper

carciofo artichoke

carne arrosto roast meat

carne trita mince

carote carrots

carpa carp

carpaccio sliced raw beef, served with olive oil, lemon juice and parmesan

cassata ice-cream cake with candied fruit

cassata alla siciliana sponge cake with ricotta and candied fruit

cassola pork, cabbage and spareribs

casserole
castagne chestnuts
cavolfiore cauliflower
cavolini di Bruxelles Brussels sprouts
cavolo cabbage
ceci chick peas
cena dinner
ciliegie cherries
cinghiale wild boar
cioccolato chocolate
cipolla onion
colazione breakfast
conchiglie pasta shells
coniglio rabbit
coniglio in umido rabbit stew
consommé clear broth made
   with meat or chicken
contorno vegetables
coperto cover charge
cosciotto d'agnello leg of lamb
costata alla fiorentina t-bone steak
costoletta cutlet
cotechino cooked spicy pork sausage
cotoletta alla milanese escalope
   of veal cooked in egg and
   breadcrumbs
cotoletta alla valdostana escalope of
   veal with ham and cheese cooked
   in egg and breadcrumbs
cozze mussels
crema custard
crepes pancakes
crespelle savoury pancake with
   white sauce and other fillings
crostini toast, croutons
crostini di fegatini di pollo fried
   chicken livers on toast

D

datteri dates
dente: al dente not overcooked
dolce cake, sweet

E

emmenthal mild, firm Swiss cheese
entrecote steak
erbe herbs

F

fagiano pheasant
fagioli beans
fagioli haricot/butter beans
fagiolini green (French) beans
fegato liver
fegato alla veneta calf liver
   cooked in butter with onions
fichi figs
finocchi fennel
fontina mild cow's cheese
formaggio cheese
forno: al forno baked
fragole strawberries
fragoline di bosco wild strawberries
frittata omelette
fritto fried
fritto misto di mare deep-fried
   seafood
frutta fruit
frutta di stagione seasonal fruit
frutti di mare seafood
funghi mushrooms
funghi champignons button
   mushrooms
funghi porcini boletus mushrooms

G

gamberetti shrimps
gamberi prawns
gamberoni king prawns
gateau gateau
gelato ice cream
ghiacciato iced, chilled
gnocchi dumplings
gnocchi alla romana milk and
   semolina dumplings

food and drink

93

gnocchi verdi **spinach dumplings**
granchio **crab, crayfish**
gratinato **sprinkled with bread-crumbs and cheese and grilled**
grigliata mista **a selection of grilled meats**

H
hamburger **hamburger**

I
impanato **cooked in egg and breadcrumbs**
insalata **salad**
insalata di riso **rice salad**
insalata mista **mixed salad**
insalata russa **diced vegetables in mayonnaise**
insalata verde **green salad**
Iva compresa **VAT included**

L
lamponi **raspberries**
lattuga **lettuce salad**
lepre **hare, rabbit**
limone **lemon**
lingua **ox tongue**
lingua salmistrata **ox tongue marinated and boiled**
lombata di vitello **loin of veal**
lumache **snails**

M
macedonia **fruit salad**
maiale **pork**
malaga **sweet, alcoholic flavour, usually of ice cream**
mandorle **almonds**
manzo **beef**
marroni **chestnuts**
mascarpone **cream cheese**
mela **apple**
melanzana **aubergine**

melanzane alla parmigiana **fried sliced aubergines baked with tomato sauce, parmesan and mozzarella**
melone **melon**
menu a prezzo fisso **set menu**
menu del giorno **menu of the day**
menu turistico **tourist menu**
meringata **meringue pie**
merluzzo **cod**
messicani in gelatina **rolls of veal with jelly**
midollo **bone marrow**
miele **honey**
minestra di fagioli **bean soup**
minestra di lenticchie **lentil soup**
minestrone **thick vegetable soup**
more **blackberries**
mortadella **mild spiced salami**
mostarda **pickled fruit**
mozzarella di bufala **moist white buffalo milk cheese**
mozzarella in carrozza **mozzarella sandwich dipped in egg and fried**

N
nocciola **hazelnut**
noce **nut**
noce moscata **nutmeg**

O
oca **goose**
olive **olives**
ossobuco **marrow-bone veal steak**
ostriche **oysters**

P
paglia e fieno **mixed green and white pasta, usually tagliatelle**
pagliarda di vitello **thin veal chop with ham**
pagliata **sweetbreads**
pancetta affumicata **smoked bacon**

pane **bread**

panettone **light, candied fruit cake, typical at Christmas**

panforte di Siena **cake with honey, candied fruits, almonds and cloves**

panino **bread roll**

panna **cream**

panna montata **whipped cream**

panzerotti **ravioli stuffed with mozzarella, tomato and ham, usually fried**

parmigiano **parmesan cheese**

pasta **dough**

patate lesse **boiled potatoes**

patate lesse con burro e prezzemolo **boiled potatoes with butter and parsley**

patatine **chips**

patatine fritte **fried potatoes**

pecorino **hard, white sheep's cheese**

pera **pear**

pesca **peach**

pescespada **swordfish**

pesto: al pesto **sauce of basil, garlic, herbs, cheese and pine nuts**

petti di pollo **chicken breast**

petti di pollo alla bolognese **chicken breast with ham and cheese**

piselli **peas**

pizza **pizza**

pizza capricciosa **pizza with tomatoes, mozzarella and mushrooms**

pizza margherita **pizza with tomatoes and mozzarella**

pizza napoletana **pizza with tomatoes, mozzarella, anchovies**

pizza quattro stagioni **four seasons pizza with a bit of everything**

pizzaiola: alla pizzaiola **with tomatoes, garlic and basil**

pizzoccheri alla valtellinese **buckwheat pasta strips with cabbage, potatoes, butter and melted cheese**

platessa **plaice**

polenta **porridge-like mixture made of maize**

pollo **chicken**

polpette **meatballs**

polpettone **meatloaf**

polpo **octopus**

pomodori **tomatoes**

pompelmo **grapefruit**

porchetta **roast pork**

porri **leeks**

pranzo **Lunch**

prezzemolo **parsley**

prosciutto **ham**

prosciutto crudo **cured ham**

prugne **plums**

punte di asparagi **asparagus tips**

purè di patate **mashed potatoes**

R

rabarbaro **rhubarb**

ragù **bolognese sauce**

ripieno **stuffed**

risi e bisi **rice and peas**

riso **rice**

risotto **rice cooked in stock**

risotto ai funghi **mushroom risotto**

risotto al nero di seppia **black risotto with cuttlefish ink**

risotto alla milanese **risotto with saffron**

robiola **creamy mild cheese**

rognone trifolato **kidney pieces cooked in oil, garlic and parsley**

rognoni **kidneys**

rosmarino **rosemary**

S

salmone salmon
salsa sauce
salsa di mela apple sauce
salsiccia sausage
saltimbocca alla romana veal stuffed
  with sage and ham and fried
salvia sage
scaloppine small slices of veal
scamorza alla brace melted
  scamorza cheese
scampi scampi
sedano celery
servizio compreso service included
sogliola alla mugnaia sole cooked in
  flour and butter
soufflé soufflé
spaghetti spaghetti
spaghetti alla carbonara with bacon,
  egg and parmesan
spaghetti alla marinara with garlic,
  basil, anchovies and tomatoes
spaghetti all'amatriciana with
  bacon, pepper and tomatoes
specialità della casa house specials
spezzatino stew, goulash
spicchi (d'aglio) cloves
spinaci spinach
stracciatella clear soup with egg
  beaten into it
strudel apple, nuts and raisins in
  layers of flaky pastry
stufato stew
suppli rice croquettes filled with
  tomato sauce
susine plums

T

tacchino turkey
tagliatelle ribbon pasta
tartufi truffles
tonno tuna fish
torta cake
torta salata savoury flan
tortellini 'hats' of pasta filled
  with meat or cheese
trippa tripe
trota trout

U

uccelli scappati pork kebabs
uova eggs
uova alla fiorentina poached eggs
  served in a bechamel sauce with
  spinach
uova strapazzate scrambled egg
uovo sodo boiled eggs
uva grapes
uvette raisins

V

vapore: al vapore steamed
verdura vegetables
verdura mista mixed vegetables
vitello veal
vitello tonnato cold braised veal
  with tuna mayonnaise
vongole clams

Z

zabaione light fluffy egg dessert
  made with Marsala wine
zampone pig's trotter filled with a
  spicy sausage
zucca pumpkin
zucchine courgettes
zuppa soup
zuppa inglese trifle
zuppa pavese egg soup

sightseeing &activities

✳ at the tourist office

sightseeing and activities

- Do you speak English? — Parla inglese? — *parla eengleze*

- Do you have... — Ha... — *a...*
  - a map of the town? — una pianta della città? — *oona pyanta della cheetta*
  - a list of hotels? — un elenco degli alberghi? — *oon elenko delyi albergee*

- Can you recommend... — Può consigliarmi... — *pwo konseelyarmee...*
  - a cheap hotel? — un albergo economico? — *oon albergo ekonomeeko*
  - a good campsite? — un buon campeggio? — *oon bwon kampejjo*
  - a traditional restaurant? — un ristorante tipico? — *oon reestorante teepeeko*

- Do you have information... — Ha informazioni... — *a eenformatsyonee...*
  - in English? — in inglese? — *een eengleze*
  - about opening times? — sugli orari di apertura? — *sulyee oraree dee apertoora*

- Can you book... — Può prenotarmi... — *pwo prenotarmee...*
  - a hotel room for me? — un albergo? — *oon albergo*
  - this day trip for me? — questa gita giornaliera? — *kwesta jeeta jornalyera*

- Where is... — Dov'è... — *dove...*
  - the old town? — il centro storico? — *eel chentro storiko*
  - the art gallery? — la galleria d'arte? — *la gallereea darte*
  - the ... museum? — il museo... ? — *eel moozeo...*

Is there...	C'è...	che...
a swimming pool	una piscina	*oona pisheena*
a bank	una banca	*oona banka*
a post office	un ufficio postale	*oon uffeecho postale*
...near here?	...qui vicino?	*...kwee veecheeno*
Can you show me on the map?	Può mostrarmelo sulla piantina?	*pwo mostrarmelo soolla pyanteena*

YOU MAY HEAR...

Da dove viene?	*da dove vyene*	Where are you from?
Quanto tempo si ferma?	*kwanto tempo see ferma*	How long are you staying?
Dove alloggia?	*dove allojja*	Where are you staying?
Che tipo di albergo desidera?	*ke teepo dee albergo dezeedera*	What kind of accommodation do you want?
È...	*e...*	It's in...
nel centro storico	*nel chentro storeeko*	the old town
in centro	*een chentro*	the town centre
Deve prendere l'autobus numero...	*deve prendere lowtoboos noomero...*	You have to take bus number...

99

✱ opening times
(see **telling the time,** page 15)

(see **telling the time,** page 15)

YOU MAY WANT TO SAY...

- **What time does the museum/palace...** Il museo/palazzo, a che ora... *eel moozeo/palatso a ke ora...*
  - **open?** apre? *apre*
  - **close?** chiude? *kyoode*

- **When does the exhibition open?** Quando apre la mostra? *kwando apre la mostra*

- **Is it open...** È aperto... *e aperto...*
  - **on Mondays?** il lunedì? *eel loonedee*
  - **at the weekend?** il fine settimana? *eel feene setteemana*

- **Can I/we visit the (monastery)?** Si può visitare il (monastero)? *see pwo veezeetare eel (monastero)*

- **Is it open to the public?** È aperto al pubblico? *e aperto al poobbleeko*

YOU MAY HEAR...

- È aperto tutti i giorni, a parte... | *E aperto toottee ee jornee a parte...* | It's open every day except...
- È aperto dalle... alle... | *e aperto dalle ... alle...* | It's open from... to...
- È chiuso il... | *e kyoozo eel...* | It's closed on...
- È chiuso... | *e kyoozo...* | It's closed for...
  - d'inverno | *deenverno* | the winter
  - per lavori | *per lavoree* | repairs

sightseeing and activities

* visiting places

YOU MAY SEE...

Aperto	Open
Chiuso (per restauri)	Closed (for restoration)
Non toccare	Do not touch
Orario visite	Opening hours
Privato	Private
Vietato fotografare con il flash	No flash photography
Vietato l'ingresso	No entry
Visite guidate	Guided tours

YOU MAY WANT TO SAY...

How much does it cost to get in?	Quanto costa/ Quant'è l'ingresso?	*kwanto kosta/ kwante leengresso*
One adult, please.	Un adulto, per favore.	*oon adoolto per favore*
Two adults, please.	Due adulti, per favore.	*doo-e adooltee per favore*
One adult and two children, please.	Un adulto e due bambini, per favore.	*oon adoolto e doo-e bambeenee per favore*
A family ticket, please.	Un biglietto familiare, per favore.	*oon beelyetto familyare per favore*
Is there a reduction for...	Ci sono sconti per...	*chee sono skontee per...*
students?	studenti?	*stoodentee*
pensioners?	pensionati?	*pensyonatee*
children?	bambini?	*bambeenee*
disabled people?	disabili?	*deezabeelee*

Is there...	C'è...	che...
wheelchair access?	accesso ai disabili?	*achesso iy deezabeelee*
an audio tour?	un'audioguida?	*oonowdyogweeda*
a picnic area?	un'area picnic?	*unarea peekneek*

Are there guided tours (in English)?	Ci sono visite guidate (in inglese)?	*chee sono veezeete gweedate (een eengleze)*

Can I/we take photos?	Si possono fare foto?	*see possono fare foto*

Can you take a photo of us, please?	Ci fa una foto, per favore?	*chee fa oona foto per favore*

When was this built?	Quando è stato/a costruito/a?	*kwando e stato/a costroo-eeto/a*

Who painted that?	Chi e il pittore?	*kee e eel peettore*

How old is it?	Di quando è?	*dee kwando e*

YOU MAY HEAR...

Costa ... euro a testa.	*kosta ... e-ooro a testa*	It costs ... euros per person.
C'è uno sconto per studenti/ anziani.	*che oono skonto per stoodentee/ anzyanee*	There's a reduction for students/ senior citizens.
I bambini sotto i ... entrano gratis.	*ee bambeene sotto ee ... entrano gratees*	Children under ... are free.
Ci sono rampe per sedie a rotelle.	*chee sono rampe per sedye a rotelle*	There are wheelchair ramps.

✳ going on tours and trips

I'd like to join the tour to...	Vorrei unirmi alla gita a...	vorre-ee ooneermee alla *jeeta* a...
What time...	A che ora...	a ke ora...
does it leave?	parte?	parte
does it get back?	torna?	torna
How long is it?	Quanto dura?	kwanto doora
Where does it leave from?	Da dove parte?	da dove parte
Does the guide speak English?	La guida parla inglese?	la gweeda parla eengleze
How much is it?	Quanto costa?	kwanto kosta
Is lunch/ accommodation included?	È incluso il pranzo/ pernottamento?	e eenkloozo eel prantso/ pernottamento
When's the next...	Quando è la prossima...	kwando e la prosseema...
boat trip?	gita in barca?	jeeta een barka
day trip?	gita giornaliera?	jeeta jornalyera
Can we hire...	Si può noleggiare...	si pwo nolejare...
a guide?	una guida?	oona gweeda
an English-speaking guide?	una guida che parla inglese?	oona gweeda ke parla eengleze
How much is it (per day)?	Quanto costa (al giorno)?	kwanto kosta al jorno

I/We'd like to see...	Mi/Ci piacerebbe vedere...	mee/chee pyacherebbe vedere...
I'm with a group.	Sono con un gruppo.	sono kon oon grooppo
I've lost my group.	Ho perso il mio gruppo.	o perso eel meeo grooppo

YOU MAY HEAR...

Parte alle...	parte alle...	It leaves at...
Ritorna alle...	reetorna alle...	It gets back at...
Parte da...	parte da...	It leaves from...
Costa ... al giorno.	kosta ... al jorno	It costs ... per day.
Come si chiama il vostro gruppo?	kome see kyama eel vostro grooppo	What's the name of your group?

✱ entertainment
(see **booking tickets**, page 107)

YOU MAY SEE...

Biglietti per lo spettacolo di oggi	Tickets for today's performance
Circo	Circus
Conservatorio/Sala a concerti	Concert hall
Fila	Row, tier
Ingresso	Entry
Ingresso vietato dopo l'inizio dello spettacolo	No entry once the performance has begun
Ippodromo	Racecourse

entertainment

Non c'è intervallo	No intervals
Palchi	Boxes
Platea	Stalls
Poltrone di platea	Orchestra stalls
Prenotazioni	Advance booking
Prima galleria (gradinata)	Dress circle
Spettacolo continuato	Continuous performance
Spettacolo pomeridiano	Matinee
Spettacolo serale	Evening performance
Teatro	Theatre
Teatro dell'Opera	Opera house
Tribuna	Stand, grandstand
Tutto esaurito	Sold out

YOU MAY WANT TO SAY...

What is there to do in the evenings here?	Cosa c'è da fare qui la sera?	*koza che da fare kwee la sera*
Is there anything for children?	C'è niente per i bambini?	*che nyente per ee bambeenee*
Is there...	C'è...	*che...*
a cinema round here?	un cinema qui vicino?	*oon cheenema kwee veecheeno*
a good nightclub round here?	una discoteca qui vicino?	*oona deeskoteka kwee veecheeno*
What's on...	Cosa danno...	*koza danno...*
tonight?	stasera?	*stasera*
tomorrow?	domani?	*domanee*

sightseeing and activities

105

At the theatre/cinema.	A teatro/Al cinema	*a te-atro/ al cheenema*
Is there a match on this weekend?	C'è la partita questo fine settimana?	*che la parteeta kwesto feene setteemana*
When does the game/performance start?	A che ora comincia la partita/lo spettacolo?	*a ke ora komeencha la parteeta/lo spettakolo*
What time does it finish?	A che ora finisce?	*a ke ora feeneeshe*
How long is it?	Quanto dura?	*kwanto doora*
Do we need to book?	Bisogna prenotare?	*beezonya prenotare*
Where can we buy tickets?	Dove si comprano i biglietti?	*dove see komprano ee beelyettee*
Is it suitable for children?	È adatto ai bambini?	*e adatto a-ee bambeenee*
Has the film got subtitles?	Il film ha i sottotitoli?	*eel feelm a ee sottoteetolee*
Is it dubbed?	È doppiato?	*e doppyato*
Who's singing?	Chi canta?	*kee kanta*
Who's playing? (music)	Chi recita?	*kee recheeta*
Who's playing? (sport)	Chi gioca?	*kee joka*

YOU MAY HEAR...

Può comprare i biglietti qui.	*pwo komprare ee beelyettee kwee*	You can buy tickets here.
Comincia alle...	*komeencha alle...*	It starts at...
Finisce alle...	*feeneeshe alle...*	It finishes at...
È meglio prenotare in anticipo.	*e melyo prenotare een anteecheepo*	It's best to book in advance.
È doppiato.	*e doppyato*	It's dubbed.
Ha i sottotitoli (in inglese).	*a ee sottoteetolee (een eengleze)*	It's got (English) subtitles.

* booking tickets

YOU MAY WANT TO SAY...

Can you get me tickets...	Può comprarmi biglietti...	*pwo komprarmee beelyettee...*
for the ballet?	per il balletto?	*per eel balletto*
for the football match?	per la partita?	*per la parteeta*
for the theatre?	per il teatro?	*per eel te-atro*
Are there any seats for Saturday?	Ci sono biglietti per sabato?	*chee sono beelyettee per sabato*
I'd like to book...	Vorrei prenotare...	*vorre-ee prenotare*
a box	un palco	*oon palko*
two seats	due posti	*doo-e postee*
In the stalls.	In platea.	*een platea*
In the dress circle.	Nella prima galleria.	*nella preema gallereea*

- **Do you have anything cheaper?** — Ha qualcosa di meno caro? — *ha kwalkoza dee meno karo*

- **Is there wheelchair access?** — È accessibile alle sedie a rotelle? — *e achesseebeele alle sedye a rotelle*

YOU MAY HEAR...

- Quanti? — *kwantee* — How many?

- Per quando? — *per kwando* — When for?

- Ha la carta di credito? — *a la karta dee kredeeto* — Do you have a credit card?

- Mi dispiace, è tutto esaurito per quella sera/quel giorno. — *mee deespyache e tootto ezowreeto per kwella sera/kwel jorno* — I'm sorry, we're sold out that night/day.

✱ at the show

YOU MAY WANT TO SAY...

- **What film/play/opera is on tonight?** — Che film/spettacolo/opera date stasera? — *ke feelm/spettakolo/opera date stasera*

- **Two tickets for tonight's performance, please.** — Due biglietti per lo spettacolo di stasera, per favore. — *doo-e beelyettee per lo spettakolo dee stasera per favore*

- **One adult and two children, please.** — Un adulto e due bambini, per favore. — *oon adoolto e doo-e bambeenee per favore*

- **How much is that?** — Quant'è? — *kwante*

We'd like seats...	Vorremmo posti...	*vorremmo postee*
at the front	davanti	*davantee*
at the back	dietro	*dyetro*
in the middle	in mezzo	*een medzo*
We've reserved seats.	Abbiamo posti prenotati.	*abbyamo postee prenotatee*
My name is...	Mi chiamo...	*mee kyamo...*
Is there an interval?	C'è un intervallo?	*che oon intervallo*
Where's...	Dov'è...	*dove...*
the dress circle?	la prima galleria	*la preema gallereea*
the bar?	il bar?	*eel bar*
Where are the toilets?	Dov'è la toilette?	*dove la twalett*
Can you stop talking, please?	Può stare zitto, per favore?	*pwo stare dzitto per favore*

✳ sports and activities

Abbonamenti	Season tickets
Campo da tennis	Tennis court
Campo di calcio	Football ground
Campo di golf	Golf course
Centro sportivo	Sports hall
Divieto di balneazione/ Vietato fare il bagno	No swimming
Divieto di pesca	No fishing
Funivia	Cable car
Noleggio	For hire

sports and activities

Noleggio sci/Affito sci	Ski hire
Pericolo	Danger
Pericolo di valanghe	Avalanche danger
Piscina	Swimming pool
Pista di sci	Ski run
Pronto soccorso	First Aid
Scuola di sci	Ski school
Seggiovia	Chair lift
Spiaggia	Beach
Vietato l'accesso	No entrance

YOU MAY WANT TO SAY...

- **Can I/we...** — Si può... — *see pwo...*
  - **go riding?** — andare a cavallo? — *andare a kavallo*
  - **go fishing?** — pescare? — *peskare*
  - **go skiing?** — sciare? — *shee-are*
  - **go swimming?** — nuotare? — *nwotare*

- **Where can I/we...** — Dove si può... — *dove see pwo...*
  - **play tennis?** — giocare a tennis? — *jokare a tennees*
  - **play golf?** — giocare a golf? — *jokare a golf*

- **I'm...** — Sono... — *sono...*
  - **a beginner** — un principiante — *oon preencheepyante*
  - **quite experienced** — abbastanza esperto — *abbastantsa esperto*

- **How much does it cost...** — Quanto costa... — *kwanto kosta...*
  - **per hour?** — all'ora? — *allora*
  - **per day?** — al giorno? — *al jorno*
  - **per week?** — alla settimana? — *alla setteemana*
  - **per round?** — per giro? — *per geero*

sightseeing and activities

- **Can I/we hire...** Si possono noleggiare... *see possono nolejare...*

    equipment? attrezzatura? *attretsatoora*
    clubs? mazze? *matse*
    rackets? racchette? *rakette*

- **Can I/we have lessons?** Si possono avere lezioni? *see possono avere letsyonee*

- **Do I/we have to be a member?** Bisogna essere soci? *bizonya essere sochee*

- **Can children do it too?** Possono farlo anche i bambini? *possono farlo anke ee bambeenee*

- **Is there a reduction for children?** Ci sono sconti per i bambini? *chee sono skontee per ee bambeenee*

- **What's...** Com'è... *come...*
    the water like? l'acqua? *lakkwa*
    the snow like? la neve? *la neve*

YOU MAY HEAR...

- Costa ... euro all'ora. *kosta ... e-ooro allora* It costs ... euros per hour.

- C'è un deposito rimborsabile di ... euro. *che oon depozeeto reemborsabeele dee ... e-ooro* There's a refundable deposit of ... euros.

- Abbiamo posti disponibili domani. *abbyamo postee deesponeebeelee domanee* We've got places tomorrow.

- Che taglia ha? *ke talya a* What size are you?

Serve...	*serve...*	You need...
una foto	*oona foto*	a photo
l'assicurazione	*lassikooratsyone*	insurance

✳ at the beach, lake or pool

YOU MAY WANT TO SAY...

Can I/we...	Si può...	*see pwo...*
swim here?	nuotare qui?	*nwotare kwee*
swim in the river?	nuotare nel fiume?	*nwotare nel fyoome*
Is it dangerous?	È pericoloso?	*e pereekolozo*
Is it safe for children?	È sicuro per i bambini?	*e seekooro per ee bambeenee*
When is high tide?	A che ora è l'alta marea?	*a ke ora e lalta marea*
Is the water clean?	È pulita l'acqua?	*e pooleeta lakkwa*

YOU MAY HEAR...

Attento/a, è pericoloso.	*attento/a e pereekolozo*	Be careful, it's dangerous.
La corrente è molto forte.	*la korrente e molto forte*	The current is very strong.
C'è molto vento.	*che molto vento*	It's very windy.

shops&services

✳ shopping

In general, shops are open from Monday to Saturday between 8.30am and 7.30pm, with a lunch break between 12.30 and 3.30pm. Food shops tend to be closed on Monday afternoons and other shops on Monday mornings. Fashion shops in town centres might operate from 10am to 6pm. To ask for something in a shop, just name it or point at it and add per favore (please).

YOU MAY SEE...

Abbigliamento	Clothes/Fashions
Abbigliamento sportivo	Sports goods
Alimentari	Groceries
Alimentari biologici	Health foods
Antiquario	Antiques
Aperto	Open
Aperto tutto il giorno	Open all day
Arredamento/Mobili	Furniture
Calzature	Shoe shop
Camerini	Fitting rooms
Cartoleria	Stationer's
Cassa	Cashier
Chiuso	Closed
Dischi	Records
Drogheria	Grocer's/drugstore
Edicola	Newsagent's
Elettrodomestici	Electrical goods
Enoteca	Off licence (Wine shop)
Entrata	Entrance

Farmacia	Chemist's
Farmacia/Medico di turno	Duty chemist/Doctor
Ferramenta	Hardware
Foto-ottica	Photo shop
Fruttivendolo	Greengrocer
Giocattoli	Toy shop
Gioielleria/Gioielliere	Jeweller's
Grandi magazzini	Department store
In offerta	On offer
Libreria	Bookshop
Macelleria/Macellaio	Butcher's
Oggetti regalo	Gift shop/Souvenirs
Orari di apertura	Business hours
Orologiaio	Watchmaker's
Ortolano	Greengrocer
Ottico	Optician
Panificio/Panettiere	Baker's
Parrucchiere	Hairdresser
Pasticceria	Cake shop
Pelletteria	Leather goods
Pescheria/Pescivendolo	Fishmonger's
Posta/Ufficio postale	Post office
Profumeria	Perfumery
Saldi	Sale
Saldi per cessata attività	Closing down sale
Salumiere	Delicatessen
Self service	Self-service shop
Si prega di non toccare	Please do not touch
Souvenir	Souvenirs
Supermercato	Supermarket
Tabaccaio/Tabaccheria	Tobacconist

shopping

Tintoria/Lavasecco	Dry cleaner's
Uscita (di sicurezza)	(Emergency) exit
Vietata l'uscita	No exit
Vietato l'ingresso	No entry

YOU MAY WANT TO SAY...

Where is...	Dov'è...	*dove...*
the main shopping street?	la via principale con i negozi?	*la **vee**-a preench-eepale kon ee negozee*
the post office?	la posta?	*la **posta***
Where can I buy...	Dove posso comprare...	*dove **posso** komprare...*
walking boots?	scarponi?	*skar**po**nee*
a map?	una piantina?	*oona pyan**tee**na*
I'd like ... please.	Vorrei ... per favore	*vorre-ee ... per favore*
that one there	quello	***kwello***
this one here	questo	***kwesto***
two of those	due di quelli	***doo*-e dee kwellee**
Have you got...?	Ha... ?	*a...*
How much does it cost?	Quanto costa?	***kwanto kosta***
How much do they cost?	Quanto costano?	***kwanto kostano***
Can you write it down, please?	Può scrivermelo, per favore?	*pwo **skree**vermelo per favore*
I'm just looking.	Sto solo guardando.	*sto **solo** gwar**dando***

shops and services

116

There's one in the window.	C'è n'è uno in vetrina.	*che ne **oo**no een ve**tree**na*
I'll take it.	Lo prendo.	*lo **prend**o*
Is there a guarantee?	C'è una garanzia?	*che **oo**na garan**tsi**a*
Can you... keep it for me? order it for me?	Può... riservarmelo? ordinarmelo?	*pwo... reezer**varm**elo ordee**narm**elo*
I/We need to think about it.	Devo/Dobbiamo pensarci.	***de**vo/dobb**ya**mo pen**sarch**ee*

YOU MAY HEAR...

Dica./Posso aiutarla?	***dee**ka/**po**sso iyoo**tarl**a*	Can I help you?
Costa ... euro.	***ko**sta ... e-**oo**ro*	It costs ... euros.
Mi dispiace, è tutto esaurito.	*mee dee**spya**che, e **too**tto ezow**ree**to*	I'm sorry, we've sold out.
Posso ordinarlo/la, se desidera.	***po**sso ordee**narl**o/la se de**zee**dera*	We can order it for you.

✶ paying

YOU MAY WANT TO SAY...

Where do I pay?	Dove si paga?	***do**ve see **pa**ga*
Do you take credit cards?	Accettate carte di credito?	*ache**tate karte** dee **kre**deeto*

shops and services

117

buying clothes and shoes

Can you wrap it, please?	Me lo incarta, per favore?	*me lo eenkarta per favore*
Can I have ... please?	Posso avere ... per favore?	*posso avere ... per favore*
the receipt	la ricevuta	*la reechevoota*
a bag	un sacchetto	*oon sakketto*
my change	il resto	*eel resto*
Sorry, I haven't got any change.	Mi dispiace, non ho spiccioli.	*mee dispyache, non o speecholee*

YOU MAY HEAR...

Glielo incarto?	*lyelo eenkarto*	Do you want it wrapped?
Come desidera pagare?	*kome dezeedera pagare*	How do you want to pay?
Posso vedere ... per favore?	*posso vedere ... per favore*	Can I see ... please?
un documento di identità	*oon dokoomento dee eedenteeta*	some ID
il suo passaporto	*eel soo-o passaporto*	your passport

✳ buying clothes and shoes
(see clothes and shoe sizes, page 21)

YOU MAY WANT TO SAY...

| I'm size... | Porto la... | *porto la...* |

- Have you got... | Ha... | a...
  the bigger size? | la taglia più grande? | *la **tal**ya pyoo **gran**de*
  the smaller size? | la taglia più piccola? | *la **tal**ya pyoo **peek**kola*
  another colour? | un altro colore? | *oon **al**tro ko**lore***

- What size is this in British sizes? | A che taglia inglese equivale? | *a ke **tal**ya een**gle**ze ek**wee**vale*

- I'm looking for... | Cercavo... | *cher**ka**vo...*
  a shirt | una camicia | *oona ka**mee**cha*
  a pair of jeans | un paio di jeans | *oon **pa**yo dee **jeenz***
  a jumper | un maglione | *oon mal**yo**ne*
  a jacket | una giacca | *oona **jak**ka*
  a skirt | una gonna | *oona **gon**na*
  a t-shirt | una maglietta | *oona mal**yet**ta*
  a hat | un cappello | *oon kap**pel**lo*

- A pair of... | Un paio di... | *oon **pi**yo dee...*
  trainers | scarpe da ginnastica | ***skar**pe da geen**nas**teeka*
  shoes | scarpe | ***skar**pe*
  sandals | sandali | ***san**dalee*
  trousers | pantaloni | *panta**lo**nee*
  boots | stivali | *stee**va**lee*

* changing rooms

- Where are the changing rooms, please? | Dove sono i camerini, per favore? | ***do**ve **so**no ee kame**ree**nee per fa**vo**re*

exchanges and refunds

Can I try this on, please?	Posso provarlo/la, per favore?	*posso provarlo/la per favore*
It doesn't fit.	Non mi va bene.	*non mee va bene*
It's too big/small.	È troppo grande/piccolo/a.	*e troppo grande/peekkolo/a*
It doesn't suit me.	Non mi sta bene.	*non mee sta bene*

YOU MAY HEAR...

Vuole provarlo/la?	*vwole provarlo/la*	Would you like to try it on?
Che taglia ha?	*ke talya a*	What size are you?
Gliene prendo un altro.	*lyene prendo oon altro*	I'll get you another one.
Mi dispiace, era l'ultimo/a.	*mee deespyache era loolteemo/a*	Sorry, that's the last one.
Le sta/stanno bene.	*le sta/stanno bene*	It suits/They suit you.

* exchanges and refunds

YOU MAY WANT TO SAY...

Excuse me, this is faulty.	Mi scusi, è difettoso/a.	*mee skoozee e deefettozo/a*
Excuse me, this doesn't fit.	Mi scusi, non va bene.	*mee skoozee non va bene*
I'd like a refund.	Vorrei un rimborso.	*vorre-ee oon reemborso*

- I'd like...   Vorrei...   *vorre-ee...*
  - **to return this**   renderlo/la   *renderlo/la*
  - **to change this**   cambiarlo/la   *kambyarlo/la*

YOU MAY HEAR...

- Ha...   a...   **Have you got...**
  - la ricevuta?   *la reechevoota*   **the receipt?**
  - la garanzia?   *la garantseea*   **the guarantee?**

- Mi dispiace, ma non facciamo rimborsi.   *mee deespyache ma non fachamo reemborsee*   **Sorry, we don't give refunds.**

- Lo può cambiare.   *lo pwo kambyare*   **You can exchange it.**

✷ bargaining

YOU MAY WANT TO SAY...

- **Is this your best price?**   È questo il suo ultimo prezzo?   *e kwesto eel soo-o oolteemo pretso*

- **It's too expensive.**   È troppo caro.   *e troppo karo*

- **Is there a reduction for cash?**   Mi fa uno sconto se pago in contanti?   *mee fa oono skonto se pago een kontantee*

- **I'll give you...**   Le do...   *le do...*

- **That's my final offer.**   Questa è la mia ultima offerta.   *kwesta e la meea oolteema offerta*

✳ at the drugstore
(see **at the chemist's**, page 134)

● For toiletries and cosmetics, you need a drogheria (drugstore). You can find some toiletries and cosmetics at a chemist's (farmacia) but these are usually medicated or for special conditions such as delicate skins or allergies.

YOU MAY WANT TO SAY...

● I need...	Ho bisogno di...	o beezonyo dee...
a shampoo	uno shampoo	oono shampoo
some shower gel	un gel doccia	oon jel docha
a deodorant	un deodorante	oon deodorante
a moisturising cream	una crema idratante	oona krema eedratante
some toothpaste	un dentrificio	oon denteefreecho
tampons	assorbenti interni	assorbentee eenternee
sanitary towels	assorbenti esterni	assorbentee esternee
toilet paper	carta igienica	karta eejeneeka
some aftersun cream	una crema doposole	oona krema doposole
some mascara	un mascara	oon maskara
a perfume	un profumo	oon profoomo
a (pink) nail varnish	uno smalto (rosa)	oono zmalto (roza)
some make-up remover	del latte detergente	del latte deterjente
some toner	del tonico	del toneeko
some foundation	del fondotinta	del fondoteenta

- I am looking for...   Cercavo...   *cherkavo...*
- I'd like...   Vorrei...   *vorre-ee...*

✳ photography

YOU MAY WANT TO SAY...

- Can you develop this film for me?   Mi sviluppa questo rullino, per favore.   *mee zveelooppa kwesto rooleeno per favore*

- I have a digital camera.   Ho una macchina fotografica digitale.   *o oona makkeena fotografeeka deegeetale*

- Can you print from this (memory stick)?   Può stamparmi questa (scheda di memoria).   *pwo stamparmee kwesta (skeda dee memorya)*

- When will it/they be ready?   Quando sarà/saranno pronti?   *kwando sara/saranno prontee*

- Do you have an express service?   Ha un servizio espresso?   *a oon serveetsyo espresso*

- Does it cost extra?   C'è un sovrapprezzo?   *che oon sovrappretso*

- I need...   Mi serve...   *mee serve...*
    - a colour film   una pellicola a colori   *oona pelleekola a koloree*
    - a black and white film   una pellicola in bianco e nero   *oona pelleekola een byanko e nero*
    - a memory stick   una scheda di memoria   *oona skeda dee memorya*

123

- **How much does it cost...** — Quanto costa... — *kwanto kosta...*
    - **per film?** — ogni rullino? — *onyee roolleeno*
    - **per print?** — ogni stampa? — *onyee stampa*

- **I'd like...** — Vorrei... — *vorre-ee...*
    - **a 24 exposure film, please** — un rullino da 24 foto, per favore — *oon roolleeno da venteekwattro foto per favore*
    - **a 36 exposure film** — un rullino da 36 foto — *oon roolleeno da trentase-ee foto*
    - **a disposable camera** — una macchina fotografica usa e getta — *oona makkeena fotografeeka ooza e jetta*

- **My camera is broken.** — Mi si è rotta la macchina fotografica. — *mee see e rotta la makkeena fotografeeka*

- **Do you do repairs?** — Fate riparazioni? — *fate reeparatsyonee*

YOU MAY HEAR...

- In che formato vuole le foto? — *een ke formato vwole le foto* — **What size do you want your prints?**

- Le vuole su carta opaca o lucida? — *le vwole soo karta opaka o lucheeda* — **Do you want them matt or glossy?**

- Torni... — *tornee...* — **Come back...**
    - domani — *domanee* — tomorrow
    - tra un'ora — *tra oonora* — in an hour

- Quante foto vuole? — *kwante foto vwole* — **How many exposures do you want?**

✳ at the tobacconist

● For cigarettes and stamps go to a tabaccaio, the sign for which is a white T on a black background. It might also sell lottery tickets and bus tickets. For scratch cards go to a newsagent.

YOU MAY WANT TO SAY...

● Can I have a packet of... ?

Posso avere un pacchetto di... ?

posso a**ve**re oon pak**ket**to dee...

● Do you have...
matches?
lighters?
cigars?

Avete...
dei fiammiferi?
degli accendini?
sigari?

avete...
de-ee fyam**mee**feree
dely achen**dee**nee
seegaree

● A stamp/Five stamps, please...

Un francobollo/
Cinque francobolli,
per favore...

oon franko**bo**llo/
cheenkwe franko**bo**llee
per fa**vo**re...

for Great Britain
for America

per la Gran Bretagna
per l'America

per la gran bre**ta**nya
per la**me**rika

✳ at the post office

● Major post offices are open from 8.30am to 5.00pm on Monday to Friday and sometimes on Saturday mornings. Post boxes are usually red, but there are some yellow ones. For a small extra charge, you can get a quicker postal service with posta prioritaria. If you only want stamps, you can get them at the tobacconist (tabaccaio – see above), and sometimes at hotels or at newspaper kiosks that sell postcards.

shops and services

YOU MAY WANT TO SAY...

A stamp/Five stamps, please...	Un francobollo/ Cinque francobolli, per favore...	oon frankobollo/ cheenkwe frankobolee per favore...
for Great Britain	per la Gran Bretagna	per la gran bretanya
for the US	per gli Stati Uniti	per lee statee ooneetee
Can I send this... registered, please? airmail, please?	Posso spedirla... raccomandata, per favore? via aerea, per favore?	posso spedeerla... rakkomandata per favore veea aerea per favore
It contains...	Contiene...	kontyene...
Do you change money here?	Cambiate valuta qui?	kambyate valoota kwee
Can I have a receipt, please?	Posso avere una ricevuta, per favore?	posso avere oona reechevoota per favore

YOU MAY HEAR...

La metta sulla bilancia?	la metta soolla beelancha	Put it on the scales, please.
Cosa c'è dentro?	koza che dentro	What's in it?
Per favore, riempia questa dichiarazione per la dogana.	per favore, ree-empya kwesta deekyaratsyone per la dogana	Please fill in this customs declaration form.

✳ at the bank

● Banks are open on weekdays from 8.30am to 1.30pm and from 3.30 to 4.30pm.

YOU MAY WANT TO SAY...

● Excuse me, where's the foreign exchange counter?
Mi scusi, dov'è lo sportello per il cambio?
mee skoozee dove lo sportello per eel kambyo

● Is there a cashpoint machine here?
C'è un bancomat qui?
che oon bankomat kwee

● The cashpoint machine has eaten my card.
Il bancomat ha trattenuto la mia carta.
eel bankomat a trattenooto la meea karta

● I've forgotten my PIN.
Ho dimenticato il codice segreto.
o deementeekato eel kodeeche segreto

● Can I check my account, please?
Mi controlla il conto, per favore?
mee kontrolla eel konto per favore

● My account number is...
Il mio numero di conto è...
eel meeo noomero dee konto e...

● My name is...
Mi chiamo...
mee kyamo...

● I'd like to...
Vorrei...
vorre-ee...

    withdraw some money
    prelevare
    prelevare

    pay some money in
    versare
    versare

    cash this cheque
    incassare questo assegno
    eenkassare kwesto assenyo

● Has my money arrived yet?
Sono arrivati i miei soldi?
sono arreevatee ee mye-ee soldee

shops and services

127

changing money

YOU MAY HEAR...

Un documento d'identità, per favore.	*oon dokoomento dee eedenteeta per favore*	Your ID, please.
Passaporto, per favore.	*passaporto per favore*	Passport, please.
Il suo saldo è...	*eel soo-o saldo e...*	Your balance is...
È in rosso di...	*e een rosso dee...*	You're overdrawn by...

✳ changing money

● The Italian unit of currency is the euro (euro), abbreviated to €. It is divided into 100 cents (centesimi).

YOU MAY WANT TO SAY...

Can I get money out on my credit card?	Posso prelevare con la mia carta di credito?	*posso prelevare kon la meea karta dee kredeeto*
Can I have ... please?	Posso avere ... per favore?	*posso avere ... per favore*
small notes	banconote da piccolo taglio	*bankonote da peekkolo talyo*
new notes	banconote nuove	*bankonote nwove*
some change	spiccioli	*speecholee*
What's the rate today...	Quant'è oggi il cambio...	*kwante ojee eel kambyo...*
for the pound?	della sterlina?	*della sterleena*
for the dollar?	del dollaro?	*del dollaro*
for the euro?	dell'euro?	*delle-ooro*

✳ telephones

● To call abroad from Italy, first dial 00 and then the code for the country – for the UK it is 44 – followed by the area code (minus the first 0) and then the number you want. For calls in Italy, the area code, inclusive of the 0, is now an integral part of the telephone number.

YOU MAY WANT TO SAY...

● Have you got change for the phone, please?	Avete moneta per il telefono, per favore?	*avete moneta per eel telefono per favore*
● The number is...	Il numero è...	*eel noomero e...*
● How much does it cost per minute?	Quanto costa al minuto?	*kwanto kosta al meenooto*
● I'd like to...	Vorrei...	*vorre-ee...*
buy a phone card	comprare una scheda telefonica	*komprare oona skeda telefoneeka*
call England	chiamare l'Inghilterra	*kyamare leengeelterra*
make a reverse charge call	fare una chiamata a carico del destinatario	*fare oona kyamata a kareeko del desteenataryo*
● What's the area code for...?	Qual'è il prefisso per... ?	*kwale eel prefeesso per...*
● What's the country code for..?	Qual'è il prefisso internazionale per... ?	*kwale eel prefeesso eenternatsyonale per...*
● Can I have an outside line?	Posso avere la linea?	*posso avere la leene-a*

telephones

Hello.	Pronto.	*pronto*
It's ... speaking	Sono...	*sono...*
Can I have extension... please?	Posso avere l'interno ... per favore?	*posso avere leenterno ... per favore*
Can I speak to...?	Posso parlare con... ?	*posso parlare kon...*
When will he/she be back?	Quando rientra?	*kwando ryentra*
I'll ring back.	Richiamerò.	*reekyamero*
Can I leave a message?	Posso lasciare un messaggio?	*posso lashare oon messajjo*
Can you say ... called?	Può dire che ha chiamato... ?	*pwo deere ke a kyamato...*
My number is...	Il mio numero è...	*eel meeo noomero e..*
Sorry, I've got the wrong number.	Mi dispiace, ho sbagliato numero.	*mee deespyache o sbalyato noomero*
It's a bad line.	La linea è disturbata.	*la leenea e deestoorbata*
I've been cut off.	È caduta la linea.	*e kadoota la leenea*

YOU MAY HEAR...

Pronto.	*pronto*	Hello.
Chi parla?	*kee parla*	Who's calling?
Mi dispiace, non c'è.	*mee dispyache non che*	I'm sorry, he/she's not here.
È occupato.	*e okkoopato*	It's engaged.

shops and services

| Non risponde. | non reesponde | There's no answer. |
| Mi dispiace, ha sbagliato numero. | mee deespyache a sbalyato noomero | Sorry, you've got the wrong number. |

✳ mobiles

● Mobile phones (cellulari or telefonini) are very popular in Italy and there are several companies who offer a temporary or prepaid account if you own a GSM, bi- or triband mobile.

YOU MAY WANT TO SAY...

Have you got...	Ha...	a...
a charger for this phone?	un caricatore per questo cellulare?	oon kareekatore per kwesto chelloolare
a SIM card for the local network?	una carta SIM per la rete locale?	oona karta seem per la rete lokale
a pay-as-you-go phone?	un telefonino a scheda?	oon telefoneeno a skeda
What's the tariff?	Quant'è la tariffa?	quante la tareeffa
Are text messages included?	Sono inclusi i messaggi?	sono eenkloozee e messajee
How do you make a local call?	Come si fa una chiamata locale?	kome see fa oona kyamata lokale
Is there a code?	C'è un codice?	che oon kodeeche
How do you send text messages?	Come si mandano i messaggi?	kome see mandano ee messajee

✳ the internet

- I'd like to...
  log on
  check my
  emails

  Vorrei...
  collegarmi
  controllare le mie
  e-mail

  vorre-ee...
  kollegarmee
  kontrollare le
  mee-e eeme-eel

- How much is it
  per minute?

  Quanto costa al
  minuto?

  kwanto kosta al
  meenooto

- I can't...
  get in
  log on

  Non posso...
  accedere
  collegarmi

  non posso...
  achedere
  kollegarmee

- It's not
  connecting.

  Non c'è la
  connessione.

  non che la
  konnessyone

- It's very slow.

  È molto lento.

  e molto lento

- Can you...
  print this?
  scan this?

  Può...
  stamparmelo?
  scansionarlo?

  pwo...
  stamparmelo
  scansyonarlo

- Do you have...
  a CD rom?
  a zip drive?
  a UBS lead?

  Avete...
  un CD rom?
  uno zip drive?
  un cavo UBS?

  avete...
  oon chee-dee-rom
  oono zeep drive
  oon kavo oo-b-s

✳ faxes

- What's your fax
  number?

  Qual è il suo numero
  di fax?

  kwale eel soo-o
  noomero dee fax

- Can you send this
  fax for me, please?

  Può spedire questo
  fax, per favore?

  pwo spedeere kwesto
  fax, per favore

- How much is it?

  Quant'è?

  kwante

health&safety

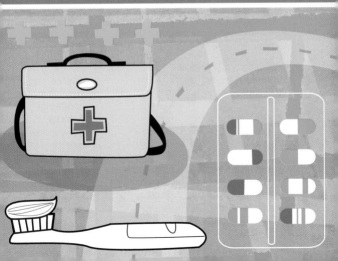

✱ at the chemist's
(see **at the drugstore**, page 122)

● The sign for a *farmacia* (chemist) is a red cross in a circle outside. Chemist shops sell mainly medicines; you can find baby products and cosmetics, too, but for these it's usually better to go to a *drogheria* (drugstore).

YOU MAY WANT TO SAY...

● Have you got something for...	Ha qualcosa per...	*a kwalkoza per...*
sunburn?	scottature?	*skottatoore*
diarrhoea?	diarrea?	*dee-arre-a*
period pains?	dolori mestruali?	*doloree mestrwalee*
headaches?	mal di testa?	*mal dee testa*
stomach ache?	mal di stomaco?	*mal dee stomako*
a sore throat?	mal di gola?	*mal dee gola*
● I need some ... please	Per favore, ho bisogno di...	*per favore o beezonyo dee...*
aspirin	aspirina	*aspeereena*
plasters	cerotti	*cherottee*
painkillers	analgesici	*analjezeechee*
insect repellent	spray antizanzare	*spriy anteedzandzare*
suntan lotion	crema da sole	*krema da sole*
travel sickness pills	pillole per il mal d'auto	*peellole per eel mal dowto*
condoms	preservativi	*preservateevee*

✱ at the doctor's
(see **medical complaints and conditions** page 137)

YOU MAY WANT TO SAY...

I need a doctor (who speaks English).	Ho bisogno di un medico (che parli inglese).	*o beezonyo dee oon medeeko (ke parlee eengleze)*
Can I make an appointment?	Posso prendere un appuntamento?	*posso prendere oon appoontamento*
I've run out of my medication.	Ho finito la mia medicina.	*o feeneeto la mee-a medeecheena*
I'm on medication for...	Sono in cura per...	*sono een koora per...*
I've been vaccinated against...	Mi sono vaccinato contro...	*mee sono vacheenato kontro...*
tetanus	il tetano	*eel tetano*
typhoid	il tifo	*eel teefo*
rabies	la rabbia	*la rabbya*
He/She has been vaccinated against...	È stato/a vaccinato/a contro...	*e stato vacheenato/a kontro...*
polio	la poliomelite	*la polyomeleete*
measles	il morbillo	*eel morbeello*
mumps	gli orecchioni	*ly orekkyonee*
Can I have a receipt for my health insurance, please?	Posso avere una ricevuta per l'assicurazione, per favore?	*posso avere oona reechevoota per lasseekooratsyone per favore*

health and safety

135

* describing your symptoms

● To indicate where the pain is you can simply point and say Mi fa male qui (It hurts here). Otherwise you'll need to look up the Italian for the appropriate part of the body, see page 139.

YOU MAY WANT TO SAY...

● I don't feel well.	Non sto bene.	*non sto **bene***
● It's my...	È il...	*e eel...*
● It hurts here.	Mi fa male qui.	*mee fa **male** kwee*

● My ... hurts.
    stomach
    head
	Mi fa male...
	lo stomaco
	la testa
		*mee fa **male**...
		lo **stom**ako
		la **testa***

● My ... hurt.
    ears
    feet
	Mi fanno male...
	le orecchie
	i piedi
		*mee **fanno male**...
		le o**rekk**ye
		ee **pye**dee*

● I feel...
    sick
    dizzy
	Ho...
	la nausea
	le vertigini
		*o...
		la **now**zea
		le ver**tee**jeenee*

● I can't...
    breathe properly
    sleep properly
	Non riesco a...
	respirare
	dormire
		*non **ryes**ko a...
		respee**ra**re
		dor**mee**re*

● I've cut/burnt myself.	Mi sono tagliato/scottato.	*mee **so**no tal**ya**to/ **skotta**to*
● I've been sick.	Ho vomitato.	*o vomee**ta**to*

✻ medical complaints and conditions

I am...	Sono...	*sono...*
asthmatic	asmatico/a	*asmateeko/a*
blind	cieco/a	*cheko/a*
deaf	sordo/a	*sordo/a*
diabetic	diabetico/a	*dyabeteeko/a*
epileptic	epilettico/a	*epeeletteeko*
HIV positive	HIV positivo	*HIV pozeeteevo*
pregnant	incinta	*eencheenta*
a wheelchair user	disabile	*deezabeele*
I have difficulty walking.	Ho difficoltà a camminare.	*o deefeekolta a camminare*
I have high/low blood pressure.	Ho la pressione alta/bassa.	*o la pressyone alta/bassa*
I have a heart condition.	Soffro di cuore.	*soffro dee kwore*
I am allergic...	Sono allergico/a...	*sono allerjeeko/a...*
to antibiotics	agli antibiotici	*alyee anteebyoteechee*
to penicillin	alla penicillina	*alla peneecheelleena*
to cortisone	al cortisone	*al korteezone*
I suffer from...	Soffro di...	*soffro dee...*
hay fever	raffreddore da fieno	*raffreddore da fyeno*
angina	angina	*anjeena*
arthritis	artrite	*artreete*
migraines	emicrania	*emeekranya*

health and safety

137

medical complaints and conditions

YOU MAY HEAR...

Dove le fa male?	*dove le fa male*	Where does it hurt?
Prende medicine?	*prende medeecheene*	Are you on medication?
È allergico a qualcosa?	*e allerjeeko a kwalkoza*	Are you allergic to anything?
Quanti anni ha?	*kwantee annee a*	How old are you?
Devo provarle la febbre.	*devo provarle la febbre*	I need to take your temperature.
Si svesta, per favore.	*see svesta per favore*	Get undressed, please.
Si sdrai lì, per favore.	*see zdriy lee per favore*	Lie down there, please.
Non è niente di serio.	*non e nyente dee seryo*	It's nothing serious.
Ha un'infezione.	*a oon eenfetsyone*	You've got an infection.
È infetto/a.	*e infetto/a*	It's infected.
Ho bisogno di un campione di sangue/urina/feci	*o beezonyo dee oon kampyone dee sangwe/ooreena/fechee*	I need a blood/urine/stool sample
Ha bisogno di raggi X.	*a beezonyo dee rajee eeks*	You need an X-ray.
Le faccio...	*le facho...*	I'm going to give you...
un'iniezione	*oon eenyetsyone*	an injection
una ricetta	*oona reechetta*	a prescription

La prenda ... volte al giorno.	*la prenda ... volte al jorno*	Take this ... times a day.
Deve riposare.	*deve reepozare*	You must rest.
Non deve bere.	*non deve bere*	You mustn't drink.
Deve andare all'ospedale.	*deve andare allospedale*	You need to go to hospital.
Ha slogato...	*a slogato...*	You've sprained your...
Ha rotto...	*a rotto*	You've broken your...
Ha...	*a...*	You've got...
l'influenza	*leenfloo-entsa*	'flu
l'appendicite	*lappendeecheete*	appendicitis
la bronchite	*la bronkeete*	bronchitis
È un infarto.	*e ooneenfarto*	It's a heart attack.

* parts of the body

ankle	la caviglia	*la kaveelya*
appendix	l'appendice	*lappendeeche*
arm	il braccio	*eel bracho*
artery	l'arteria	*larterya*
back	la schiena	*la skyena*
bladder	la vescica	*la vesheeka*
blood	il sangue	*eel sangwe*
body	il corpo	*eel korpo*
bone	l'osso	*losso*
bottom	il sedere	*eel sedere*

bowels	l'intestino	*leentesteeno*
breast	il seno	*eel seno*
buttock	la natica	*la nateeka*
cartilage	la cartilagine	*la karteelajeene*
chest	il torace	*eel torache*
chin	il mento	*eel mento*
collar bone	l'osso del collo	*losso del kollo*
ear	l'orecchio	*lorekkyo*
elbow	il gomito	*eel gomeeto*
eye	l'occhio	*lokkyo*
face	la faccia/il viso	*la facha/eel veezo*
finger	il dito	*eel deeto*
foot	il piede	*eel pyede*
genitals	i genitali	*ee jeneetalee*
gland	la ghiandola	*la gee-andola*
hair	i capelli	*ee kapellee*
hand	la mano	*la mano*
head	la testa	*la testa*
heart	il cuore	*eel kwore*
heel	il calcagno	*eel kalkanyo*
hip	il fianco	*eel fyanko*
jaw	la mandibola	*la mandeebola*
joint	l'articolazione	*larteekolatsyone*
kidney	i reni	*ee renee*
knee	il ginocchio	*eel jeenokkyo*
leg	la gamba	*la gamba*
ligament	il legamento	*eel legamento*
lip	il labbro	*eel labbro*
liver	il fegato	*eel fegato*
lung	il polmone	*eel polmone*
mouth	la bocca	*la bokka*
muscle	il muscolo	*eel mooskolo*
nail	l'unghia	*loongya*
neck	il collo	*eel kollo*

nerve	il nervo	eel **nervo**
nose	il naso	eel **naso**
penis	il pene	eel **pene**
private parts	gli organi sessuali	lyee **organee** sessualee
rib	la costola	la **kostola**
shoulder	la spalla	la **spalla**
skin	la pelle	la **pelle**
spine	la spina dorsale	la **speena** dorsale
stomach	lo stomaco	lo **stomako**
tendon	il tendine	eel **tendeene**
testicle	il testicolo	eel **testeekolo**
thigh	la coscia	la **kosha**
throat	la gola	la **gola**
thumb	il pollice	eel **polleeche**
toe	il dito del piede	eel **deeto** del **pyede**
tongue	la lingua	la **leengwa**
tonsils	le tonsille	le **tonseelle**
tooth	il dente	eel **dente**
vagina	la vagina	la **vajeena**
vein	la vena	la **vena**
wrist	il polso	eel **polso**

✳ at the dentist's

YOU MAY WANT TO SAY...

● I need a dentist (who speaks English).	Ho bisogno di un dentista (che parli inglese).	o beezonyo dee oon denteesta (ke parlee eengleze)
● I've got toothache.	Ho mal di denti.	o mal dee dentee
● It really hurts.	Mi fa davvero male.	mee fa davvero male

at the dentist's

It's my wisdom tooth.	È il dente del giudizio.	*e eel dente del judeetsyo*
I've lost...	Ho perso...	*o perso...*
a filling	un'otturazione	*oon ottooratsyonee*
a crown/cap	una capsula	*oona kapsoola*
I've broken a tooth.	Ho rotto un dente.	*o rotto oon dente*
Can you fix it temporarily?	Può curarlo in modo provvisorio?	*pwo koorarlo een modo provveezoryo*
How much will it cost?	Quanto costerà?	*kwanto kostera*

YOU MAY HEAR...

Apra bene.	*apra bene*	Open wide.
Chiuda bene.	*kyooda bene*	Close firmly.
Ha bisogno di un'otturazione.	*a beezonyo dee oon ottooratsyone*	You need a filling.
Devo estrarlo.	*devo estrarlo*	I'll have to take it out.
Le faccio...	*le facho...*	I'm going to give you...
un'iniezione	*oon eenyetsyone*	an injection
un'otturazione provvisoria	*oon ottooratsyone provveezorya*	a temporary filling
una capsula provvisoria	*oona capsoola provveezorya*	a temporary crown

142

* emergencies

● In an emergency, you can dial 113 and ask to be put through to la Polizia (Police), i Carabinieri (Military Police), un'ambulanza (Ambulance) or i Vigili del fuoco (Fire Brigade).

YOU MAY WANT TO SAY...

I need... a doctor an ambulance the fire brigade the police	Ho bisogno... di un medico di un' ambulanza dei vigili del fuoco della polizia	o beezonyo... dee oon medeeko dee oon amboolantsa de-ee veejeelee del fwoko della poleetsee-a
● Immediately!	Subito!	soobeeto
● It's very urgent!	È molto urgente!	e molto oorjente
● Help!	Aiuto!	iyooto
● Please help me/us!	Per favore mi/ci aiuti!	per favore mee/chee iyootee
● There's a fire.	C'è un incendio.	che oon eenchendyo
● There's been an accident.	C'è stato un incidente.	che stato oon eencheedente
● I've been attacked/mugged.	Sono stato aggredito/scippato.	sono stato aggredeeto/ sheeppato
● I have to use the phone.	Devo usare il telefono.	devo oozare eel telefono
● I'm lost.	Mi sono perso/a.	mee sono perso/a

- I've lost my... | Ho perso... | *o perso*
  - son | mio figlio | ***mee**-o **fil**yo*
  - daughter | mia figlia | ***mee**-a **fil**ya*
  - friends | i miei amici | *ee **mye**-ee a**mee**cee*

- Stop! | Fermo/a! | ***fer**mo/a*

✳ police

YOU MAY WANT TO SAY...

- Sorry, I didn't realise it was against the law. | Mi dispiace, non sapevo che fosse illegale. | *mee dee**spya**che non sa**pe**vo ke **fo**sse eelle**ga**le*

- Here are my documents. | Ecco i miei documenti. | ***ek**ko ee **mye**-ee doko**men**tee*

- I haven't got my passport on me. | Non ho con me il mio passaporto. | *non o kon me eel **mee**-o passa**por**to*

- I don't understand. | Non capisco. | *non ka**pees**ko*

- I'm innocent. | Sono innocente. | ***so**no eenno**chen**te*

- I need a lawyer (who speaks English). | Ho bisogno di un avvocato (che parli inglese). | *o bee**zon**yo dee oon avvo**ka**to (ke **par**lee een**gle**ze)*

- I want to contact my embassy/consulate. | Voglio contattare la mia ambasciata/il mio consolato. | ***vol**yo kontat**ta**re la **mee**-a amba**sha**ta/eel **mee**-o konso**la**to*

- Give me back my passport, please. | Mi ridia il mio passaporto, per favore. | *mee ree**dee**-a eel **mee**-o passa**por**to per fa**vo**re*

YOU MAY HEAR...

Deve pagare una multa.	*deve pagare oona moolta*	You have to pay a fine.
Documenti, per favore.	*dokoomentee per favore*	Your documents, please.
È in arresto.	*e een arresto*	You're under arrest.

* reporting crime

YOU MAY WANT TO SAY...

I want to report a theft.	Voglio denunciare un furto.	*volyo denoonchare oon foorto*
My ... has been stolen.	Mi hanno rubato...	*mee anno roobato...*
purse	il borsellino	*eel borselleeno*
wallet	il portafoglio	*eel portafolyo*
Our car has been stolen.	Ci hanno rubato la macchina.	*chee anno roobato la makkeena*
Our car has been broken into.	Ci hanno scassinato la macchina.	*chee anno skasseenato la makkeena*
I've been...	Sono stato ...	*sono stato...*
mugged	scippato	*sheeppato*
attacked	aggredito	*aggredeeto*
I've lost my...	Ho perso...	*o perso...*
credit cards	le mie carte di credito	*le mee-e karte dee kredeeto*
luggage	la valigia	*la valeeja*

health and safety

YOU MAY HEAR...

Quando è successo?	*kwando e soochesso*	When did it happen?
Dove?	*dove*	Where?
Cos'è successo?	*koze soochesso*	What happened?
Dovete riempire questo modulo.	*dovete ree-empeere kwesto modoolo*	You have to fill in this form.
Me lo/la/li descriva.	*me lo/la/lee deskreeva*	What did he/she/they look like?

YOU MAY WANT TO SAY...

It happened...	È successo...	*e soochesso...*
(ten) minutes ago	(dieci) minuti fa	*(dyechee) meenootee fa*
this morning	stamattina	*stamatteena*
on the beach	sulla spiaggia	*soolla spyaja*
He/She had blonde hair.	Era biondo/a.	*era byondo/a*
He/She had a knife.	Aveva un coltello.	*aveva oon koltello*
He/She was...	Era...	*era...*
tall	alto	*alto/a*
young	giovane	*jovane*
short	basso/a	*basso/a*
He/She was wearing...	Indossava...	*eendossava...*
jeans	i jeans	*ee jeens*
a shirt	una camicia	*oona kameecha*

basic grammar

✳ nouns

All Italian nouns (words for people and things) have a gender – masculine or feminine.

Most nouns ending in –o are masculine. The few exceptions include la mano (hand) and la radio (radio).

Most nouns ending in –a are feminine. Exceptions include il cinema (cinema). Nouns ending in –ione are also generally feminine.

Some nouns ending in –e are masculine and others are feminine – the dictionary at the end of the book indicates the gender.

A masculine plural noun can refer to a mixture of masculine and feminine:
i bambini (children, i.e. sons and daughters)
gli italiani (Italian men, or the Italians)

✳ plurals

All masculine nouns ending in –o form their plural with –i:
ragazzo (boy) ragazzi (boys)

Most feminine nouns ending in –a form their plural with –e:
ragazza (girl) ragazze (girls)

The exceptions are feminine nouns with a stressed final vowel. These do not change in the plural:
la città/le città (town/towns)
la difficoltà/le difficoltà (difficulty/difficulties)

Most nouns ending in –e form their plural with –i:
giornale (newspaper) giornali (newspapers)

Many nouns ending in –co, –go, –ca, –ga form their plural in
–chi, –ghi, –che, –ghe.

buco (hole)   buchi (holes)
fungo (mushroom)   funghi (mushrooms)
banca (bank)   banche (banks)
stringa (shoelace)   stringhe (shoelaces)

A notable exception to this is amico (male friend), which
becomes amici.

✳ indefinite article (a, an)

The indefinite article 'a' or 'an' has different forms in Italian.
un is used with masculine nouns, una with feminine nouns:
un giorno (a day) una macchina (a car)

uno is used with masculine nouns beginning with a z or with
an s followed by a consonant:
uno zio (an uncle) uno specchio (a mirror)

un' is used with feminine nouns beginning with a vowel:
un'arancia (an orange)

✳ definite article (the)

The definite article 'the' has different forms for masculine
and feminine, and also for singular and plural.

In the masculine singular, il is used for nouns beginning with
a consonant. Lo is used for nouns beginning with z or s +
consonant, and l' is used for nouns beginning with a vowel.

In the masculine plural, i is used for nouns beginning with a consonant and gli for nouns beginning with a vowel or z or s + consonant:

il ragazzo (the boy)	i ragazzi (the boys)
l'amico (the friend)	gli amici (the friends)
lo zio (the uncle)	gli zii (the uncles)

In the feminine singular, la is used for nouns beginning with a consonant and l' before nouns beginning with a vowel.

In the feminine plural, le is used in all cases:

la ragazza (the girl)	le ragazze (the girls)
l'amica (the friend)	le amiche (the friends)

✳ adjectives

Adjectives 'agree with' the nouns they are describing – they have different endings for masculine and feminine, singular and plural.

Many adjectives end in −o for masculine and −a for feminine and change the endings in the plural in the same way as nouns do:

un ragazzo stupido	dei ragazzi stupidi
una macchina rossa	macchine rosse

Some adjectives, including those ending in −e, have only one ending in the singular for both masculine and feminine. In the plural both masculine and feminine adjectives end in −i:

un ragazzo intelligente	ragazzi intelligenti
una ragazza intelligente	ragazze intelligenti

Adjectives ending in −co, −go, −ca, −ga behave in the same way as nouns with those endings when it comes to forming the plural (see page 148). Some −co endings are an exception to this rule: e.g. simpatico/simpatici.

✳ position of adjectives

Most adjectives come after the noun:
vino bianco (white wine)
una macchina nuova (a new car)

Some common adjectives always come before the noun. They include molto (much), poco (little), pochi, poche (few), troppo (too much), tanto (so much), questo (this), quello (that):

molte ragazze (many girls)   poche donne (few women)
questo ragazzo (this boy)   troppa pasta (too much pasta)

✳ comparatives and superlatives

'More' is più and comes before the adjective.
più interessante (more interesting)
più grande (bigger)
più vecchio (older)

'Less' is meno:
meno importante (less important)
meno complicato (less complicated)
meno caro (less expensive)

The comparatives of 'good' and 'bad' are meglio (better) and peggio (worse).

'Than', as in 'more than' and 'less than', is di, if you are comparing two different things:
questa casa è più grande dell'altra (this car is bigger than the other)

To say 'the most' or 'the least', put the definite article il or la before più or meno:
la più bella città (the most beautiful city)

il/la più grande del mondo (the biggest in the world)

Meno tends to come after the noun:
il ristorante meno caro (the cheapest restaurant)

If you want to say that something is 'very...' add -issimo,
-issima, -issimi, -issime to the stem of the adjective (the
ending depends on whether the adjective is masculine or
feminine and singular or plural).
l'Italia è bellissima (Italy is very beautiful)
il portiere è gentilissimo (the porter is very kind)

✷ possessives (my, your, his, her, etc.)

Possessive adjectives 'agree with' the nouns they refer to.
The forms are as follows:

	SINGULAR		PLURAL	
	m	f	m	f
my	mio	mia	miei	mie
your	tuo	tua	tuoi	tue
your (formal)	suo	sua	suoi	sue
his/her	suo	sua	suoi	sue
our	nostro	nostra	nostri	nostre

Possessives are usually preceded by the definite article,
unless you're talking about a member of the family:

la mia macchina (my car) il tuo amico (your friend)
la nostra casa (our house) il suo portafoglio (his, her
                            or your wallet)
mio fratello (my brother) tua sorella (your sister)

To indicate possession, the word di (of) is used.
il fratello di John (John's brother)
la casa di John e Susan (John and Susan's house)

✳ demonstratives (this, that)

	SINGULAR		PLURAL	
	m	f	m	f
this, these	questo	questa	questi	queste
that, those	quello	quella	quei/quegli	quelle

All these words are also used as demonstrative pronouns
('this one', 'that one', etc.)

✳ prepositions

The following are four of the most common prepositions
in Italian: a (to, at), in (in), di (of), su (on).

When these prepositions are followed by a definite article
(il, lo, la, l' in the singular, and i, le, gli in the plural) they
combine with the article to make one word:

al mercato	(a+il)	at/to the market
sul treno	(su+il)	on the train
del ragazzo	(di+il)	of the boy
nella città	(in+la)	in the city
all'ospedale	(a+l')	at/to the hospital
nell'acqua	(in+l')	in the water
ai negozi	(a+i)	at/to the shops
delle donne	(di+le)	of the women
negli studi	(in+gli)	in the studies

✳ subject pronouns (I, you, he, she, etc.)

io	I
tu	you (informal)
lei	you (formal)
lui	he

lei	she
noi	we
voi	you (informal, plural)
loro	you (formal, plural)
loro	they

These pronouns are not much used in Italian, as the verb endings show who the subject is (see verbs below). Lei (you) tends to be used more often than the others, for politeness.

✴ words for 'you'

In English there is only one way of addressing people – using the word 'you'. In Italian there are two ways – one is more polite/formal and the other is more casual/informal.

The informal way with tu (singular) or voi (plural) is used among people of similar ages and between family and friends. The formal way (with lei, and loro plural) is normal in all other cases, but it is used less often than it used to be.

In this book we use the informal, singular way of saying 'you', tu, unless otherwise specified.

✴ verbs

Italian verbs have different endings according to the subject of the verb and the tense. There are three main groups of verbs, with different sets of endings for each group. In dictionaries, verbs are listed in the infinitive form which ends in -are, -ere, -ire.

Below are the regular endings for the present tense of these three groups. The Italian present tense is also used to translate the English '–ing' form: parlo means both 'I speak' and 'I am speaking'.

	-ARE	**-ERE**	**-IRE**
	parlare	vedere	partire
	(to speak)	(to see)	(to leave)
io	parlo	vedo	parto
tu	parli	vedi	parti
lui, lei	parla	vede	parte
noi	parliamo	vediamo	partiamo
voi	parlate	vedete	partite
loro	parlano	vedono	partono

There are some verbs in the −ire group that have different
endings. These include: capire (to understand), finire
(to finish) and preferire (to prefer):

io	capisco
tu	capisci
lui, lei	capisce
noi	capiamo
voi	capite
loro	capiscono

✳ 'to be' and 'to have'

Both these verbs are irregular:

	ESSERE		**AVERE**	
	(to be)		(to have)	
io	sono	I am	ho	I have
tu	sei	you are	hai	you have
lui, lei	è	he, she is	ha	he, she has
noi	siamo	we are	abbiamo	we have
voi	siete	you are	avete	you have
loro	sono	they are	hanno	they have

✳ other irregular verbs

Other common verbs that are irregular include:

SAPERE	ANDARE	POTERE	VOLERE
(to know)	(to go)	(to be able)	(to want)
so	vado	posso	voglio
sai	vai	puoi	vuoi
sa	va	può	vuole
sappiamo	andiamo	possiamo	vogliamo
sapete	andate	potete	volete
sanno	vanno	possono	vogliono

✳ other verb tenses

A few verbs in other tenses you might find useful:

andare	I have been/I went	sono andato/a
	we have been/ we went	siamo andati/e
	I used to go	andavo
	we used to go	andavamo
essere	I have been/I was	sono stato/a
	we have been/ we were	siamo stati/e
	I used to be	ero
	we used to be	eravamo
avere	I have had/I had	ho avuto
	we have had/ we had	abbiamo avuto
	I used to have	avevo
	we used to have	avevamo
venire	I have come/I came	sono venuto/a
	we have come/ we came	siamo venuti/e
	I used to come	venivo
	we used to come	venivamo

When talking about the future, you can often use the present tense:

Domani gioco a tennis (Tomorrow I am playing tennis)

✳ negatives

To make a verb negative, you simply put non before it.

Non ho bambini (I don't have children)
Non capisco (I don't understand)
Il signor Rossi non c'è (Mr Rossi isn't in)

Italian has double negatives:

Non ho niente (I have nothing); niente literally means nothing.
Non ho visto nessuno (I haven't seen anyone); nessuno means no-one.

✳ questions

To ask a question, use a question word ('why', 'when', 'who', etc.) plus the verb. If there is no question word, simply put a question in your voice by making it go up at the end of the sentence.

Quando viene? (When is he coming?)
Chi parla? (Who is speaking?)
Dove vai? (Where are you going?)
Dov'è la stazione? (Where is the station?)
Perché? (Why?)
Ha bambini? (Have you got any children?)

English – Italian dictionary

There's a list of **car parts** on page 57 and **parts of the body** on page 139. See also the **menu reader** on page 90, and **numbers** on page 12.

Italian nouns are given with their gender in brackets: (m) for masculine and (f) for feminine, (m/f) for those which can be either, (pl) for plural.

Adjectives which have different endings for masculine and feminine are shown like this: bianco/a (i.e. bianco for masculine, bianca for feminine). See **basic grammar**, page 149 for further explanation.

A

a, an un (m) una (f) *oon, oona*

abbey abbazia (f) *abbatsee-a*

about *(relating to)* su *soo*
  (approximately) circa *cheerka*

above sopra *sopra*

abroad all'estero *alestero*

abscess ascesso (m) *ashesso*

to accept *(take)* accettare *achettare*

accident incidente (m) *eencheedente*

accommodation alloggio (m) *alodjo*

account *(bank)* conto (m) *konto*

ache dolore (m) *dolore*

acid *(adj.)* acido/a *acheedo/a*

across attraverso *attraverso (opposite)*
  dall'altro lato di *dallaltro lato dee*

adaptor riduttore (m) *reedoottore*

address indirizzo (m) *eendeereetso*

admission ammissione (f) *ammeessyone*

admission charge entrata (f) *entrata*

adopted adottato/a *adottato/a*

adult adulto/a *adoolto/a*

advance avanzamento (m) *avantsamento*
  » **in advance** in anticipo *een anteecheepo*

advertisement, advertising pubblicità (f) *poobbleecheeta*

aerial aereo/a *aereo*

aeroplane aeroplano (m) *aeroplano*

afraid: I'm afraid ho paura *ho powra*

after(wards) dopo *dopo*

afternoon pomeriggio (m) *pomereejo*

aftershave dopobarba (m) *dopobarba*

again ancora *ankora*

against contro *kontro*

age età (f) *eta*

agency agenzia (f) *ajentseea*

ago fa *fa*

to agree essere d'accordo *essere dakkordo*

AIDS AIDS *aeeds*

air aria (f) *arya*
  » **by air** per aereo *per a-ereo*
  » **(by) air mail** via aerea *vee-a a-erea*

air conditioning aria (f) condizionata *arya kondeetsyonata*

air force aviazione (f) militare *avyatseeone meeleetare*

airline linea (f) aerea *leenea a-erea*

airport aeroporto (m) *a-eroporto*

aisle passaggio (m) *passajo*

alarm allarme (m) *alarme*

alarm clock sveglia (f) *svelya*

alcohol alcool (m) *alko-ol*

alcoholic *(content)* alcolicità (f) *alkoleecheeta* *(person)* alcolista (m/f) *alkoleesta*

alive vivo/a *veevo/a*

all tutto/a *tootto/a*

allergic to allergico/a a *allerjeeko/a a*

alley vicolo (m) *veekolo*

to allow permettere *permettere*

allowed permesso *permesso*

all right *(OK)* va bene *va bene*

alone solo/a *solo/a*

along lungo *loongo*

already già *ja*

also anche *anke*

although benché *benke*

always sempre *sempre*

ambassador ambasciatore (m), ambasciatrice (f) *ambashatore, ambashatreeche*

ambition ambizione (f) *ambeetsyone*

ambulance ambulanza (f) *amboolantsa*

among tra *tra*

amount *(money)* importo (m) *eemporto*

amusement park parco (m) dei divertimenti *parko de-ee deeverteementee*

anaesthetic *(local)* anestetico (m) locale *anesteteeko lokale* *(general)* anestetico (m) generale *anesteteeko jenerale*

and e *e*

angry arrabbiato/a *arrabyato/a*

animal animale (m) *aneemale*

anniversary anniversario (m) *aneeversaryo*

annoyed seccato/a *sekato/a*

another un altro/un'altra *oonaltro/a*

answer risposta (f) *reesposta*

antibiotic antibiotico (m) *anteebeeoteeko*

antifreeze anticongelante (m) *anteekonjelante*

antique pezzo (m) di antiquariato *petso dee anteekwaryato*

antiseptic antisettico (m) *anteesetteeko*

anxious preoccupato/a *preokoopato/a*

any ne *ne*

anyone qualcuno *kwalkoono*

anything qualcosa *kwalkoza*

anything else qualcos'altro *kwalkozaltro*

anyway in ogni modo *een onyee modo*

anywhere da qualche parte *da kwalke parte*

apart *(from)* a parte *a parte*

apartment appartamento (m) *apartamento*

appendicitis appendicite (f) *apendecheete*

apple mela (f) *mela*

appointment appuntamento (m) *apoontamento*

approximately circa *cheerka*

arch arco (m) *arko*

archaeology archeologia (f) *arkeeolojeea*

architect architetto (m) *arkeetetto*

area area (f) *area*

argument discussione (f) *deeskoosyone*

arm braccio (f) *bracho*

armbands *(swimming)* braccioli (m/pl) *bracholee*

army esercito (m) *esercheeto*

around intorno a *eentorno a*

to arrange *(fix)* organizzare *organeetsare*

arrest: under arrest arresto: in arresto *arresto: een arresto*

arrival arrivo (m) *arreevo*

to arrive arrivare *arreevare*

art arte (f) *arte*

» **art gallery** galleria (f) d'arte *galleree-a darte*

» **fine arts** belle arti (f/pl) *belle artee*

arthritis artrite (f) *artreete*

article articolo (m) *arteekolo*

artificial artificiale *arteefeechale*

artist artista (m/f) *arteesta*

as *(like)* come *kome*

ash cenere (f) *chenere*
ashtray portacenere (m) *portachenere*
to ask chiedere *kyedere*
aspirin aspirina (f) *aspeereena*
assistant assistente (m/f) *aseestente*
asthma asma (f) *asma*
at a *a*
athletics atletica (f) *atleteeka*
atmosphere atmosfera (f) *atmosfera*
to attack aggredire *aggredeere*
  (mug) scippare *sheeppare*
attendant (bathing) bagnaiolo (m)
  banyiyolo
attractive attraente *attra-ente*
auction vendita (f) all'asta *vendeeta*
  alasta
aunt zia *dzeea*
automatic automatico/a *owtomateeko/a*
autumn autunno (m) *owtoonno*
avalanche valanga (f) *valanga*
to avoid evitare *eveetare*
awful terribile *tereebeele*

B

baby neonato/a (m/f) *neonato/a*
baby food cibo (m) per neonati *cheebo*
  per neonatee
baby wipes salvietta (f) detergente
  salvyetta deterjente
baby's bottle biberon (m) *beeberon*
babysitter baby-sitter (m/f)
  babeeseetter
back (reverse side) rovescio (m) *rovesho*
back: at the back fondo: in fondo *fondo:*
  in fondo
backwards all'indietro *aleendyetro*
bacon pancetta (f) *panchetta*
bad cattivo/a *katteevo/a*
bag borsa (f) *borsa*
baggage bagagli (m/pl) *bagalyee*
baker's panetteria (f) *panettereea*
balcony (theatre etc.) galleria (f)
  gallereea
bald calvo/a *kalvo/a*

ball palla (f) *palla*
ballet balletto (m) *balletto*
banana banana (f) *banana*
band (music) banda (f) *banda*
bandage benda (f) *benda*
bank (money) banca (f) *banka*
bar bar (m) *bar*
bargain affare (m) *affare*
baseball baseball (m) *besbol*
basement piano (m) interrato
  pyano eenterrato
basin (sink) lavabo (f) *lavabo*
basket cesto (m) *chesto*
basketball pallacanestro (f)
  pallakanestro
bath bagno (m) *banyo*
to bathe bagnarsi *banyarsee*
bathing costume costume (m)
  da bagno *kostoome da banyo*
bathroom stanza (f) da bagno
  stantsa da banyo
battery pila (f) *peela*
bay baia (f) *biya*
to be essere *essere*
beach spiaggia (f) *spyajja*
beans fagioli (m/pl) *fajolee*
beard barba (f) *barba*
beautiful bello/a *bello/a*
because perché *perke*
bed letto (m) *letto*
bedroom camera (f) da letto
  kamera da letto
bee ape (f) *ape*
beef manzo (m) *mantso*
beer birra (f) *beerra*
before prima di *preema dee*
to begin cominciare *komeenchare*
beginner principiante (m/f)
  preencheepyante
beginning inizio (m) *eeneetsyo*
behind dietro *dyetro*
beige beige *bej*
to believe credere *kredere*
bell campana (f) *kampana*

to belong to appartenere a *appartenere a*

below sotto *sotto*

belt cintura (f) *cheentoora*

bend curva (f) *koorva*

berry bacca (f) *bakka*

berth *(on ship)* cuccetta (f) *koochetta*

besides inoltre *eenoltre*

best il/la migliore *eel/la meelyore*

better meglio *melyo*

between tra *tra*

beyond oltre *oltre*

bib bavaglia (m) *bavalya*

Bible Bibbia (f) *beebbya*

bicycle bicicletta (f) *beecheekletta*

big grande *grande*

bigger più grande *pyoo grande*

bill conto (m) *konto*

bin *(rubbish)* bidone (m) della spazzatura *beedone della spatsatoora*

bin liners sacchetti (m/pl) per l'immondizia *sakkettee per leemondeetsya*

binding *(ski)* attacco (m) degli sci *attakko delyee shee*

binoculars binocolo (m) *beenokolo*

bird uccello (m) *oochello*

birthday compleanno (m) *kompleanno*

biscuit biscotto (m) *beeskotto*

bit pezzo (m) *petso*

to bite mordere *mordere*

bitter amaro/a *amaro*

black nero/a *nero*

black coffee caffè nero *kaffe nero*

blackcurrant ribes (m) nero *reebes nero*

blanket coperta (f) *koperta*

to bleed sanguinare *sangweenare*

blind persiana (f) *persyana*

blister vescica (f) *vesheeka*

to block *(road)* bloccare *blokkare*

blocked bloccato/a *blokkato/a*

    (road) chiuso/a *kyoozo/a*

blonde biondo/a *byondo/a*

blood sangue (f) *sangwe*

blouse camicetta (f) *cameechetta*

to blow soffiare *soffyare*

to blow-dry asciugare con il phon *ashoogare kon eel fon*

blue blu *bloo*

to board imbarcarsi *eembarkarsee*

boarding card carta (f) d'imbarco *karta deembarko*

boat barca (f) *barka*

boat trip gita (f) in barca *jeeta een barka*

body corpo (m) *korpo*

to boil bollire *bolleere*

boiled egg uovo (m) sodo *oo-ovo sodo*

boiler scaldabagno (m) *skaldabanyo*

bomb bomba (f) *bomba*

bone osso (m) *osso*

book libro (m) *leebro*

to book prenotare *prenotare*

booking prenotazione (f) *prenotatsyone*

booking office *(rail)* biglietteria (f) *beelyetereea (theatre)* botteghino (m) *bottegeeno*

bookshop libreria (f) *leebrereea*

boot *(shoe)* scarpone (f) *skarpone*

border *(frontier)* frontiera (f) *frontyera*

boring noioso/a *noyozo/a*

both entrambi *entrambee*

bottle bottiglia (f) *botteelya*

bottle opener apribottiglie (m) *apreebotteelye*

bottom fondo *fondo*

bow *(ship)* prua (f) *prooa*

bowl ciotola (f) *chotola*

box scatola (f) *skatola*

    (theatre) palco (m) *palko*

box office botteghino (m) *bottegeeno*

boy, boyfriend ragazzo (m) *ragatso*

bra reggiseno (m) *rejeeseno*

bracelet braccialetto (m) *brachaletto*

brain cervello (m) *chervello*

branch *(bank etc.)* filiale (f) *feelyale*

brand marca (f) *marka*

brandy brandy (m) *brandy*

brass ottone (m) *ottone*

brave coraggioso/a *korajoso*

bread pane (m) *pane*

» **wholemeal bread** pane (m) integrale *pane eentegrale*

bread roll panino (m) *paneeno*

to break *(inc. limb)* rompere *rompere*

to break down essere in panne *essere een panne*

break down truck carro (m) attrezzi *karro attretsee*

breakfast colazione (f) *kolatsyone*

breast seno (m) *seno*

to breathe respirare *respeerare*

bridge ponte (m) *ponte*

briefcase cartella (f) *kartella*

bright *(colour)* vivo/a *veevo/a* *(light)* brillante *breellante*

to bring portare *portare*

British britannico/a *breetanneeko/a*

broad largo/a *largo/a*

brochure opuscolo (m) *opooskolo*

broken rotto/a *rotto/a*

bronchitis bronchite (f) *bronkeete*

bronze bronzo (m) *brondzo*

brooch spilla (f) *speella*

broom scopa (f) *skopa*

brother fratello (m) *fratello*

brother-in-law cognato (m) *konyato*

brown bruno/a *broono/a*

bruise livido (m) *leeveedo*

brush spazzola (f) *spatsola*

bucket secchio (m) *sekkyo*

buffet buffet (m) *boofe*

to build costruire *kostroo-eere*

builder costruttore (m) *kostroottore*

building edificio (m) *edeefeecho*

bulb *(light)* lampadina (f) *lampadeena*

bull toro (m) *toro*

bumper *(car)* paraurti (m) *para-oortee*

burn *(on skin)* ustione (f) *oostyone*

burnt *(food)* bruciacchiato *broochakkyato*

bus autobus (m) *owtoboos*

» **by bus** in autobus *een owtoboos*

bus-driver autista (m) *owteesta*

bush cespuglio (m) *chespoolyo*

business affari (m/pl) *affaree*

» **on business** per affari *per affaree*

bus station autostazione (f) *owtostatsyone*

bus stop fermata (f) d'autobus *fermata dowtoboos*

busy occupato/a *okoopato/a*

but ma *ma*

butane gas gas (m) butano *gas bootano*

butcher's macelleria (f) *machellereea*

butter burro (m) *boorro*

butterfly farfalla (f) *farfalla*

button bottone (m) *bottone*

to buy comprare *komprare*

by *(author etc.)* di *dee*

C

cabin cabina (f) *kabeena*

cable car funivia (f) *fooneevee-a*

café bar *bar*

cake torta (f) *torta*

cake shop pasticceria (f) *pasteechereea*

calculator calcolatrice (f) *kalkolatreeche*

call *(phone)* telefonata (f) *telefonata*

to call chiamare *kyamare*

» **to be called** chiamarsi *kyamarsee*

calm calmo/a *kalmo/a*

camera macchina (f) fotografica *makkeena fotografeeka*

to camp campeggiare *kampejare*

camp bed letto (m) da campo *letto da kampo*

camping campeggio (m) *kampejo*

campsite campeggio (m) *kampejo*

can *(to be able)* potere *potere*

can *(tin)* lattina (f) *latteena*

can opener apriscatole (m) *apreeskatole*

to cancel annullare *anoollare*

cancer cancro (m) *kankro*

candle candela (f) *kandela*

canoe canoa (f) *kanoa*

capital *(city)* capitale (f) *kapeetale*
captain *(boat)* capitano (m) *kapeetano*
car macchina (f) *makkeena*
» **by car** in macchina *een makkeena*
car hire autonoleggio (m) *owtonolejo*
car park parcheggio (m) *parkejo*
carafe caraffa (f) *karaffa*
caravan roulotte (f) *roolot*
caravan site campeggio (m) per roulotte *kampejo per roolot*
cardigan cardigan (m) *kardeegan*
care: I don't care non m'importa *non meemporta*
career carriera (f) *karryera*
careful attento/a *attento/a*
carpet tappeto (m) *tappeto*
carriage *(rail)* carrozza (f) *karrotsa*
to carry portare *portare*
to carry on *(walking/driving)* continuare *konteenooare*
car wash autolavaggio (m) *owtolavajo*
case: in case in caso *een kazo*
cash contanti (m/pl) *kontantee*
» **to pay cash** pagare in contanti *pagare een kontantee*
to cash incassare *eenkassare*
cash desk cassa (f) *kassa*
cashier cassiere/a *kassyere/a*
cassette cassetta (f) *kassetta*
castle *(palace)* castello (m) *kastello* *(fortress)* fortezza (f) *fortetsa*
cat gatto (m) *gatto*
to catch *(train/bus)* prendere *prendere*
cathedral duomo (m) *dwomo*
Catholic cattolico/a *kattoleeko/a*
to cause provocare *provokare*
caution cautela (f) *kowtela*
cave grotta (f) *grotta*
CD CD (m) *cheedee*
ceiling soffitto (m) *soffeetto*
cellar cantina (f) *kanteena*
cemetery cimitero (m) *cheemeetero*
centimetre centimetro (m) *chenteemetro*

central centrale *chentrale*
central heating riscaldamento (m) centralizzato *reeskaldamento chentraleetsato*
centre centro (m) *chentro*
century secolo (m) *sekolo*
certain certo *cherto*
certainly certamente *chertamente*
certificate certificato (m) *cherteefeekato*
chain catena (f) *katena*
chair sedia (f) *sedya*
chair lift seggiovia (f) *sejoveea*
chalet chalet (m) *shale*
champagne champagne (m) *shampan*
change *(small coins)* spiccioli (m/pl) *speecholee*
to change *(clothes)* cambiarsi *kambyarsee* *(money, trains)* cambiare *kambyare*
changing room *(shop)* camerino (m) *kamereeno*
chapel cappella (f) *kappella*
charcoal carbone (m) *karbone*
charge *(money)* spesa (f) *speza*
charter flight volo (m) charter *volo charter*
cheap a buon mercato *a bwon merkato*
to check controllare *kontrollare*
check-in *(desk)* accettazione (f) *achettatsyone*
cheek guancia (f) *gwancha*
cheeky sfacciato/a *sfachato/a*
cheers! cin cin!/salute! *cheen cheen/saloote*
cheese formaggio (m) *formajo*
chef chef (m) *shef*
chemist chimico (m) –a (f) *keemeeko/a*
cheque assegno (m) *assenyo*
chess scacchi (m/pl) *skakkee*
chewing gum gomma (f) da masticare/cicca *gomma da masteekare/cheekka*
chicken pollo (m) *pollo*
chickenpox varicella (f) *vareechella*
child bambino (m) –a (f) *bambeeno/a*
children bambini (m/pl) *bambeenee*

chin mento (m) *mento*

china porcellana (f) *porchellana*

chips patatine (f/pl) fritte *patateene freette*

chocolate cioccolato (m) *chokkolato*

to choose scegliere *shelyere*

Christian cristiano/a *kreestyano/a*

Christian name nome (m) *nome*

Christmas Natale (m) *natale*

Christmas Day giorno (m) di Natale *jorno dee natale*

Christmas Eve vigilia (f) di Natale *veejeelya dee natale*

church chiesa (f) *kyeza*

cigar sigaro (m) *seegaro*

cigarette sigaretta (f) *seegaretta*

cigarette paper cartina (f) per sigarette *karteena per seegarette*

cinema cinema (m) *cheenema*

circle cerchio (m) *cherkyo* (theatre) galleria (f) *galleree-a*

city città (f) *cheetta*

civil servant funzionario (m) *foontsyonaryo*

class classe (f) *klasse*

classical music musica (f) classica *moozeeka klasseeka*

claustrophobia claustrofobia (f) *klowstrofobya*

to clean pulire *pooleere*

clean pulito/a *pooleeto/a*

cleaner addetto (m) –a (f) alle pulizie *addetto/a alle pooleetsee-e*

cleansing lotion latte (m) detergente *latte deterjente*

clear chiaro/a *kyaro/a*

clever intelligente *eentelleejente*

cliff scogliera (f) *skolyera*

climate clima (m) *kleema*

to climb scalare *skalare*

climber scalatore (m) –trice (f) *skalatore, skalatreeche*

clinic clinica (f) *kleeneeka*

cloakroom guardaroba (m) *gwardaroba*

clock orologio (m) *orolojo*

close (by) vicino *veecheeno*

to close chiudere *kyoodere*

closed chiuso/a *kyoozo/a*

cloth stoffa (f) *stoffa*

clothes vestiti (m/pl) *vesteetee*

clothes pegs mollette (f/pl) da bucato *mollette da bookato*

cloud nuvola (f) *noovola*

cloudy nuvoloso/a *noovolozo/a*

club club (m) *kloob*

coach pullman (m) *poolman* (railway) carrozza (f) *karrotsa*

coast costa (f) *kosta*

coat mantello (m) *mantello*

coathanger gruccia, appendiabiti (f) *groocha, appendee-abeetee*

cocktail cocktail (m) *koktael*

coffee caffè (m) *kaffe*

coin moneta (f) *moneta*

cold freddo/a *freddo/a* (illness) raffreddore (m) *raffreddore*

collar collo (m) *kollo*

colleague collega (m/f) *kollega*

to collect collezionare *kolletsyonare*

collection (postal) levata (f) *levata* (rubbish) raccolta (f) *rakkolta*

college scuola (f) superiore *skwola sooperyore*

colour colore (m) *kolore*

comb pettine (m) *petteene*

to come venire *veneere*

to come back tornare *tornare*

to come in entrare *entrare*

comedy commedia (f) *kommedya*

comfortable comodo/a *komodo/a*

comic (magazine) giornalino (m) *jornaleeno*

commercial commerciale *komerchale*

common (usual) comune *komoone* (shared) in comune *in komoone*

communism comunismo (m) *komooneesmo*

company società *sochee-eta*

compared with paragonato/a a *paragonato/a a a*

compartment scompartimento (m) *skomparteemento*

compass bussola (f) *boossola*

to complain lamentarsi *lamentarsee*

complaint reclamo (m) *reklamo*

complete *(finished)* completo/a *kompleto/a*

complicated complicato/a *kompleekato/a*

compulsory obbligatorio/a *obleegatoryo*

composer compositore (m) –trice (f) *kompozeetore, kompozeetreeche*

computer computer (m) *kompyooter*

concert concerto (m) *koncherto*

concert hall sala (f) dei concerti *sala de-ee konchertee*

concussion commozione (f) cerebrale *kommotsyone cherebrale*

condition *(state)* condizione (f) *kondeetsyone*

conditioner balsamo (m) *balsamo*

condom preservativo (m) *prezervateevo*

conference congresso (m) *kongresso*

confirm confermare *konfermare*

conjunctivitis congiuntivite (f) *konjoonteeveete*

connection connessione (f) *konessyone*

conscious cosciente *koshente*

conservation conservazione (f) *konservatsyone*

conservative conservatore *konservatore*

constipation stitichezza (f) *steeteeketsa*

consulate consolato (m) *konsolato*

consultant consulente (m/f) *konsoolente*

contact lenses lenti (f/pl) a contatto *lentee a kontatto*

continent continente (m) *konteenente*

contraceptive contraccettivo (m) *kontrachetteevo*

contract contratto (m) *kontratto*

control *(passport)* controllo (m) *kontrollo*

convent convento (m) *konvento*

convenient comodo/a *komodo/a*

cook cuoco (m) –a (f) *kwoko/a*

to cook cucinare *koocheenare*

cooked cotto/a *kotto/a*

cooker fornello (m) *fornello*

cool fresco/a *fresko/a*

cool box frigo (m) portatile *freego portateele*

copy copiare *kopyare*

cork tappo (m) *tappo*

corkscrew cavatappi (m) *kavatappee*

corner angolo (m) *angolo*

correct corretto/a *korretto/a*

corridor corridoio (m) *koreedoyo*

cosmetics trucco (m) *trookko*

to cost costare *kostare*

cot lettino (m) *letteeno*

cotton *(material)* cotone (m) *kotone* *(thread)* cotone (m) *kotone*

cotton wool cotone (m) idrofilo *kotone eedrofeelo*

couchette cuccetta (f) *koochetta*

to cough tossire *tosseere*

to count contare *kontare*

counter *(post office)* banco (m) *banko*

country *(nation)* paese (m) *pa-eze*

countryside campagna (f) *kampanya*

couple *(pair)* coppia (f) *koppya*

course *(lessons)* corso (m) *korso*

court *(law)* tribunale (m) *treeboonale* *(tennis)* campo (m) *kampo*

cousin cugino/a (m/f) *koojeeno/a*

cover *(lid)* coperchio (m) *koperkyo*

cow mucca (f) *mookka*

crab granchio (m) *grankyo*

cramp crampo (m) *krampo*

crazy pazzo/a *patso/a*

cream panna (f) *panna* *(lotion)* crema (f) *krema* *(colour)* crema *krema*

credit card carta (f) di credito *karta di kredeeto*

crisps patatine (f/pl) *patateene*

cross croce (f) *kroche*

to **cross** *(border)* passare *passare*

cross-country skiing sci di fondo *shee dee fondo*

crossing *(sea)* traversata (f) *traversata*

crossroads incrocio (m) *eenkrocho*

crowd folla (f) *folla*

crowded affollato/a *affollato/a*

crown corona (f) *korona*

cruise crociera (f) *krochera*

crutch gruccia (f) *groocha*

to **cry** piangere *pyanjere*

crystal cristallo (m) *kreestallo*

cup tazza (f) *tatsa*

cupboard armadio (m) *armadyo*

cure *(remedy)* cura (f) *koora*

to **cure** guarire *gwareere*

curly ricciuto/a *reechooto/a*

current attuale *attwale*

curtain tenda (f) *tenda*

curve curva (f) *koorva*

cushion cuscino (m) *koosheeno*

customs dogana (f) *dogana*

cut taglio (m) *talyo*

to **cut** tagliare *talyare*

to **cut oneself** tagliarsi *talyarsee*

cutlery posate (f/pl) *pozate*

cycling ciclismo (m) *cheekleesmo*

cyclist ciclista (m/f) *cheekleesta*

cystitis cistite (f) *cheesteete*

D

daily quotidiano/a *kwoteedyano/a*

damage danno (m) *danno*

to **damage** danneggiare *dannejare*

damp umido/a *oomeedo/a*

dance ballo (m) *ballo*

to **dance** ballare *ballare*

danger pericolo (m) *pereekolo*

dangerous pericoloso *pereekoloso*

dark buio (m) *booyo*

date *(day)* data (m) *data*

daughter figlia (f) *feelya*

daughter-in-law nuora (f) *nwora*

day giorno (m) *jorno*

  » **day after tomorrow** dopodomani *dopodomanee*

  » **day before yesterday** l'altro ieri *laltroyeree*

dead morto/a *morto/a*

deaf sordo/a *sordo/a*

dear *(loved)* caro/a *karo/a*

  (expensive) caro/a *karo/a*

death morte (f) *morte*

debt debito (m) *debeeto*

decaffeinated decaffeinato/a *dekaffe-eenato/a*

deck ponte (m) *ponte*

deckchair sedia (f) a sdraio *sedya a zdriyo*

to **decide** decidere *decheedere*

to **declare** dichiarare *deekyarare*

deep profondo/a *profondo/a*

deer cervo (m) *chervo*

defect difetto (m) *deefetto*

definitely definitivamente *defeeneeteevamente*

to **defrost** scongelare *skongelare*

degree *(temperature)* grado (m) *grado (university)* laurea (f) *lowrea*

delay ritardo (m) *reetardo*

delicate delicato/a *deleekato/a*

delicious delizioso/a *deleetsyoso*

to **deliver** consegnare *konsenyare*

delivery consegna (f) *konsenya*

demonstration *(example)* dimostrazione (f) *deemostratsyone*

denim jeans (m) *jeens*

dentist dentista (m/f) *denteesta*

denture dentiera (f) *dentyera*

deodorant deodorante (m) *deodorante*

to **depart** *(bus, train, plane)* partire *parteere*

department reparto (m) *reparto*

department store grande magazzino (m) *grande magatseeno*

departure (bus, car, train, plane) partenza (f) *partentsa*

departure lounge sala (f) delle partenze *sala delle partentse*

deposit deposito (m) *depozeeto*

desert deserto (m) *dezerto*

to **describe** descrivere *deskreevere*

description descrizione (f) *deskreetsyone*

design (dress) disegno (m) *deezenyo*

designer (of clothes) stilista (m/f) *steeleesta*

dessert dessert (m) *desser*

destination destinazione (f) *desteenatsyone*

detail dettaglio (m) *dettalyo*

detergent detersivo (m) *deterseevo*

to **develop** sviluppare *sveelooppare*

diabetic diabetico/a *dyabeteeko/a*

to **dial** comporre *komporre*

dialling code prefisso (m) *prefeesso*

dialling tone segnale (m) di libero *senyale dee leebero*

diamond diamante (m) *dyamante*

diarrhoea diarrea (f) *dyarrea*

diary agenda (f) *agenda*

dice dadi (m/pl) *dadee*

dictionary dizionario (m) *deetsyonaryo*

to **die** morire *moreere*

diesel diesel *deezel*

diet dieta (m) *dyeta*

different diverso/a *deeverso/a*

difficult difficile *deeffeecheele*

digital digitale *deejeetale*

digital camera fotocamera (f) digitale *fotokamera deejeetale*

dining room sala (f) da pranzo *sala da prantso*

dinner cena (f) *chena*

direct (train) diretto *deeretto*

direction direzione (f) *deeretsyone*

directory elenco telefonico (m) *elenko telefoneeko*

dirty sporto/a *sporko/a*

disabled disabile *dizabile*

disappointed deluso/a *deloozo/a*

disco(theque) discoteca (f) *deeskoteka*

discount sconto (m) *skonto*

dish piatto (m) *pyatto*

dishwasher lavastoviglie (f) *lavastoveelye*

disinfectant disinfettante (m) *deeseenfettante*

dislocated slogato/a *zlogato/a*

disposable monouso/a *mono-oozo/a*

disposable nappies pannolini usa e getta *pannoleenee ooza e jetta*

distance distanza (f) *deestantsa*

distilled water acqua (f) distillata *akwa deesteellata*

district quartiere (m) *kwartyere*

to **dive** tuffarsi *tooffarsee*

diversion deviazione (f) *deevyatsyone*

diving immersione (f) *eemmersyone*

divorced divorziato/a *deevortsyato/a*

dizzy stordito/a *stordeeto/a*

to **do** fare *fare*

doctor dottore (m) dottoressa (f) *dottore, dottoressa*

document documento (m) *dokoomento*

dog cane (m) *kane*

dollar dollaro (m) *dollaro*

dome cupola (f) *koopola*

donkey asino (m) *aseeno*

door porta (f) *porta*

double doppia (f) *doppya*

double bed letto (m) matrimoniale *letto matreemonyale*

down (movement) giù *joo*

to **download** scaricare *skareekare*

drama dramma (m) *dramma*

draught (air) corrente (f) d'aria *korrente darya*

draught beer birra (f) alla spina *beerra alla speena*

to **draw** disegnare *deesenyare*

drawer cassetto (m) *kassetto*

drawing disegno (m) *deesenyo*

dreadful orrendo/a *orrendo/a*

dress abito (m) *abeeto*

to dress, get dressed vestirsi *vesteersee*

dressing *(medical)* fasce (f/pl) *fashe*
  (salad) condimento (m)
  kondeemento

drink bevanda (f) *bevanda*

to drink bere *bere*

to drip gocciolare *gocholare*

to drive guidare *gweedare*

driver autista (m/f) *owteesta*

driving licence patente (f) di guida
  patente dee gweeda

to drown affogare *affogare*

drug droga (f) *droga*

drum tamburo (m) *tambooro*

drunk ubriaco/a *oobree-ako/a*

dry asciutto/a *ashootto/a*
  (wine) secco/a *sekko/a*

dry-cleaner's tintoria (f) *teentoree-a*

dubbed doppiato/a *doppyato/a*

duck anatra (f) *anatra*

dull *(weather)* coperto *koperto*

dumb muto/a *mooto/a*

dummy *(baby's)* succhiotto (m)
  sookkyotto

during durante *doorante*

dustbin pattumiera (f) *pattoomyera*

dusty polveroso/a *polveroso/a*

duty *(tax)* dazio (m) *dadzyo*

duty-free esente da dazio *esente da
  dadzyo*

duvet piumone (m) *pyoomone*

DVD DVD (m) *devede*

dyslexic dislessico/a *deeslesseeko/a*

E

each ognuno *onyoono*

ear orecchio (m) *orekkyo*

earache mal (m) d'orecchi *mal dorekkee*

eardrops gocce (f/pl) per le orecchie
  goche per le orekkye

earlier prima *preema*

early presto *presto*

to earn guadagnare *gwadanyare*

earring orecchino (m) *orekkeeno*

earth terra (f) *terra*

earthquake terremoto (m) *terremoto*

east est (m) *est*

eastern orientale *oryentale*

Easter Pasqua (f) *paskwa*

easy facile *facheele*

to eat mangiare *manjare*

economical economico/a *ekonomeeko*

economy economia (f) *ekonomeea*

edible commestibile *kommesteebeele*

either uno dei due *oono de-ee doo-e*

either... or... sia... che... *seea... ke...*

elastic band elastico (m) *elasteeko*

election elezione (f) *eletsyone*

electric elettrico/a *elettreeko*

electrician elettricista (m)
  elettreecheesta

electricity elettricità (f) *elettreecheeta*
  (wiring) impianto (m) *eempyanto*

electronic elettronico/a *elettroneeko/a*

email email (f) *ee-me-eel*

to email inviare un'email *eenvyare
  unee-me-eel*

to embark *(boat)* imbarcare *eembarkare*

embarrassing imbarazzante
  eembaratsante

embassy ambasciata (f) *ambashata*

emergency emergenza (f) *emerjendza*

empty vuoto *vwoto*

to empty svuotare *svvotare*

end fine (f) *feene*

to end finire *feeneere*

energy energia (f) *enerjeea*

engaged *(to be married)* fidanzato/a
  feedantsato/a
  (occupied) occupato/a *okkoopato/a*

engine motore (m) *motore*

engineer ingegnere (m) *eenjenyere*

England Inghilterra (f) *eengeelterra*

English inglese *eengleze*

to enjoy oneself divertirsi *deeverteersee*

enough abbastanza *abbastandza*

to enter entrare *entrare*

entertainment divertimento (m) *deeverteemento*

enthusiastic entusiasta *entoozyasta*

entrance entrata (f) *entrata*

envelope busta (f) *boosta*

environment ambiente (m) *ambyente*

environmentally friendly ambientalista *ambyentaleesta*

equal uguale *oogwale*

equipment attrezzatura (f) *attretsatoora*

escalator scala (f) mobile *skala mobeele*

especially soprattutto *soprattootto*

essential essenziale *essentsyale*

estate agent agente (m) immobiliare *ajente eemobeelyare*

even *(including)* anche *anke*
  (not odd) pari *paree*

evening sera (f) *sera*

every ogni *onyee*

everyone tutti *toottee*

everything tutto *tootto*

everywhere ovunque *ovoonkwe*

exactly esattamente *ezattamente*

examination esame (m) *ezame*

example esempio (m) *ezempyo*
  » **for example** per esempio *per ezempyo*

excellent eccellente *echelente*

except a parte *aparte*

excess baggage eccedenza (f) di bagaglio *echedentsa dee bagalyo*

to exchange scambiare *skambyare*
  (money) cambiare *kambyare*

exchange rate tasso (m) di cambio *tasso dee kambyo*

excited eccitato/a *echeetato/a*

exciting eccitante *echeetante*

excursion escursione (f) *eskoorsyone*

excuse me scusi *skoozee*

executive esecutivo/a *ezekooteevo/a*

exercise esercizio (m) *ezercheetsyo*

exhibition mostra (f) *mostra*

exit uscita (f) *oosheeta*

to expect aspettarsi *aspettarsee*

expensive caro/a *karo/a*

experience esperienza (f) *esperyentsa*

expert perito (m) –a (f) *pereeto/a*

to explain spiegare *spyegare*

explosion esplosione *esplozyone*

to export esportare *esportare*

express esprimere *espreemere*

extension cable prolunga (f) *proloonga*

external esterno *esterno*

extra supplementare *soopplementare*

eye occhio (m) *okkyo*

eyebrows sopracciglia (f/pl) *sopracheelya*

eyelashes ciglia (f/pl) *cheelya*

F

face faccia (f) *facha*

face cream crema (f) per il viso *krema per eel veezo*

face powder cipria (f) *cheeprya*

facilities servizi (m/pl) *serveetsee*

fact fatto (m) *fatto*
  » **in fact** difatti *deefattee*

factory fabbrica (f) *fabbreeka*

to fail *(exam/test)* essere bocciato/a *essere bochato/a*

failure fallimento (m) *faleemento*

to faint svenire *sveneere*

fair *(hair)* biondo/a *byondo/a*

fair giusto/a *joosto/a*

fairly abbastanza *abastantsa*

faith fede (f) *fede*

fake falso/a *falso/a*

to fall *(down/over)* cadere *kadere*

false falso/a *falso/a*

familiar familiare *fameelyare*

family famiglia (f) *fameelya*

fan *(air)* ventilatore (m) *venteelatore*
  (supporter) tifoso/з *teefoso/a*

fantastic fantastico/ *fantasteeko/a*

far *(away)* lontano/a *lontano/a*

fare tariffa (f) *tareefa*

farm fattoria (f) *fattoreea*

farmer agricoltore (m) *agreekoltore*

fashion moda (f) *moda*

fashionable/in fashion alla moda *alla moda*

fast veloce *veloche*

fat (noun) grasso (m) *grasso*
(adj.) grasso/a *grasso/a*

fatal mortale *mortale*

father padre (m) *padre*

father-in-law suocero (m) *soo-ochero*

fault difetto (m) *deefetto*

faulty difettoso/a *deefettoso/a*

favourite preferito/a *prefereeto/a*

fax fax (m) *faks*

feather penna (f) *penna*

fed up: to be fed up essere stufo/a *essere stoofo/a*

fee onorario (m) *onoraryo*

to feed (inc. baby) nutrire *nootreere*

to feel sentire *senteere*
(ill/well) sentirsi *senteersee*

female, feminine femminile *femeeneele*

ferry traghetto (m) *tragetto*

festival festa (f) *festa*

to fetch andare a prendere *andare a prendere*

fever febbre (f) *febbre*

few: a few poco/a *poko/a*

fiancé(e) fidanzato/a (m/f) *feedantsato/a*

field campo (m) *kampo*

to fight combattere *kombattere*

file (documents) archivio (m) *arkeevyo*
(nail/DIY) lima (f) *leema*

to fill riempire *ryempeere*

filling (dental) otturazione (f) *ottooratsyone*

film film (m) *feelm*

to finance finanziare *feenantsyare*

to find trovare *trovare*

fine (OK) ottimo *otteemo*
(penalty) multa (f) *moolta*
(weather) bello/a *bello/a*

finger dito (m) *deeto*

to finish finire *feeneere*

fire fuoco (m) *fwoko*

fire brigade vigili (m/pl) del fuoco *veejeelee del fwoko*

fire extinguisher estintore (m) *esteentore*

firework fuoco (m) d'artificio *fwoko darteefeecho*

firm (company) ditta (f) *deetta*

first primo/a *preemo/a*

first aid pronto soccorso (m) *pronto sokkorso*

first aid kit cassetta (f) di pronto soccorso *kassetta dee pronto sokkorso*

fish pesce (m) *peshe*

to fish/go fishing pescare *peskare*

fishing rod canna (f) da pesca *kanna da peska*

fishmonger's pescivendolo/a *pesheevendolo*

fit (healthy) in forma *een forma*

fitting room sala (f) di prova *sala dee prova*

to fix (mend) riparare *reeparare*

fizzy gassato/a *gazzato/a*

flag bandiera (f) *bandyera*

flash (camera) flash (m) *flash*

flat (apartment) appartamento (m) *appartamento*

flat (level) piano/a *pyano*

flavour aroma (f) *aroma*

flaw difetto (f) *deefetto*

flea market mercato (m) delle pulci *merkato delle poolchee*

flight volo (m) *volo*

flippers pinne (f/pl) *peenne*

flood inondazione (f) *eenondatsyone*

floor pavimento (m) *paveemento*
» **on the first floor** al primo piano (m) *al preemo pyano*
» **ground floor** pianterreno (m) *pyanterreno*

flour farina (f) *fareena*

flower fiore (m) *fyore*

flu influenza (f) *eenfloo-entsa*

fluent *(language)* corrente *korrente*

fluid fluido (m) *floo-eedo*

fly mosca (f) *moska*

fly sheet volantino (m) *volanteeno*

fly spray insetticida (m) spray *eensetteecheeda spraee*

to **fly** volare *volare*

fog nebbia (f) *nebbya*

folding *(e.g. chair)* pieghevole *pyegevole*

folk music musica (f) folcloristica *moozeeka folkloreesteeka*

to **follow** seguire *segweere*

following *(next)* di seguito *dee segweeto*

food cibo (m) *cheebo*

food poisoning intossicazione (f) alimentare *eentosseekatsyone aleementare*

foot piede (m) *pyede*

» **on foot** a piedi *a pyedee*

football calcio (m) *kalcho*

footpath sentiero (m) per pedoni *sentyero per pedonee*

for per *per*

forbidden vietato/a *vyetato/a*

foreign straniero/a *stranyero/a*

foreigner straniero (m) –a (f) *stranyero/a*

forest foresta (f) *foresta*

to **forget** dimenticare *deementeekare*

to **forgive** perdonare *perdonare*

fork forchetta *forketta*

form scheda (f) *skeda*

fortnight due settimane (f) *doo-e setteemane*

fortress fortezza (f) *fortetsa*

forward in avanti *een avantee*

forwarding address indirizzo (m) d'inoltro *eendeereetso deenoltro*

fountain fontana (f) *fontana*

fox volpe (f) *volpe*

fracture frattura (f) *frattoora*

fragile fragile *frajeele*

freckles lentiggini (f) *lenteejeenee*

free gratuito/a *gratweeto* *(unoccupied)* libero/a *leebero/a*

freedom libertà (f) *leeberta*

to **freeze** congelare *konjelare*

freezer congelatore (m) *konjelatore*

frequent frequente *frekwente*

fresh fresco/a *fresko/a*

fridge frigorifero (m) *freegoreefero*

fried fritto/a *freetto/a*

friend amico (m) –a (f) *ameeko/a*

frightened spaventato/a *spaventato/a*

frog rana (f) *rana*

from di *dee*

front fronte (f) *fronte*

» **in front of** davanti a *davantee a*

frontier frontiera (f) *frontyera*

frost brina (f) *breena*

frozen ghiacciato/a *gyachato*

fruit frutta (f) *frootta*

to **fry** friggere *freejjere*

frying pan padella (f) *padella*

fuel carburante (m) *karboorante*

full pieno/a *pyeno/a*

full board pensione (f) *pensyone*

full up *(booked up)* completo/a *kompleto*

fun: to have fun divertirsi *deeverteersee*

funeral funerale (m) *foonerale*

funfair luna park (m) *loona park*

funny *(amusing)* buffo/a *boofo/a* *(peculiar)* strano/a *strano/a*

fur pelliccia (f) *pelleecha*

furniture mobili (m/pl) *mobeelee*

further on più lontano *pyoo lontano*

fuse fusibile (m) *foozeebeele*

fusebox scatola (f) dei fusibili *skatola de-ee foozeebeelee*

G

gallery galleria (f) *gallereea*

gambling gioco (m) d'azzardo *joko dadzardo*

game *(match)* partita (f) *parteeta* *(hunting)* cacciagione (f) *kachajone*

garage *(for parking)* garage (m) *garaj* *(for petrol)* stazione (f) di servizio *statsyone dee serveetsyo*

garden giardino (m) *jardeeno*

gardener giardiniere (m) –a (f) *jardeenyere/a*

garlic aglio (m) *alyo*

gas gas (m) *gaz*

gas bottle/cylinder bombola (f) del gas *bombola del gaz*

gas refill ricambio (m) del gas *reekambyo del gaz*

gate cancello (m) *kanchello* (airport) uscita (f) *oosheeta*

gay (homosexual) gay *ge-ee*

gel (hair) gel (m) *jel*

general generale *jenerale*

» **in general** in genere *een jenere*

generous generoso/a *jeneroso/a*

gentle dolce *dolche*

gentleman gentiluomo (m) *jenteelwomo*

gentlemen signori (m/pl) *seenyoree* uomini (m/pl) *womeenee*

genuine genuino/a *jenoo-eeno*

German tedesco (m) –a (f) *tedesko/a*

Germany Germania (f) *jermanya*

to get ottenere *ottenere*

» **to get off** (bus) scendere *shendere*

» **to get on** (bus) salire *saleere*

gift regalo (m) *regalo*

gin gin (m) *jeen*

girl, girlfriend ragazza (f) *ragatsa*

to give dare *dare*

to give back restituire *resteetoo-eere*

glass (pane) vetro (m) *vetro* (tumbler) bicchiere (m) *beekkyere*

glasses occhiali (m/pl) *okkyalee*

gloves guanti (m/pl) *gwantee*

glue colla (f) *kolla*

to go andare *andare*

» **to go away** andar via *andar veea*

» **to go down** scendere *shendere*

» **to go in** entrare *entrare*

» **to go out** uscire *oosheere*

» **let's go!** andiamo! *andyamo*

goal scopo (m) *skopo* (football) rete (f) *rete*

goat capra (f) *kapra*

God Dio (m) *dee-o*

goggles (swimming) occhialini (m/pl) *okkyaleenee* (ski) occhiali da sci *okkyalee da schee*

gold oro (m) *oro*

golf golf (m) *golf*

golf clubs mazze (f/pl) da golf *matse da golf*

golf course campo (m) di golf *kampo dee golf*

good buono/a *bwono/a*

» **good day** buongiorno *bwonjorno*

» **good evening** buonasera *bwonasera*

» **good morning** buongiorno *bwonjorno*

» **good night** buonanotte *bwonanotte*

goodbye arrivederci *areevederchee* (casual) ciao *chow*

government governo (m) *governo*

gramme grammo (m) *grammo*

grammar grammatica (f) *grammateeka*

grandchildren nipoti (m/pl) *neepotee*

granddaughter nipote (f) *neepote*

grandfather nonno (m) *nonno*

grandmother nonna (f) *nonna*

grandparents nonni (m/pl) *nonnee*

grandson nipote (m) *neepote*

grass erba (f) *erba*

grateful riconoscente *reekonoshente*

greasy unto/a *oonto/a*

great! magnifico! *manyeefeeko*

green verde *verde*

greengrocer's fruttivendolo *frootteevendolo*

to greet accogliere *akkolyere*

grey grigio/a *greejo/a*

grilled alla griglia *alla greelya*

grocer's drogheria (f) *drogereea*

ground terra (f) *terra*

groundsheet telone (m) impermeabile *telone eempermee-abeele*

ground floor pianterreno (m) *pyanterreno*

group gruppo (f) *grooppo*

guarantee garanzia (f) *garantseea*

guest ospite (m/f) *ospeete*

guest house pensione (f) *pensyone*

guide guida (f) *gweeda*

guided tour visita (f) guidata *veezeeta gweedata*

guidebook guida (f) turistica *gweeda tooreesteeka*

guilty colpevole *kolpevole*

guitar chitarra (f) *keetarra*

gun arma (f) da fuoco *arma da fwoko*

H

habit abitudine (f) *abeetoodeene*

hail grandine (f) *grandeene*

hair capelli (m/pl) *kapellee*

hairbrush spazzola (f) per capelli *spatsola per kapellee*

haircut taglio (m) dei capelli *talyo de-ee kapellee*

hairdresser parrucchiere (m) –a (f) *parrookkyere/a*

hairdryer asciugacapelli (m) *ashoogakapellee*

half metà (f) *meta; (adj)* mezzo/a *medzo*

» **half board** mezza pensione (f) *medza pensyone*

» **half price** a metà prezzo *a meta predzo*

» **half an hour** mezz'ora *medzora*

» **half past (two)** (le due) e mezza *le doo-e e medza*

hall *(in house)* atrio (m) *atreeo*

ham prosciutto (m) *proshootto*

hamburger hamburger (m) *amboorger*

hammer martello (m) *martello*

hand mano (f) *mano*

hand cream crema per le mani *krema per le manee*

hand luggage bagaglio (m) a mano *bagalyo a mano*

hand made fatto a mano *fatto a mano*

handbag borsetta (f) *borsetta*

handkerchief fazzoletto (m) *fatsoletto*

handle maniglia (f) *maneelya*

to hang up *(telephone)* attaccare *attakkare*

hangover sbronza (f) *sbrontsa*

to happen avvenire *avveneere*

happy allegro/a *allegro/a*

harbour porto (m) *porto*

hard duro/a *dooro/a*
    (difficult) difficile *deeffeecheele*

hard drive disco (m) rigido *deesko reejeedo*

hardware shop negozio di ferramenta (f) *negotsyo dee ferramenta*

to hate odiare *odyare*

to have avere *avere*

hay fieno (m) *fyeno*

hayfever raffreddore (m) da fieno *raffreddore da fyeno*

he lui *loo-ee*

head testa (f) *testa (boss)* capo (m) *kapo*

headache mal (m) di testa *mal dee testa*

headphones cuffia (f) *kooffya*

to heal guarire *gwareere*

health salute (f) *saloote*

healthy sano/a *sano/a*

to hear sentire *senteere*

hearing udito (m) *oodeeto*

hearing aid apparecchio (m) acustico *apparekkyo akoosteeko*

heart cuore (m) *kwore*

heart attack infarto (m) cardiaco *eenfarto kardeeako*

heat calore (m) *kalore*

heater stufetta (f) *stoofetta*

heating riscaldamento (m) *reeskaldamento*

heavy pesante *pezante*

heel tallone (m) *tallone*
    (shoe) tacco (m) *takko*

height altezza (f) *altetsa*

helicopter elicottero (m) *eleekottero*

hello salve *salve*

helmet *(motorbike)* casco (m) *kasko*

help aiuto (m) *iyooto*

help! aiuto! *iyooto*

to help aiutare *iyootare*

her *(adj)* suo/a *soo-o/a*
  (pronoun) lei *le-ee*

herb erba (f) *erba*

herbal tea tisana *teezana*

here qui *kwee*

hers suo/a *soo-o/a*

hiccups: to have hiccups avere il singhiozzo (m) *avere eel seengyotso*

high alto *alto*

high chair seggiolone (m) *sejjolone*

to hijack dirottare *deerottare*

hill collina (f) *kolleena*

him lui *loo-ee*

to hire noleggiare *nolejare*

his suo/a *soo-o/a*

history storia (f) *storya*

to hit colpire *kolpeere*

to hitchhike fare l'autostop (m) *fare lowtostop*

HIV HIV *akkaeevee*

HIV positive HIV positivo *akka-ee-vee pozeeteevo*

hobby passatempo (m) *passatempo*

to hold tenere *tenere*

hole buco (m) *booko*

holiday vacanza (f) *vakantsa*
  » on holiday in vacanza *een vakantsa*

holy santo/a *santo/a*

home casa (f) *kaza*
  » at home a casa *a kaza*

homeopathic omeopatico/a *omeopateeko*

to be homesick avere la nostalgia *avere la nostaljeea*

homosexual omosessuale *omosessoo-ale*

honest onesto/a *onesto/a*

honeymoon viaggio (m) di nozze *vyajo dee notse*

to hope sperare *sperare*
  » I hope so spero di sì *spero dee see*

horrible orribile *orreebeele*

horse cavallo (m) *kavallo*

hospital ospedale (m) *ospedale*

host ospite (m) *ospeete*

hot caldo/a *kaldo/a*
  (spicy) piccante *peekante*

hotel albergo (m) *albergo*

hour ora (f) *ora*

half-hour mezz'ora *medzora*

house casa (f) *kasa*

how quanto *kwanto*
  » how far? quanto lontano? *kwanto lontano*
  » how long? quanto tempo? *kwanto tempo*
  » how many? quanti? *kwantee*
  » how much? quanto? *kwanto*

human umano/a *oomano/a*

hungry affamato/a *affamato/a*
  » to be hungry aver fame *aver fame*

to hunt cacciare *kachare*

hunting caccia (f) *kacha*

hurry: to be in a hurry aver fretta *aver fretta*

to hurt far male *far male*
  » it hurts fa male *fa male*

husband marito (m) *mareeto*

hydrofoil aliscafo (m) *aleeskafo*

I

I io *ee-o*

ice ghiaccio (m) *gyacho*

ice rink pista di pattinaggio (f) *peesta dee patteenajjo*

icy ghiacciato/a *gyachato*

idea idea (f) *eede-a*

if se *se*

ill malato/a *malato/a*

illness malattia (f) *malatteea*

to imagine immaginare *eemajeenare*

imagination immaginazione (f) *eemajeenatsyone*

immediately immediatamente *eemmedyatamente*

immersion heater boiler (m) *bo-eeler*

impatient impaziente *eempatsyente*

important importante *eemportante*

impossible impossibile *eemposseebeele*

impressive impressionante *eempressyonante*

in in *een*

included incluso/a *eenkloozo/a*

independent indipendente *eendeependente*

indigestion indigestione (f) *eendeejestyone*

indoors dentro *dentro*

industry industria (f) *eendoostreea*

infected infetto/a *eenfetto/a*

infection infezione (f) *eenfetsyone*

infectious contagioso/a *kontajoso/a*

inflamed infiammato/a *eenfyammato/a*

influenza influenza (f) *eenfloo-entsa*

informal informale *eenformale*

information informazione (f) *eenformatsyone*

information desk/office ufficio (m) informazioni *ooffeecho eenformatsyonee*

injection iniezione (f) *eenyetsyone*

to **injure** ferire *fereere*

injured ferito *fereeto*

injury ferita (f) *fereeta*

innocent innocente *eennochente*

insect insetto (m) *eensetto*

insect bite puntura d'insetto *poontoora deensetto*

insect repellent insettifugo (m) *eensetteefoogo*

inside dentro *dentro*

to **insist** insistere *eenseestere*

instant coffee caffè (m) solubile *kaffe soloobeele*

instead of invece di *eenveche dee*

instructor istruttore (m) *eestroottore*

insulin insulina (f) *eensooleena*

insurance assicurazione (f) *asseekooratsyone*

insurance policy polizza (f) d'assicurazione *poleetsa dasseekooratsyone*

to **insure** assicurare *asseekoorare*

intelligent intelligente *eentelleejente*

interest *(rate)* interesse (m) *eenteresse*

interested interessato/a *eenteressato/a*

interesting interessante *eenteressante*

international internazionale *eenternatsyonale*

Internet Internet (m) *eenternet*

Internet connection collegamento (m) Internet *kollegamento eenternet*

interpreter interprete (m/f) *eenterprete*

interval *(theatre etc.)* intervallo (m) *eentervallo*

interview intervista (f) *eenterveesta*

into in *een*

to **introduce** presentare *prezentare*

invitation invito (m) *eenveeto*

to **invite** invitare *eenveetare*

iodine iodio (m) *yodeeo*

Ireland Irlanda (f) *eerlanda*

Irish irlandese *eerlandese*

iron *(metal)* ferro (m) *ferro*; *(for clothes)* ferro da stiro *ferro da steero*

is è *e*

» **is there?** c'è? *che*

Islamic islamico/a *eezlameeko/a*

island isola (f) *eezola*

it esso/a *esso/a*

itch prurito (m) *prooreeto*

J

jacket giacca (f) *jakka*

jam marmellata (f) *marmellata*

jar barattolo (m) *barattolo*

jaw mascella (f) *mashella*

jazz jazz (m) *jaz*

jeans jeans (m/pl) *jeens*

jelly gelatina (f) *jelateena*

jellyfish medusa (f) *medoosa*

jetty gettata (f) *jettata*

jeweller's gioielleria (f) *joyellereea*

Jewish ebreo/a *ebre-o/a*

job lavoro (m) *lavoro*

to **jog** fare jogging *fare joggeeng*

joke battuta (f) *battoota*
journey viaggio (m) *vyajjo*
judge giudice (m) *joodeeche*
jug brocca (f) *brokka*
juice sugo (m) *soogo*
to jump saltare *saltare*
jump leads cavi (m/pl) di avviamento *kavee dee aveeamento*
jumper golf (m) *golf*
junction *(road)* incrocio (m) *eenkrocho*
just *(only)* soltanto *soltanto*

K

to keep tenere *tenere*
kettle bollitore (m) *bolleetore*
key chiave (f) *kyave*
key ring anello (m) portachiavi *anello portakyavee*
kidney rene (m) *rene*
to kill uccidere *oocheedere*
kilo(gram) chilo(grammo) (m) *keelo; keelogrammo*
kilometre chilometro (m) *keelometro*
kind *(sort)* genere (m) *jenere* *(generous)* gentile *jenteele*
king re (m) *re*
kiss bacio (m) *bacho*
to kiss baciare *bachare*
kitchen cucina (f) *koocheena*
knee ginocchio (m) *jeenokkyo*
knickers mutande (f/pl) *mootande*
knife coltello (m) *koltello*
to knock bussare *boossare*
knot nodo (m) *nodo*
to know *(someone)* conoscere *konoshere* *(something)* sapere *sapere*
   » **I don't know** non lo so *non lo so*

L

label etichetta (f) *eteeketta*
ladder scala (f) *skala*
ladies signore (f/pl) *seenyore*
lady signora (f) *seenyora*
lager birra (f) bionda *beerra byonda*

lake lago (m) *lago*
lamb *(meat)* agnello (m) *anyello*
lamp lampada (f) *lampada*
lamp post lampione (m) *lampyone*
land terreno (m) *terreno*
to land atterrare *atterrare*
landlady proprietaria (f) *propryetareea*
landlord proprietario (m) *propryetareeo*
language lingua (f) *leengwa*
large grande *grande*
last ultimo/a *oolteemo/a*
to last durare *doorare*
late in ritardo *een reetardo*
later dopo *dopo*
laugh risata (f) *reezata*
to laugh ridere *reedere*
launderette lavanderia (f) a gettoni *lavandereea a jettonee*
laundry lavanderia (f) *lavandereea*
lawyer avvocato (m) *avvokato*
laxative lassativo (m) *lassateevo*
lazy pigro/a *peegro/a*
lead piombo (m) *pyombo*
lead-free senza piombo *sentsa pyombo*
leaf foglio (m) *folyo*
leaflet volantino (m) *volanteeno*
to lean out sporgersi *sporjersee*
to learn imparare *eemparare*
least: at least almeno *almeno*
leather pelle (f) *pelle*
to leave lasciare *lashare* *(to go away)* partire *parteere*
left sinistro/a *seeneestro/a*
left luggage *(office)* deposito (m) bagagli *depozeeto bagalyee*
leg gamba (f) *gamba*
legal legale *legale*
lemon limone (m) *leemone*
lemonade limonata (f) *leemonata*
to lend prestare *prestare*
length lunghezza (f) *loongetsa*
lens *(camera)* lente (f) *lente*
lesbian lesbica (f) *lezbeeka*
less meno *meno*

lesson lezione (f) *letsyone*

to let *(allow)* permettere *permettere*
(rent) affittare *affeettare*

letter lettera (f) *lettera*

letterbox buca (f) delle lettere **boo**ka
delle *lettere*

lettuce lattuga (f) *lattooga*

leukemia leucemia (f) *leoochemeea*

level *(height, standard)* livello (m)
leevello; *(flat)* piano/a *pyano/a*

level crossing passaggio (m) a livello
passajjo a leevello

library biblioteca (f) *beeblyoteka*

licence *(driving)* patente (f) *patente*
(fishing etc) permesso (m) *permesso*

lid coperchio (m) *koperkyo*

to lie down sdraiarsi *zdriyarsee*

life vita (f) *veeta*

lifebelt salvagente (m) *salvajente*

lifeboat battello (m) di salvataggio
battello dee salvatajjo

lifeguard bagnino/a (m/f) *banyeeno/a*

lifejacket giubbotto (m) di salvataggio
joobbotto dee salvatajjo

lift ascensore (m) *ashensore*

light luce (f) *looche*

light bulb lampadina (f) *lampadeena*

light *(coloured)* chiaro/a *kyaro/a*
(weight) leggero/a *lejero/a*

to light *(fire)* accendere *achendere*

lighter *(cigarette)* accendino (m)
achendeeno

lighter fuel gas (m) per accendini *gaz per
achendeenee*

lightning fulmine (m) *foolmeene*

like *(similar to)* come *kome*

to like *(food, people)* piacere *pyachere*
» I like mi piace *mee pyache*

likely probabile *probabeele*

limited limitato/a *leemeetato/a*

line linea (f) *leenea*

lion leone (m) *leone*

lips labbra (f/pl) *labbra*

lipstick rossetto (m) *rossetto*

liqueur liquore (m) *leekwore*

liquid liquido/a *leekweedo/a*

list elenco (m) *elenko*

to listen ascoltare *askoltare*

litre litro (m) *leetro*

litter rifiuti (m/pl) *reefyootee*

little poco/a *poko/a*
» **a little** un po' *oon po*

to live vivere *veevere*
(dwell) abitare *abeetare*

liver fegato (m) *fegato*

living-room salotto (m) *salotto*

loan prestito (m) *presteeto*

local locale *lokale*

lock serratura (f) *serratoora*

to lock chiudere a chiave *kyoodere a kyave*

locker armadietto (m) *armadyetto*

London Londra (f) *Londra*

lonely solitario/a *soleetaryo/a*

long lungo/a *loongo/a*

long-distance *(telephone call)* telefonata (f)
interurbana *telefonata eenteroorbana*

look sguardo (m) *zgwardo*

to look (at) guardare *gwardare*

to look for cercare *cherkare*

loose sciolto/a *sholto/a*

lorry camion (m) *kamyon*

to lose perdere *perdere*

lost property office ufficio (m) oggetti
smarriti *ooffeecho ojjettee smarreetee*

a lot *(of)* molto/a *molto*

lotion lozione (f) *lotsyone*

lottery lotteria (f) *lottereea*

loud forte *forte*

lounge salotto (m) *salotto*

love amore (m) *amore*

to love amare *amare*

low basso/a *basso/a*

low-fat sgrassato/a *sgrassato/a*

lucky fortunato/a *fortoonato/a*

luggage bagagli (m/pl) *bagalyee*

lump *(swelling)* protuberanza (f)
protooberantsa

lunch pranzo (m) *prantso*

M

machine macchina (f) *makkeena*

mad pazzo/a *patso/a*

madam signora *seenyora*

magazine rivista (f) *reeveesta*

mail corriere (m) *korryere*

main principale *preencheepale*

to make fare *fare*

make-up trucco (m) *trooko*

male maschio (m) *maskyo*

man uomo (m) *womo*

to manage *(cope)* cavarsela *kavarsela*

manager direttore (m) –trice (f) *deerettore, deerettreeche*

many molti *moltee*

» not many pochi *pokee*

map cartina (f) *karteena*

marble marmo (m) *marmo*

margarine margarina (f) *margareena*

market mercato (m) *merkato*

married sposato/a *spozato/a*

» to get married sposarsi *spozarsee*

mascara mascara (m) *maskara*

masculine maschile *maskeele*

mask maschera (f) *maskera*

mass *(church)* messa (f) *messa*

match fiammifero (m) *fyammeefero*

  (game) partita (f) *parteeta*

material materiale (m) *materyale*

matter: it doesn't matter non importa *non eemporta*

» what's the matter? cosa c'è? *koza che?*

mattress materasso (m) *materasso*

» air mattress materasso (m) pneumatico *materasso pneoomateeko*

mature *(cheese)* maturo *matooro*

me me *me*

meadow prato (m) *prato*

meal pranzo (m) *prantso*

mean: what does this mean? che significa? *ke seenyeefeeka?*

meanwhile intanto *eentanto*

measles morbillo (m) *morbeello*

» German measles rosolia (f) *rozolya*

to measure misurare *meezoorare*

measurement misura (f) *meezoora*

meat carne (f) *karne*

» cold meats salumi *saloomee*

mechanic meccanico (m) *mekkaneeko*

medical medico/a *medeeko/a*

medicine *(drug)* medicina (f) *medeecheena*

medieval medievale *medee-evale*

Mediterranean Mediterraneo (m) *medeeterraneo*

medium *(size)* media *medya*

  (steak) a puntino *a poonteeno*

  (wine) semisecco, *semeesekko*

meeting riunione (f) *ryoonyone*

member socio (m) *sochyo*

memory memoria (f) *memorya*

memory stick *(for camera)* scheda (f) di memoria *skeda dee memorya*

men uomini (m/pl) *womeenee*

to mend riparare *reeparare*

menu *(à la carte)* menu (m) a scelta *menu a shelta*

  (set) menu (m) fisso *menu feesso*

message messaggio (m) *messajjo*

metal metallo (m) *metallo*

meter contatore (m) *kontatore*

metre metro (m) *metro*

microwave oven forno (m) a microonde (f) *forno a meekro-onde*

midday mezzogiorno (m) *medzojorno*

middle mezzo (m) *medzo*

middle-aged di mezza età (f) *dee medza eta*

midnight mezzanotte (f) *medzanotte*

migraine emicrania (f) *emeekranya*

mild mite *meete*

milk latte (m) *latte*

mind: do you mind if...? le dispiace se...? *le deespyache se...*

» I don't mind non mi dispiace *non mee deespyache*

mine *(of me)* mio/a *mee-o/a*

minibus minibus (m) *meeneeboos*

mini-disc minidisco (m) *meeneedeesko*

minister ministro (m) *meeneestro*

minute minuto (m) *meenooto*

mirror specchio (m) *spekkyo*

Miss Signorina (f) *seenyoreena*

to miss *(bus etc)* perdere *perdere*

 (nostalgia) mancare *mankare*

mist nebbia (f) *nebbya*

mistake errore (m) *errore*

 » **to make a mistake** sbagliarsi
 sbalyarsee

mixed misto/a *meesto/a*

mixture miscela (f) *meeshela*

mobile *(phone)* telefonino (m)
 telefoneeno; cellulare (m) *chelloolare*

model modello (m) *modello*

modern moderno/a *moderno/a*

moisturiser idratante (m) *eedratante*

moment attimo (m) *atteemo*

monastery monastero (m) *monastero*

money soldi (m/pl) *soldee*

month mese (m) *meze*

monument monumento (m)
 monoomento

moon luna (f) *loona*

moped ciclomotore (m) *cheeklomotore*

more di più *dee pyoo*

morning mattina (f) *matteena*

mortgage mutuo (m) *mootwo*

mosque moschea (f) *moskea*

mosquito zanzara (f) *dzandzara*

mosquito net zanzariera (f) *dzandzaryera*

most (of) la maggior parte *la majjor
 parte*

mother madre (f) *madre*

mother-in-law suocera (f) *soo-ochera*

motor motore (m) *motore*

motorbike motocicletta (f)
 motocheekletta

motorboat motoscafo (m) *motoskafo*

motor racing corse (f/pl)
 automobilistiche *korse
 owtomobeeleesteeke*

motorway autostrada (f) *owtostrada*

mountain montagna (f) *montanya*

mountaineering alpinismo (m)
 alpeeneezmo

moustache baffi (m/pl) *baffee*

mouth bocca (f) *bokka*

to move muovere *mwovere*

Mr Signor *seenyor*

Mrs Signora *seenyora*

much molto *molto*

mug *(cup)* tazza (f) *tatsa*

mullah mullah (m) *moola*

to murder assassinare *assasseenare*

museum museo (m) *mooze-o*

music musica (f) *moozeeka*

musical musicale *moozeekale*

musician musicista (m/f) *moozeecheesta*

Muslim mussulmano/a *moossoolmano/a*

must: you must dovere: devi *dovere:
 devee*

my mio/a *mee-o/a*

mystery mistero (m) *meestero*

N

nail unghia (f) *oongya*

nail clippers tronchesine (f/pl)
 tronkeseene

nail file lima (f) da unghie *leema da
 oongye*

naked nudo/a *noodo/a*

name nome (m) *nome*

napkin tovagliolo (m) *tovalyolo*

nappy pannolino (m) *pannoleeno*

national nazionale *natsyonale*

nationality nazionalità (f) *natsyonaleeta*

natural naturale *natoorale*

naturally naturalmente *natooralmente*

naughty birichino/a *beereekeeno/a*

navy marina (f) militare *mareena
 meeleetare*

navy blue blu marino *bloo mareeno*

near vicino *veecheeno*

nearby qui vicino *kwee veecheeno*

nearest più vicino *pyoo veecheeno*

nearly quasi *kwazee*

necessary necessario/a *nechessaryo/a*

necklace collana (f) *kollana*

to need avere bisogno di *avere beezonyo dee*

needle ago (m) *ago*

negative *(photo)* negativo (m) *negateevo*

neighbour vicino (m) *veecheeno*

neither... nor... né... né... *ne... ne...*

nephew nipote (m) *neepote*

nervous ansioso/a *ansyozo/a*

net rete (f) *rete*

never mai *ma-ee*

new nuovo/a *nwovo/a*

New Year's Day capodanno (m) *kapodanno*

news notizie (f/pl) *noteetsye*

newspaper giornale (m) *jornale*

newspaper kiosk edicola (f) *edeekola*

next prossimo/a *prosseemo/a*

next to accanto a *akkanto a*

nice simpatico/a *seempateeko/a*

niece nipote (f) *neepote*

night notte (f) *notte*

nightclub locale (m) notturno *lokale notturno*

no no *no*

nobody nessuno/a *nessoono/a*

noise rumore (m) *roomore*

noisy rumoroso/a *roomoroso/a*

non-alcoholic analcolico/a *analkoleeko/a*

none nessuno/a *nessoono/a*

non-smoking per non fumatori *per non foomatoree*

normal normale *normale*

normally normalmente *normalmente*

north nord (m) *nord*

nose naso (m) *nazo*

nosebleed emorragia (f) nasale *emorrajee-a nazale*

not non *non*

note *(bank)* banconota (f) *bankonota*

notepad bloc-notes (m) *bloknotes*

nothing niente *nyente*

» **nothing else** nient'altro *nyentaltro*

now adesso *adesso*

nowhere da nessuna parte *da nessoona parte*

nuclear power energia (f) nucleare *enerjeea nookleare*

number numero (m) *noomero*

nurse infermiera (f) *eenfermyera*

nursery slope pista (f) per principianti *peesta per preencheepyantee*

nut noce (f) *noche*

O

oar remo (m) *remo*

object *(thing)* oggetto (m) *ojjetto*

obvious evidente *eveedente*

occasionally ogni tanto *onyee tanto*

occupied occupato/a *okkoopato/a*

odd strano/a *strano/a*

　(not even) dispari *deesparee*

of di *dee*

» **of course** certo *cherto*

off *(TV, light)* spento/a *spento/a; (milk)* andato/a a male *andato/a a male*

offended offeso/a *offezo/a*

offer offerta (f) *offerta*

» **special offer** offerta (f) speciale *offerta spechale*

office ufficio (m) *ooffeecho*

officer ufficiale (m) *ooffeechale*

official ufficiale *ooffeechale*

often spesso *spesso*

» **how often?** quanto spesso? *kwanto spesso?*

oil olio (m) *olyo*

OK okay *okay*

old vecchio/a *vekkyo/a*

old-fashioned superato/a *sooperato/a*

olive oliva (f) *oleeva*

olive oil olio (m) d'oliva *olyo doleeva*

on *(prep)* su *soo*

　(TV, light) acceso/a *acchezo/a*

once una volta (f) *oona volta*

only soltanto *soltanto*

open aperto/a *aperto/a*

to **open** aprire *apreere*

opera opera (f) *opera*

operation intervento (m) chirurgico *eentervento keeroorjeeko*

opinion opinione (f) *opeenyone*

» **in my opinion** a mio parere (m) *a meeo parere*

opposite opposto/a *opposto/a*

optician ottico (m) *otteeko*

or o *o*

orange *(fruit)* arancia (f) *arancha* *(colour)* arancione *aranchone*

to **order** comandare *komandare*

ordinary ordinario/a *ordeenaryo/a*

to **organise** organizzare *organeetsare*

original originale *oreejeenale*

originally originalmente *oreejeenalmente*

other altro/a *altro/a*

our, ours nostro *nostro*

out (of) fuori *fworee*

outdoors, outside all'aperto *allaperto*

over finito *feeneeto*

overcast coperto/a *koperto/a*

to **overtake** sorpassare *sorpassare*

to **owe** dovere *dovere*

owner proprietario/a (f) *propryetaryo/a*

ozone-friendly che rispetta l'ozono *ke reespetta lozono*

P

package tour viaggio (m) organizzato *vyajjo organeetsato*

packet pacchetto (m) *paketto*

paddle *(canoeing)* pagaia (f) *pagiya*

padlock lucchetto (m) *looketto*

page pagina (f) *pajeena*

pain dolore (m) *dolore*

painful doloroso/a *doloroso/a*

painkiller analgesico (m) *analjeseeko*

paint vernice (f) *verneeche*

to **paint** *(picture)* dipingere *deepeenjere*

painter pittore (m) *peettore*

painting pittura (f) *peettoora*

pair paio (m) *piyo*

palace palazzo (m) *palatso*

pale pallido/a *paleedo/a*

pants mutande (f/pl) *mootande*

paper carta (f) *karta*

paraffin paraffina (f) *parafeena*

paralysed paralizzato/a *paraleetsato/a*

parcel pacco (m) *pakko*

pardon? prego? *prego*

parents genitori (m/pl) *jeneetoree*

park parco (m) *parko*

to **park** parcheggiare *parkejare*

parking parcheggio (m) *parkejo*

parking meter parchimetro (m) *parkeemetro*

parliament parlamento (m) *parlamento*

part parte (f) *parte*

particular: in particular in particolare *een parteekolare*

partly parzialmente *partsyalmente*

partner socio (m) *socho*

party festa (f) *festa*

to **pass** *(on road, salt etc.)* passare *passare*

passenger passeggero (m) *passejero*

passion passione (f) *passyone*

passport passaporto (m) *passaporto*

passport control controllo (m) dei passaporti *kontrollo de-ee passaportee*

past passato (m) *passato*

» **in the past** nel passato *nel passato*

pasta pasta (f) *pasta*

pastry pasta (f) *pasta*

path sentiero (m) *sentyero*

patient *(hospital)* paziente (m/f) *patsyente*

pattern trama (f) *trama*

pavement marciapiede (m) *marchapyede*

to **pay** pagare *pagare*

» **to pay cash** pagare in liquido *pagare een leekweedo*

peace pace (f) *pache*

peanut arachide (f) *arakeede*

pedal pedale (m) *pedale*

pedestrian pedone (m) *pedone*

pedestrian crossing attraversamento (m) pedonale *attraversamento pedonale*

to **peel** sbucciare *sboochare*

peg picchetto (m) *peeketto*

pen penna (f) *penna*

pencil matita (f) *mateeta*

penknife temperino (m) *tempereeno*

penicillin penicillina (f) *peneecheeleena*

pensioner pensionato (m) –a (f) *pensyonato*

people gente (f) *jente*

pepper pepe (m) *pepe*

per per *per*

perfect perfetto/a *perfetto/a*

performance spettacolo (m) *spettakolo*

perfume profumo (m) *profoomo*

perhaps forse *forse*

period *(menstrual)* mestruazioni (f/pl) *mestrooatsyonee*

period pains dolori mestruali *doloree mestrualee*

permit permesso (m) *permesso*

to **permit** permettere *permettere*

personal personale (m) *personale*

petrol benzina (f) *bentseena*

petrol can latta (f) per la benzina *latta per la bentseena*

petrol station stazione (f) di rifornimento *statsyone dee reeforneemento*

to **photocopy** fotocopiare *fotokopeeare*

photo foto (f) *foto*

photographer fotografo (m) –a (f) *fotografo/a*

phrase book frasario (m) *frazaryo*

piano pianoforte (m) *pyanoforte*

to **pick** *(choose)* scegliere *shelyere*

picnic picnic (m) *peekneek*

picture pittura (f) *peetoora*

piece pezzo (m) *petso*

pier pontile (m) *ponteele*

pig maiale (m) *miyale*

pill pillola (f) *peelola*

» **the pill** la pillola (f) *la peelola*

pillow cuscino (m) *koosheeno*

pillowcase federa (f) *federa*

pilot pilota (m) *peelota*

pilot light fiammella (f) d'emergenza *fyammella demerjenza*

pin spillo (m) *speello*

pink roso/a *rozo/a*

pipe *(smoking)* pipa (f) *peepa* *(drain)* tubo (m) *toobo*

place luogo (m) *loo-ogo* *(seat)* posto (m) *posto*

plain semplice *sempleeche*

plan piano (m) *pyano* (m)

plane aereo (m) *aereo*

plant pianta (f) *pyanta*

plaster *(sticking)* cerotto (m) *cherotto*

plastic plastica (f) *plasteeka*

plastic bag sacchetto (m) di plastico *saketto dee plasteeko*

plate piatto (m) *pyatto*

platform binario (m) *beenareeo*

play *(theatre)* commedia (f) *kommedya*

to **play** giocare *jokare*

pleasant piacevole *pyachevole*

please per favore *per favore*

plenty (of) parecchio/a *parekkyo/a*

plug *(bath)* tappo (m) *tappo* *(electrical)* spina (f) *speena*

plumber idraulico (m) *eedrowleeko*

pneumonia polmonite (f) *polmoneete*

pocket tasca (f) *taska*

point punto (m) *poonto*

poison veleno (m) *veleno*

poisonous velenoso/a *velenoso/a*

pole palo (m) *palo*

police polizia (f) *poleetseea*

police car auto (f) della polizia *owto della poleetseea*

police station commissariato (m) *commeessaryato*

polish lucido (m) *loocheedo*

polite cortese *korteze*

politician politico (m) *poleeteeko*

politics politica (f) *poleeteeka*

polluted inquinato/a *eenkweenato/a*

pollution inquinamento (m) *eenkweenamento*

pool *(swimming)* piscina (f) *peesheena*

poor povero/a *povero/a*

pop *(music)* pop-music (f) *popmoozeek*

Pope Papa (m) *papa*

popular popolare *popolare*

pork maiale (m) *miyale*

port *(harbour)* porto (m) *porto*

(wine) Porto (m) *porto*

portable portatile *portateele*

porter portiere (m) *portyere*

portion porzione (f) *portsyone*

portrait ritratto (m) *reetratto*

positive *(sure)* sicuro/a *seekooro/a*

possible possibile *posseebeele*

» **as ... as possible** al più ... possibile *al pyoo ... posseebeele*

possibly possibilmente *posseebeelmente*

post *(mail)* posta (f) *posta*

to **post** imbucare *eembookare*

postbox casetta (f) delle lettere *kassetta delle lettere*

postcard cartolina (f) *kartoleena*

postcode codice (m) di avviamento postale *kodeeche dee aveeamento postale*

poster affissione (f) *affeessyone*

post office ufficio (m) postale *ooffeecho postale*

to **postpone** rinviare *reenvee-are*

pot pentola (f) *pentola*

potato patata (f) *patata*

potato crisps patatine (f/pl) *patateene*

pottery ceramica (f) *cherameeka*

potty *(child's)* vasino (m) *vaseeno*

pound *(sterling)* sterlina (f) *sterleena*

to **pour** versare *versare*

powder polvere (f) *polvere*

powdered milk latte (m) in polvere *latte een polvere*

power potere (m) *potere*; *(physical strength)* forza (f) *fortsa*

power cut interruzione (f) di corrente *eenterrootsyone dee korrente*

pram carrozzina (f) *karrotseena*

to **prefer** preferire *prefereere*

pregnant incinta *eencheenta*

to **prepare** preparare *preparare*

prescription ricetta (f) *reechetta*

present *(gift)* regalo (m) *regalo*

pretty grazioso/a *gratsyoso/a*

price prezzo (m) *pretso*

priest prete (m) *prete*

prime minister primo ministro (m) *preemo meeneestro*

prince principe (m) *preencheepe*

princess principessa (f) *preencheepessa*

print *(photo)* stampato (m) *stampato*

to **print** stampare *stampare*

prison prigione (f) *preejone*

private privato/a *preevato/a*

prize premio (m) *premyo*

probably probabilmente *probabeelmente*

problem problema (m) *problema*

profession professione (f) *professyone*

profit profitto (m) *profeetto*

programme programma (m) *programma*

prohibited proibito (m) *proeebeeto*

to **promise** promettere *promettere*

properly correttamente *korrettamente*

property proprietà (f) *propree-eta*

protestant protestante *protestante*

public pubblico (m) *poobbleeko*

(adj.) pubblico/a *poobbleeko/a*

public holiday festa (f) nazionale *festa natsyonale*

to **pull** tirare *teerare*

to **pump up** gonfiare *gonfyare*

puncture gomma (f) *gomma*

pure puro/a *pooro/a*

purple viola *vyola*

purse borsellino (m) *borselleeno*
to push spingere *speenjere*
push-chair passeggino (m) *passejeeno*
to put down posare *pozare*
to put on *(clothes)* indossare *eendossare*
pyjamas pigiama (m) *peejama*

Q

quality qualità (f) *kwaleeta*
quarter quarto (m) *kwarto*
quay banchina (f) *bankeena*
queen regina (f) *rejeena*
question domanda (f) *domanda*
queue coda (f) *koda*
quick(ly) presto *presto*
quiet taciturno/a *tacheetoorno/a*
quite abbastanza *abbastantsa*

R

rabbi rabbino (m) *rabbeeno*
rabbit coniglio (m) *koneelyo*
rabies rabbia (f) *rabbya*
racecourse ippodromo (m) *eeppodromo*
racing *(horse)* corse (f/pl) ippiche *korse eeppeeke;* *(motor)* corse (f/pl) automobilistiche *korse owtomobeeleesteeke*
racket *(tennis)* racchetta (f) *rakketta*
radiator radiatore (m) *radyatore*
radio radio (f) *radyo*
radio station stazione (f) radio *statsyone radeeo*
raft zattera (f) *dzattera*
railway ferrovia (f) *ferroveea*
railway station stazione (f) ferroviaria *statsyone ferrovyarya*
rain pioggia (f) *pyojja*
» **it's raining** piove *pyove*
raincoat impermeabile (m) *eemperme-abeele*
rare raro/a *raro/a*
rare *(steak)* al sangue *al sangwe*
rash *(spots)* sfogo (m) *sfogo*

rate *(speed)* ritmo (m) *reetmo*
(tariff) tariffa (f) *tareeffa*
rather *(quite)* piuttosto *pyoottosto*
raw crudo/a (m) *kroodo/a*
razor rasoio (m) *razo-yo*
razor blade lametta (f) *lametta*
to reach raggiungere *rajoonjere*
to read leggere *lejjere*
reading lettura (f) *lettoora*
ready pronto *pronto*
real *(authentic)* autentico/a *owtenteeko/a*
really veramente *veramente*
rear retro (m) *retro*
reason ragione (f) *rajone*
receipt ricevuta (f) *reechevoota*
receiver *(telephone)* ricevitore (m) *reecheveetore*
reception ricezione (f) *reechetsyone*
receptionist receptionist (m/f) *reechepshoneest*
recipe ricetta (f) *reechetta*
to recognise riconoscere *reekonoshere*
to recommend raccomandare *rakkomandare*
to recover *(from an illness)* guarire *gwareere*
red rosso/a *rosso/a*
reduction riduzione (f) *reedootsyone*
to refill riempire *ryempeere*
refrigerator frigorifero (m) *freegoreefero*
refugee rifugiato (m) *reefoojato*
refund rimborso (m) *reemborso*
to refund rimborsare *reemborsare*
region regione (f) *rejone*
to register registrare *rejeestrare*
registered letter lettera (f) raccomandata *lettera rakkomandata*
registration number numero (m) di targa *noomero dee targa*
registration document *(car)* libretto (m) di circolazione *leebretto dee cheerkolatsyone*
relation parente (m/f) *parente*
relatively relativamente *relateevamente*

religion religione (f) *releejone*
to remain rimanere *reemanere*
to remember ricordare *reekordare*
to remove togliere *tolyere*
   (tooth) estrarre *estrarre*
rent affitto (m) *affeetto*
to rent prendere in affitto *prendere een affeetto*
to repair riparare *reeparare*
to repeat ripetere *reepetere*
reply risposta (f) *reesposta*
to reply rispondere *reespondere*
report rapporto (m) *rapporto*
to report rapportare *rapportare*
to rescue salvare *salvare*
reservation *(hotel etc)* prenotazione (f) *prenotatsyone*
to reserve prenotare *prenotare*
reserved riservato/a *reezervato/a*
responsible responsabile *responsabeele*
to rest riposo (m) *reepozo*
restaurant ristorante (m) *reestorante*
result risultato (m) *reesooltato*
retired in pensione *een pensyone*
return ritorno (m) *reetorno;* *(ticket)* andata e ritorno *andata e reetorno*
to return tornare *tornare*
to reverse *(car)* fare marcia indietro *fare marcha eendyetro*
reverse-charge call chiamata (f) a carico del destinatario *kyamata a kareeko del desteenataryo*
rheumatism reumatismo (m) *reoomateezmo*
rice riso (m) *reezo*
rich ricco/a *reekko/a*
to ride *(horse)* cavalcare *kavalkare* *(bike)* andare a bicicletta (f) *andare a beecheekletta*
right destro/a *destro/a* *(correct)* giusto *joosto*
  » **to be right** avere ragione *avere rajone*
  » **right-hand** destro/a *destro/a*
ring *(jewellery)* anello (m) *anello*

ripe maturo/a *matooro/a*
river fiume (m) *fyoome*
road strada (f) *strada*
roadworks lavori (m/pl) stradali *lavoree stradalee*
roast arrosto/a *arrosto/a*
to rob rubare *roobare*
robbery rapina (f) *rapeena*
roof tetto (m) *tetto*
room stanza (f) *stantsa* *(space)* posto (m) *posto*
rope corda (f) *korda*
rose rosa (f) *roza*
rotten marcio/a *marcho/a*
rough *(surface)* ruvido/a *rooveedo/a* *(sea)* agitato/a *ajeetato/a*
round rotondo/a *rotondo/a*
roundabout rotatoria (f) *rotatorya*
row *(theatre etc.)* fila (f) *feela*
to row remare *remare*
rowing boat barca (f) a remi *barka a remee*
royal reale *re-ale*
rubber gomma (f) *gomma*
rubbish rifiuti (m/pl) *reefyootee*
rucksack zaino (m) *dza-eeno*
rude sgarbato/a *zgarbato/a*
ruins rovine (f/pl) *roveene*
rum rum (m) *room*
to run correre *korrere*
rush hour ora (f) di punta *ora dee poonta*
rusty arrugginito/a *arroojeeneeto/a*

S

sad triste *treeste*
safe *(strongbox)* cassaforte (f) *kassaforte*
safe sicuro/a *seekooro/a*
safety pin spilla (f) di sicurezza *speella dee seekooretsa*
sail vela (f) *vela*
to sail navigare *naveegare*
sailing navigazione *naveegatsyone*
sailing boat barca (f) a vela *barka a vela*

saint santo (m) *santo*

salad insalata (f) *eensalata*

sale *(bargains)* sconti (m/pl) *skontee*

salmon salmone (m) *salmone*

salt sale (m) *sale*

salty salato/a *salato/a*

same stesso/a *stesso/a*

sample campione (m) *kampyone*

sand sabbia (f) *sabbya*

sandals sandali (m/pl) *sandalee*

sandwich tramezzino (m) *trametseeno*

sandy sabbioso/a *sabbyoso /a*

sanitary towels assorbenti (m/pl) *assorbentee*

sauce sugo (m) *soogo*

saucepan tegame (m) *tegame*

saucer piattino (m) *pyatteeno*

sauna sauna (f) *sowna*

to save *(money)* risparmiare *reesparmyare*

to say dire *deere*

to scald scottare *skottare*

scales bilancia (m) *beelancha*

scarf sciarpa (f) *sharpa*

scene scena (f) *shena*

scenery paesaggio (m) *paezajjo*

scent profumo (m) *profoomo*

school scuola (f) *skwola*

scissors forbici (m/pl) *forbeechee*

scooter scooter (m) *skooter*

score punteggio (m) *poontejjo*

Scotland Scozia (f) *skotsya*

Scottish scozzese *skotseze*

scratch graffio (m) *graffyo*

screen schermo (m) *skermo*

screw vite (f) *veete*

screwdriver cacciavite (m) *kachaveete*

sculpture scultura (f) *skooltoora*

sea mare (m) *mare*

seafood frutti (m/pl) di mare *froottee dee mare*

seasickness mal (m) di mare *mal dee mare*

season stagione (f) *stajone*

season ticket abbonamento (m) *abbonamento*

seat sedile (m) *sedeele*

seatbelt cintura (f) di sicurezza *cheentoora dee seekooretsa*

second *(time period)* secondo (m) *sekondo; (adj.)* secondo/a *sekondo/a*

secret segreto (m) *segreto*

section sezione (f) *setsyone*

sedative sedativo (m) *sedateevo*

to see vedere *vedere*

to seem sembrare *sembrare*

self-catering flat appartamento (m) indipendente *appartamento eendeependente*

self-service self-service (m) *selfservees*

to sell vendere *vendere*

to send mandare *mandare*

senior citizen anziano (m) –a (f) *antsyano/a*

sensible assennato/a *assennato/a*

sentence frase (m) *fraze*

separate(d) separato/a *separato/a*

septic tank fossa (f) settica *fossa setteeka*

serious serio/a *seryo/a* *(grave)* grave *grave*

to serve servire *serveere*

service *(charge)* servizio (m) *serveetsyo* *(church)* messa (f) *messa*

several parecchi *parekkee*

to sew cucire *koocheere*

sex *(gender)* sesso (m) *sesso* *(intercourse)* sesso (m) *sesso*

shade *(not sunny)* ombra (f) *ombra*

shadow ombra (f) *ombra*

shampoo shampoo (m) *shampo*

sharp affilato/a *affelato/a*

shave rasatura (f) *rasatoora*

to shave rasare *razare*

shaving cream/foam crema/schiuma (f) da barba *krema/skyooma da barba*

she lei *le-ee*

sheep pecora (f) *pekora*

sheet lenzuolo (m) *lentswolo*

shelf scaffale (m) *skaffale*

shell *(egg, nut)* guscio (m) *goosho*

shelter riparo (m) *reeparo*

shiny lucente *loochente*

ship nave (f) *nave*

shirt camicia (f) *kameecha*

shock *(electrical)* scossa (f) *skossa*
   (emotional) shock (m) *shok*

shoe(s) scarpa (f) –e (f/pl) *skarpa/e*

shoelace stringa (f) *streenga*

shoe polish lucido (m) da scarpe *loocheedo da skarpe*

shoe repairer's calzoleria *kaltsolereea*

shoe shop negozio (m) di calzature *negotsyo dee kalzatoore*

shop negozio (m) *negotsyo*

shop assistant commesso (m) –a (f) *komesso/a*

shopping: to go shopping fare la spesa *fare la speza*

shopping centre centro (m) commerciale *chentro komerchale*

short corto/a *korto/a*

shorts calzoncini (m/pl) *kalzoncheenee*

shout grido (m) *greedo*

show spettacolo (m) *spettakolo*

to show mostrare *mostrare*

shower doccia (f) *docha*

to shrink restringersi *restreenjersee*

shrunk ristretto/a *reestretto/a*

shut chiuso/a *kyoozo/a*

to shut chiudere *kyoodere*

shutter battente (m) *battente*

sick malato/a *malato/a*
   » **to feel sick** stare male *stare male*
   » **to be sick** essere malato *essere malato*

side lato (m) *lato*

sieve setaccio (m) *setacho*

sight *(vision)* vista (f) *veesta*; *(tourist)* luogo d'interesse *lwogo deenteresse*

sightseeing giro (m) turistico *jeero tooreesteeko*

sign segno (m) *senyo*

to sign firmare *feermare*

signal segnale (m) *senyale*

signature firma (f) *feerma*

silent silenzioso/a *seelentsyoso*

silk seta (f) *seta*

silver argento (m) *arjento*

SIM card carta (f) SIM *karta seem*

similar simile *seemeele*

simple semplice *sempleeche*

since da allora *da allora*

to sing cantare *kantare*

single *(room)* singola *seengola*; *(ticket)* di sola andata *dee sola andata*; *(unmarried: man)* celibe *cheleebe* *(unmarried: woman)* nubile *noobeele*

sink lavandino (m) *lavandeeno*

sir signore (m) *seenyore*

sister sorella (f) *sorella*

sister-in-law cognata (f) *konyata*

to sit *(down)* sedersi *sedersee*

size *(clothes, shoes)* misura (f) *meesoora*

skates *(ice)* pattini (m/pl) *patteenee* *(roller)* pattini (m/pl) a rotelle *patteenee a rotelle*

to skate pattinare *patteenare*

to ski sciare *shee-are*

skiing lo sci *lo shee*
   » **cross-country skiing** sci (m) di fondo *shee dee fondo*
   » **downhill skiing** sci (m) alpino *shee alpeeno*

ski boots scarponi da sci *skarponee da shee*

ski-lift sciovia (f) *sheeoveea*

ski-run/slope pista (f) da sci *peesta da shee*

ski sticks racchette (f/pl) da sci *rakette da shee*

skimmed milk latte (m) scremato *latte skremato*

skin pelle (f) *pelle*

skirt gonna (f) *gonna*

sky cielo (m) *chelo*

to sleep dormire *dormeere*

sleeper/sleeping-car carrozza (f) letto *karotsa letto*

sleeping bag sacco (m) a pelo *sakko a pelo*

sleeve manica (f) *maneeka*

slice fetta (f) *fetta*

sliced affettato/a *affettato/a*

slim snello/a *znello/a*

slippery scivoloso/a *sheevoloso*

slow lento/a *lento/a*

slowly lentamente *lentamente*

small piccolo/a *peekkolo/a*

smell odore (m) *odore*

to smell puzzare *putsare*

smile sorriso (m) *sorreeso*

to smile sorridere *sorreedere*

smoke fumo (m) *foomo*

to smoke fumare *foomare*

smooth liscio/a *leesho/a*

to sneeze starnutire *starnooteere*

snorkel respiratore (m) a tubo *respeeratore a toobo*

snow neve (f) *neve*

to snow nevicare *neveekare*

so allora *allora*
(therefore) dunque *doonkwe*

soap sapone (m) *sapone*

sober sobrio/a *sobryo/a*

socialism socialismo *sochaleesmo*

sock calza (f) *kaltsa*

socket presa (f) di corrente *presa dee korente*

soft morbido/a *morbeedo/a*

soft drink analcolico (m) *analkoleeko*

soldier soldato (m) *soldato*

sold out esaurito/a *ezowreeto/a*

solicitor procuratore (m) legale *prokooratore legale*

solid solido/a *soleedo/a*

some alcuno/a *alkoono/a*

somehow in qualche modo *een kwalke modo*

someone qualcuno *kwalkoono*

something qualcosa *kwalkoza*

sometimes qualche volta *kwalke volta*

somewhere da qualche parte *da kwalke parte*

son figlio (m) *feelyo*

song canto (m) *kanto*

son-in-law genero (m) *jenero*

soon presto *presto*

sore doloroso *doloroso*

sorry: I'm sorry mi dispiace *mee deespyache*

sort genere (m) *jenere*

sound suono (m) *swono*

soup zuppa (f) *dzooppa*

sour aspro/a *aspro/a*

south sud (m) *sood*

souvenir ricordo (m) *reekordo*

space spazio (m) *spatsyo*

spade vanga (f) *vanga*

spanner chiave (f) inglese *kyave eengleze*

spare di ricambio *dee reekambyo*

spare time tempo (m) libero *tempo leebero*

spare tyre gomma (f) di scorta *gomma dee skorta*

sparkling *(water)* gasata *gazata*

to speak parlare *parlare*

special speciale *spechale*

special offer in offerta *een offerta*

specialist specialista (m/f) *spechaleesta*

speciality specialità (f) *spechaleeta*

spectacles occhiali (m/pl) *okyalee*

speed velocità (f) *velocheeta*

speed limit limite (m) di velocità *leemeete dee velocheeta*

to spend *(money)* spendere *spendere*
(time) passare *passare*

spice spezie (f/pl) *spetsye*

spicy piccante *peekkante*

spirits liquori (m/pl) *leekworee*

splinter scheggia (f) *skejja*

to spoil guastare *gwastare*

sponge *(bath)* spugna (f) *spoonya*

spoon cucchiaio (m) *kookya-yo*

sport sport (m) *sport*

spot pallino (m) *palleeno*
    (place) locale (m) *lokale*
to **sprain** storcersi *storchersee*
sprained storto/a *storto/a*
spray spruzzo (m) *sprootso*
spring (season) primavera (f) *preemavera*
square piazza (f) *pyatsa*
    (shape) quadrato (m) *kwadrato*
stadium stadio (m) *stadyo*
stain macchia (f) *makkya*
stairs scalinata (f) *skaleenata*
stalls (theatre) poltrone (f/pl) *poltrone*
stamp (postage) francobollo (m) *frankobollo*
stand (stadium) tribuna (f) coperta *treeboona koperta*
to **stand up** alzarsi *altsarsee*
star stella (f) *stella*
start inizio (m) *eeneetsyo*
to **start** cominciare *komeenchare*
starter (food) antipasto (m) *anteepasto*
state stato (m) *stato*
station stazione (f) *statsyone*
stationer's cartoleria (f) *kartolereea*
statue statua (f) *statooa*
to **stay** (live) abitare *abeetare*
    (remain) rimanere *reemanere*
to **steal** rubare *roobare*
steam vapore (m) *vapore*
steamer piroscafo (m) *peeroskafo*
steel acciaio (m) *achiyo*
steep ripido/a *reepeedo/a*
step (footstep) passo (m) *passo*
    (stairs) scalino (m) *skaleeno*
step-brother fratellastro (m) *fratellastro*
step-children figliastri *feelyastree*
step-father patrigno (m) *patreenyo*
step-mother matrigna (f) *matreenya*
step-sister sorellastra (f) *sorellastra*
stereo stereo (m) *stereo*
stick bastone (m) *bastone*
to **stick: it's stuck** è bloccato e *blokatto*
sticky adesivo/a *adeseevo/a*

sticky tape Scotch (m) *skoch*
stiff rigido/a *reejeedo/a*
still (yet) sempre *sempre*
still (non-fizzy) naturale *natoorale*
sting puntura (f) *poontoora*
to **sting** pungere *poonjere*
stock exchange Borsa (f) *borsa*
stockings calze (f) *kaltse*
stolen rubato/a *roobato/a*
stomach stomaco (m) *stomako*
stomach ache mal (m) di stomaco *mal dee stomako*
stone pietra (f) *pyetra*
stop (bus) fermata *fermata*
to **stop** fermare *fermare*
    stop! fermo! *fermo*
stopcock rubinetto (m) principale *roobeenetto preencheepale*
story storia (f) *storya* (f)
stove stufa (f) *stoofa*
straight diritto/a *deereetto/a*
straight on sempre dritto *sempre dreetto*
strange strano/a *strano/a*
stranger sconosciuto/a *skonoshooto/a*
strap cinghia (f) *cheengya*
straw (drinking) cannuccia (f) *kanoocha*
stream ruscello (m) *rooshello*
street strada (f) *strada*
stretcher lettiga (f) *letteega*
strike sciopero (m) *shopero*
   » **on strike** in sciopero *een shopero*
string spago (m) *spago*
striped a strisce (f/pl) *a streeshe*
strong forte (f) *forte*
student studente (m) –essa (f) *stoodente, stoodentessa*
to **study** studiare *stoodyare*
stupid stupido/a *stoopeedo/a*
style stile (m) *steele*
subtitles sottotitoli (m/pl) *sottoteetolee*
suburb sobborgo (m) *sobborgo*
success successo (m) *soochesso*
such tale *tale*

suddenly d'improvviso *deemproveezo*

sugar zucchero (m) *dzookero*

suit completo (m) *kompleto*

suitcase valigia (f) *valeeja*

summer estate (f) *estate*

sun sole (m) *sole*

to **sunbathe** prendere il sole *prendere eel sole*

sunburn scottatura (f) *skottatoora*

sunglasses occhiali (m/pl) da sole *okyalee da sole*

sunny pieno/a di sole *pyeno/a dee sole*

sunshade parasole (m) *parasole*

sunstroke colpo (m) di sole *kolpo dee sole*

suntan abbronzatura (f) *abbrontsatoora*

suntan lotion lozione (f) abbronzante *lotsyone abbrontsante*

suntan oil olio (m) abbronzante *olyo abbrontsante*

supermarket supermercato (m) *soopermerkato*

supper cena (f) *chena*

supplement supplemento (m) *soopplemento*

to **suppose: I suppose so** suppongo di sì *sooppongo dee see*

suppository supposta (f) *soopposta*

sure sicuro/a *seekooro/a*

surface superficie (f) *sooperfeeche*

surname cognome (m) *konyome*

surprise sorpresa (f) *sorpreza*

surprised sorpreso/a *sorprezo/a*

to **sweat** sudare *soodare*

sweatshirt felpa (f) *felpa*

to **sweep** spazzare *spatsare*

sweet dolce *dolche*

sweetener dolcificante (m) *dolcheefeekante*

sweets caramelle (f/pl) *karamelle*

swelling gonfiore (m) *gonfyore*

to **swim** nuotare *nwotare*

swimming nuoto (m) *nwoto*

swimming pool piscina (f) *peesheena*

swimming trunks calzoncini (m/pl) da bagno *kalzoncheenee da banyo*

swimsuit costume (m) da bagno *kostoome da banyo*

switch interruttore (m) *eenterrootore*

to **switch off** spegnere *spenyere*

to **switch on** accendere *achendere*

swollen gonfiato/a *gonfyato/a*

symptom sintomo (m) *seentomo*

synagogue sinagoga (f) *seenagoga*

synthetic sintetico/a *seenteteeko*

system sistema (m) *seestema*

T

table tavolo (m) *tavolo*

tablet tavoletta (f) *tavoletta*

table tennis tennis (m) da tavolo/ping pong *tennees da tavolo/peeng pong*

tailor sarto (m) *sarto*

to **take** prendere *prendere*; (photo) scattare *skattare*; (exam) sostenere *sostenere*; (time) metterci *metterchee*

taken (seat) occupato/a *okkoopato/a*

to **take off** (clothes) togliere *tolyere* (plane) decollare *dekollare*

talcum powder talco (m) *talko*

to **talk** parlare *parlare*

tall alto/a *alto/a*

tampons assorbenti (m/pl) interni *assorbentee eenternee*

tap rubinetto (m) *roobeenetto*

tape (cassette) cassetta (f) *kasetta*

tape measure metro (m) a nastro *metro a nastro*

taste gusto (m) *goosto*

to **taste** assaggiare *assajare*

tax imposta (f), tassa (f) *eemposta, tassa*

taxi taxi (m) *taksee*

taxi rank posteggio (m) dei taxi *postejjo de-ee taksee*

tea tè (m) *te*

teabag bustina (f) da tè *boosteena da te*

to **teach** insegnare *eensenyare*

teacher professore (m) –essa (f) *professore, professoressa*

team squadra (f) *skwadra*

tear *(rip)* strappo (m) *strappo*
(cry) lacrima (f) *lakreema*
» **in tears** in lacrime (f/pl) *een lakreeme*

teaspoon cucchiaino (m) *kookkya-eeno*

teat *(for baby's bottle)* tettarella (f) *tettarella*

tea towel strofinaccio (m) *strofeenacho*

technical tecnico/a *tekneeko/a*

technology tecnologia (f) *teknolojee-a*

teenager adolescente (m/f) *adoleshente*

telephone telefono (m) *telefono*

telephone card scheda (f) telefonica *skeda telefoneeka*

telephone directory elenco (m) telefonico *elenko telefoneeko*

to telephone telefonare *telefonare*

television televisione (f) *televeezyone*

to tell (to) dire (a) *deere (a)*

temperature temperatura (f) *temperatoora*
» **to have a temperature** avere la febbre (f) *avere la febbre*

temporary temporaneo/a *temporaneo/a*

tender tenero/a *tenero/a*

tennis tennis (m) *tennees*

tennis court campo (m) di tennis *kampo dee tennees*

tent tenda (f) *tenda*

tent peg picchetto (m) da tenda *peekketto da tenda*

tent pole palo (m) della tenda *palo della tenda*

terminal *(airport)* terminal (m) *termeenal*

terminus capolinea (m) *kapoleenea*

terrace terrazzo (m) *terratso*

terrible terribile (m) *terreebeele*

terrorist terrorista (m/f) *terroreesta*

text message SMS (m) *esemes*

than di *dee*

thank you (very much) grazie (molto) *gratsye molto*

that (one) quello/a *kwello/a*

the il/la *eel/la*

theatre teatro (m) *te-atro*

their loro *loro*

theirs loro *loro*

them li/le *lee/le*

then allora *allora*

there là/lì *la/lee*

there is/are c'è/ci sono *che/chee sono*

therefore dunque *doonkwe*

thermometer termometro (m) *termometro*

these questi/e *kwestee/e*

they loro *loro*

thick spesso/a *spesso/a*

thief ladro (m) *ladro*

thin magro/a *magro/a*

thing cosa (f) *koza*

to think pensare *pensare*
(believe) credere *kredere*

third terzo/a *tertso*

thirsty assetato/a *assetato/a*
» **I'm thirsty** ho sete *osete*

this (one) questo/a *kwesto/a*

those quelli/e *kwellee/e*

thread filo (m) *feelo*

throat lozenges/pastilles pastiglie (f/pl) *pasteelye*

through attraverso *attraverso*

to throw gettare *jettare*

to throw away buttar via *bootar vee-a*

thumb pollice (m) *polleeche*

thunder tuono (m) *twono*

ticket biglietto (m) *beelyetto*

ticket office biglietteria (f) *beelyetterya*

tide *(high/low)* marea (f) *marea*

tidy in ordine *een ordeene*

tie cravatta (f) *kravatta*

to tie legare *legare*

tight *(clothes)* stretti *strettee*

tights collant (m) *kollan*

till *(until)* fino a *feeno a*

time tempo (m) *tempo; (once etc.)* una
  volta *oona volta; (on clock)* ora (f) *ora*
timetable *(train)* orario (m) *oraryo*
tin scatola (f) *skatola*
tin foil stagnola (f) *stanyola*
tinned in scatola *een skatola*
tin-opener apriscatole (m) *apreeskatole*
tip *(in restaurant etc.)* mancia (f) *mancha*
tired stanco/a *stangko/a*
tissues fazzoletti (m/pl) di carta
  fatsoletti dee karta
to a *a*
tobacco tabacco (m) *tabakko*
tobacconist's tabaccaio (m) *tabakkiyo*
toboggan toboga (m) *toboga*
today oggi *ojjee*
toiletries articoli (m/pl) da toilette
  arteekolee da toylette
toilets gabinetti (m/pl) *gabbeenettee*
toilet paper carta (f) igienica *karta
  eejeneeka*
toll pedaggio (m) *pedajo*
tomato pomodoro (m) *pomodoro*
tomorrow domani *domanee*
tongue lingua (f) *leengwa*
tonight stasera *stasera*
too troppo/a *troppo (as well)* anche *anke*
tool strumento (m) *stroomento*
tooth dente (f) *dente*
toothache mal (m) di denti *mal dee
  dentee*
toothbrush spazzolino (m) *spatsoleeno*
toothpaste dentifricio (m)
  denteefreecho
toothpick stuzzicadenti (m)
  stootseekadentee
top *(mountain)* cima (f) *cheema*
  » **on top of** in cima di *een cheema dee*
torch torcia (f) *torcha*
torn strappato/a *strappato/a*
total totale *totale*
totally totalmente *totalmente*
to touch toccare *tokare*
  tough *(meat)* duro *dooro*

tour giro (m) *jeero*
to tour girare per *jeerare per*
tourism turismo (m) *tooreesmo*
tourist turista (m/f) *tooreesta*
tourist office ufficio (m) turistico
  ooffeecho tooreesteeko
to tow trainare *triynare*
towards verso *verso*
towel asciugamano (m) *ashoogamano*
tower torre (f) *torre*
town città (f) *cheeta*
town centre centro (m) *chentro*
town hall municipio (m) *mooneecheepyo*
toy giocattolo (m) *jokatolo*
track pista (f) *peesta*
tracksuit tuta (f) *toota*
traditional tradizionale *tradeetsyonale*
traffic traffico (m) *traffeeko*
traffic jam ingorgo (m) *eengorgo*
traffic lights semaforo (m) *semaforo*
trailer rimorchio (m) *reemorkyo*
train treno (m) *treno*
  » **by train** per treno *per treno*
trainers scarpe (f/pl) da ginnastica
  skarpe da jeennasteeka
tram tram (m) *tram*
tranquiliser tranquillante (m)
  trankweellante
to translate tradurre *tradoorre*
translation traduzione (f) *tradootsyone*
to travel viaggiare *vyajjare*
  travel agency agenzia (f) viaggi
  ajentseeya vyajjee
  traveller's cheques traveller's cheques
  traveller's chekes
  travel sickness mal (m) d'auto *mal dowto*
  tray vassoio (m) *vassoyo*
  treatment cura (f) *koora*
  tree albero (m) *albero*
  trip gita (f) *jeeta*
  trousers pantaloni (m/pl) *pantalonee*
  trout trota (f) *trota*
  true vero/a *vero/a*
  » **that's true** è vero *e vero*

to try provare *provare*
to try on provare *provare*
  T-shirt maglietta (f) *malyetta*
  tube *(pipe)* tubo (m) *toobo*
    (underground) metro (f) *metro*
  tuna tonno (m) *tonno*
  tunnel galleria (f) *gallereea*
  turn: it's my turn tocca a me *tokka a me*
to turn girare *jeerare*
  to turn off *(tap)* chiudere *kyoodere*
  turning *(side road)* svolta (f) *svolta*
  twice due volte (f/pl) *doo-e volte*
  twin beds letti (m/pl) gemelli *lettee jemellee*
  twins gemelli (m/pl) –e (f/pl) *jemellee/–e*
  twisted *(ankle)* slogato/a *slogato/a*
  type *(sort)* tipo (m) *teepo*
to type battere a macchina (f) *battere a makkeena*
  typical tipico/a *teepeeko/a*

U

  USB lead cavo (m) USB *kavo oo-es-bee*
  ugly brutto/a *brootto/a*
  ulcer ulcera (f) *oolchera*
  umbrella ombrello (m) *ombrello*
  uncle zio (m) *dzee-o*
  uncomfortable scomodo/a *skomodo/a*
  under sotto/a *sotto/a*
  underground *(tube)* metropolitana (f) *metropoleetana*
  underpants mutande (f/pl) *mootande*
  underpass sottopassaggio (m) *sottopassajjo*
to understand capire *kapeere*
  underwater subacqueo/a *soobakweo/a*
  underwear biancheria (f) intima *byankereea eenteema*
to undress *(oneself)* spogliarsi *spolyarsee*
  unemployed disoccupato/a *deezokoopato/a*
  unfortunately purtroppo *poortroppo*
  unhappy infelice *eenfeleeche*

  uniform uniforme (f) *ooneeforme*
  university università (f) *ooneeverseeta*
  unleaded petrol benzina (f) senza piombo *bentseena sentsa pyombo*
  unless a meno che *a meno ke*
  unpack disfare una valigia *deesfare oona valeeja*
  unpleasant sgradevole *zgradevole*
to unscrew svitare *zveetare*
  until fino a *feeno a*
  unusual insolito *eensoleeto*
  unwell indisposto/a *eendeesposto/a*
  up su *soo*
  upper superiore *sooperyore*
  upstairs di sopra *dee sopra*
  urgent urgente *oorjente*
  urine urina (f) *ooreena*
  us noi *no-ee*
to use servirsi di *serveersee dee*
  useful utile *ooteele*
  useless inutile *eenooteele*
  usually di solito *dee soleeto*

V

  vacant libero/a *leebero*
  vacuum cleaner aspirapolvere (m) *aspeerapolvere*
  valid valido/a *valeedo/a*
  valley valle (f) *valle*
  valuable prezioso/a *pretsyoso/a*
  valuables oggetti (m/pl) di valore *ojjettee dee valorè*
  van furgone (m) *foorgone*
  vanilla vaniglia (f) *vaneelya*
  vase vaso (m) *vazo*
  VAT IVA *eeva*
  vegan vegano (m) –a (f) *vegano/a*
  vegetables verdura (f) *verdoora*
  vegetarian vegetariano/a *vejetaryano/a*
  vehicle veicolo (m) *ve-eekolo*
  very molto *molto*
  vest maglia (f) *malya*
  vet veterinario (m) *vetereenaryo*
  via via *vee-a*

video video (m) *veedeo*
view vista (f) *veesta*
villa villa (f) *veella*
village paese (m) *piyese*
vinegar aceto (m) *acheto*
vineyard vigneto (m) *veenyeto*
virgin vergine (f) *verjeene*
visa visto (m) *veesto*
visit visita (f) *veezeeta*
to visit visitare *veezeetare*
visitor visitatore (m) –trice (f) *veezeetatore; veezeetatreeche*
vitamin vitamina (f) *veetameena*
voice voce (f) *voche*
volleyball pallavolo (f) *pallavolo*
voltage tensione (f) *tensyone*
to vote votare *votare*

W

wage stipendio (m) *steependyo*
waist vita (f) *veeta*
waistcoat panciotto (m) *panchotto*
to wait (for) aspettare *aspettare*
waiter cameriere (m) *kameryere*
waiting room sala (f) d'attesa *sala datteza*
waitress cameriera (f) *kameryera*
Wales Galles (m) *galles*
walk cammino (m) *kammeeno*
to walk camminare *kammeenare*
to go for a walk fare una passeggiata (f) *fare oona passejjata*
walking stick bastone (m) da passeggio *bastone da passejjo*
wall (inside) parete (f) *parete* (outside) muro (m) *mooro*
wallet portafoglio (m) *portafolyo*
to want desiderare *dezeederare*
war guerra (f) *gwerra*
warm caldo/a *kaldo/a*
to wash lavare *lavare*
washable lavabile *lavabeele*
wash-basin lavandino (m) *lavandeeno*
washing bucato (m) *bookato*

washing machine lavatrice (f) *lavatreeche*
washing powder detersivo (m) in polvere *deterseevo een polvere*
washing-up piatti (m/pl) sporchi *pyattee sporkee*
washing-up liquid detersivo (m) per piatti *deterseevo per pyattee*
wastepaper basket cestino (m) *chesteeno*
watch (clock) orologio (m) *orolojo*
to watch guardare *gwardare*
water acqua (f) *akwa*
water heater scaldabagno (m) *skaldabanyo*
waterfall cascata (f) *kaskata*
waterproof impermeabile *eemperme-abeele*
water-skiing sci (m) acquatico *shee akwateeko*
water-skis sci (m/pl) acquatici *shee akwateechee*
wave onda (f) *onda*
way (path) via (f) *vee-a*
wax cera (f) *chera*
we noi *noy*
weather tempo (m) *tempo*
weather forecast previsioni (f/pl) del tempo *preveezyone del tempo*
web (internet) Web (m) *web*
wedding nozze (f/pl) *notse*
week settimana (f) *setteemana*
weekday giorno (m) lavorativo *jorno lavorateevo*
weekend fine (f) settimana *feene setteemana*
weekly settimanale *setteemanale*
to weigh pesare *pezare*
weight peso (m) *pezo*
well bene *bene*
well done (steak) ben cotto *ben kotto*
Welsh gallese *galleze*
west ovest (m) *ovest*
western occidentale *ocheedentale*
wet bagnato/a *banyato/a*

wetsuit muta (f) *moota*

what che *ke*

what? come? *kome*

wheel ruota (f) *rwota*

wheelchair sedia (f) a rotelle *sedya a rotelle*

when quando *kwando*

when? quando? *kwando*

whenever ogni volta che *onyee volta ke*

where dove *dove*

where? dove? *dove*

which che *ke*

which? quale? *kwale*

while mentre *mentre*

white bianco/a *byanko/a*

who che *ke*

who? chi? *kee*

whole intero/a *eentero/a*

why? perché? *perke*

wide largo/a *largo/a*

widow vedova (f) *vedova*

widower vedovo (m) *vedovo*

wife moglie (f) *molye*

wild selvatico/a *selvateeko/a*

to **win** vincere *veenchere*

wind vento (m) *vento*

windmill mulino (m) a vento *mooleeno a vento*

window finestra (f) *feenestra*
(shop) vetrina (f) *vetreena*

to **windsurf** fare del windsurf (m) *fare del weendsoorf*

windy ventoso/a *ventoso/a*

wine vino (m) *veeno*

wine merchant enoteca (f) *enoteka*

wing ala (f) *ala*

winter inverno (m) *eenverno*

with con *kon*

without senza *sentsa*

woman donna (f) *donna*

wonderful meraviglioso/a *meraveelyoso/a*

wood legno (m) *lenyo*

wool lana (f) *lana*

word parola (f) *parola*

work lavoro (m) *lavoro*

to **work** (job) lavorare *lavorare*
(function) funzionare *foontsyonare*

world (noun) mondo (m) *mondo*
(adj.) mondiale *mondyale*

worried preoccupato/a *preokkoopato/a*

worse peggio/a *pejjo/a*

worth: to be worth valere *valere*
» it's not worth it non vale la pena *non vale la pena*

wound ferita (f) *fereeta*

to **wrap (up)** avvolgere *avvoljere*

wrong zbagliato/a *sbalyato/a*

to **write** scrivere *skreevere*

writer scrittore (m) –trice (f) *skreettore, skreettreeche*

writing paper carta (f) da scrivere *karta da skreevere*

X

X-ray raggio X (m) *rajo eeks*

Y

yacht yacht (m) *yot*

to **yawn** sbadigliare *zbadeelyare*

year anno (m) *anno*

yellow giallo/a *jallo/a*

yes si *see*

yesterday ieri *yeree*

yet ancora *ankora*

yoghurt yogurt (m) *yogoort*

you (formal) lei *le-ee*; (informal) tu *too*; (plural) voi *voy*; (plural formal) loro *loro*

young giovane *jovane*

your tuo/vostro/suo *too-o, vostro, soo-o*

yours tuo/vostro/suo *too-o, vostro, soo-o*

youth giovane (m) *jovane*

youth hostel ostello *ostello*

Z

zip lampo (f) *lampo*

zoo zoo (m) *dzoo*

Italian – English dictionary

A

a at, to
abbastanza enough, fairly; quite
abbazia (f) abbey
abbonamento (m) season ticket
abbronzatura (f) suntan
abitare to live *(dwell)*
abito (m) dress
abitudine (f) habit
accanto a next to
accendere to light *(fire)*; to switch on *(light)*
accendino (m) lighter *(cigarette)*
acceso/a on *(TV, light)*
accettare to accept *(take)*
accettazione (f) check-in *(desk)*
accogliere to greet
accordo: essere d'accordo to agree
aceto (m) vinegar
acido/a acid *(adj.)*
acqua (f) water
acqua (f) di colonia toilet water
acqua (f) distillata distilled water
addetto (m) –a (f) alle pulizie cleaner
adesivo/a sticky
adesso now
adolescente (m/f) teenager
adulto/a adult
aereo (m) plane
aereo: per aereo by air
aeroplano (m) aeroplane
aeroporto (m) airport
affamato/a hungry
affare (m) bargain
affari (m/pl) business
» per affari on business
affettato/a sliced
affilato/a sharp
affissione (f) poster
affittare to let; to rent
affitto (m) rent
affitto: prendere in affitto to rent

affogare to drown
affollato/a crowded
agenda (f) diary
agente (m) immobiliare estate agent
agenzia (f) agency
agenzia (f) viaggi travel agency
aggredire to attack *(mug)*
agire to act *(take action)*
agitato/a rough *(sea)*
aglio (m) garlic
agnello (m) lamb *(meat)*
ago (m) needle
agricoltore (m) farmer
AIDS AIDS
aiutare to help
aiuto (m) help
aiuto! help!
al più … possibile as … as possible
al più presto possibile as soon as possible
ala (f) wing
albergo (m) hotel
albero (m) tree
alcol (m) alcohol
alcolico/a alcoholic *(content)*
alcolista (m/f) alcoholic *(person)*
alcuno/a some
alimentare to feed
aliscafo (m) hydrofoil
allarme (m) alarm
allegro/a happy
allergico/a a allergic to
alloggio (m) accommodation
allora so, then
allora: da allora since
almeno at least
alpinismo (m) mountaineering
altezza (f) height
alto/a tall, high
altra: un'altra another
altri others
altro/a other

altro: un altro another
alzarsi to stand up
amare to love
amaro/a bitter
ambasciata (f) embassy
ambasciatore (m), ambasciatrice (f) ambassador
ambiente (m) environment
ambientalista environmentally friendly
ambizione (f) ambition
ambizioso/a ambitious
ambulanza (f) ambulance
amici (m/pl) friends
amico (m) –a (f) friend
ammissione (f) admission
amore (m) love
analcolico (m) soft drink
analcolico/a non-alcoholic
analgesico (m) painkiller
anatra (f) duck
anche also, too *(as well)*; even *(including)*
ancora again; yet
andar via to go away
andare to go
andare a bicicletta (f) to ride *(bike)*
andare a trovare to go round *(visit)*
andata e ritorno return *(ticket)*
andata: di sola andata single *(ticket)*
andiamo! let's go!
anello (m) ring *(jewellery)*
anestetico (m) anaesthetic
angolo (m) corner
animale (m) animal
anniversario (m) anniversary
anno (m) year
annullare to cancel
ansioso/a nervous
antibiotico (m) antibiotic
anticipo: in anticipo in advance
anticongelante (m) antifreeze
antipasto (m) starter *(food)*
antisettico (m) antiseptic
anziano (m) – a (f) senior citizen

ape (f) bee
aperto/a open
aperto: all'aperto outdoors, outside
apparecchio (m) acustico hearing aid
appartamento (m) apartment, flat
appartamento (m) indipendente self-catering flat
appartenere a to belong to
appendicite (f) appendicitis
appuntamento (m) appointment
apribottiglie (m) bottle-opener
aprire to open
apriscatole (m) can-opener
arachide (f) peanut
arancia (f) orange *(fruit)*
arancione orange *(colour)*
architetto (m) architect
archivio (m) archive
arco (m) arch
area (f) area
argento (m) silver
aria (f) air
aria (f) condizionata air conditioning
arma (f) da fuoco gun
armadietto (m) locker
armadio (m) cupboard
aroma (f) flavour
arrabbiato/a angry
arrivare to arrive
arrivederci goodbye
arrivo (m) arrival
arrosto (m) roast
arrugginito/a rusty
arte (f) art
articoli (m/pl) da toilette toiletries
articolo (m) article
artificiale artificial
artista (m/f) artist
artrite (f) arthritis
ascensore (m) lift
ascesso (m) abscess
asciugamano (m) towel
asciutto/a dry
ascoltare to listen

asino (m) donkey
asma (f) asthma
aspettare to wait (for)
aspettarsi to expect
aspirapolvere (m) vacuum cleaner
aspirina (f) aspirin
aspro/a sour
assaggiare to taste
assegno (m) cheque
assennato/a sensible
assetato/a thirsty
assicurare to insure
assicurato/a insured
assicurazione (f) insurance
assistente (m/f) assistant
assorbenti (m/pl) sanitary towels
assorbenti (m/pl) interni tampons
atletica (f) athletics
atmosfera (f) atmosphere
atrio (m) hall *(in house)*
attaccare to attack
attaccare to hang up *(telephone)*
attacco (m) degli sci binding *(ski)*
attento/a careful
atterrare to land
attimo (m) moment
attraente attractive
attraversamento (m) pedonale
   pedestrian crossing
attraverso across, through
attrezzatura (f) equipment
attuale current
autentico/a real *(authentic)*
autista (m/f) driver
auto (f) della polizia police car
autobus (m) bus
autobus: in autobus by bus
autolavaggio (m) car wash
automatico/a automatic
autonoleggio (m) car hire
autore (m) –trice (f) author
autostazione (f) bus station
autostop: fare l'autostop (m) to hitchhike
autostrada (f) motorway

autunno (m) autumn
avanti: in avanti forward
avanzamento (m) advance
avanzare to advance
avere to have
avvenire to happen
avvolgere to wrap (up)

B

baciare to kiss
bacio (m) kiss
baffi (m/pl) moustache
bagagli (m/pl) baggage, luggage
bagaglio (m) a mano hand luggage
bagnarsi to bathe
bagnato/a wet
bagnaiolo (m) attendant *(bathing)*
bagnino/a (m/f) lifeguard
bagno (m) bath
bagno: fare il bagno to have a bath
baia (f) bay
ballare to dance
balletto (m) ballet
ballo (m) dance
balsamo (m) conditioner
bambini (m/pl) children
bambino (m) –a (f) child
bambola (f) doll
banana (f) banana
banca (f) bank *(money)*
banchina (f) quay
banco (m) counter *(post office)*
banconota (f) note *(bank)*
banda (f) band *(music)*
bandiera (f) flag
bar (m) bar, café
barattolo (m) jar
barba (f) beard
barca (f) boat
baseball (m) baseball
basso/a low
bastone (m) stick
battente (m) shutter
battuta (f) joke
bavaglia (m) bib

beige beige
belle arti (f/pl) fine arts
bello/a beautiful, fine *(weather)*
ben cotto well done *(steak)*
benché although
benda (f) bandage
bene well
benzina (f) petrol
benzina (f) senza piombo unleaded petrol
bere to drink
bevanda (f) drink
biancheria (f) intima underwear
bianco/a white
biberon (m) baby's bottle
biblioteca (f) library
bicchiere (m) glass *(tumbler)*
bicicletta (f) bicycle
bidone (m) della spazzatura bin *(rubbish)*
bidone (m) per la benzina can *(petrol)*
biglietteria (f) booking office *(rail)*
biglietteria (f) ticket office
biglietto ticket
bilancia (f) scales
binario (m) platform
binocolo (m) binoculars
biondo/a blonde
biondo/a fair *(hair)*
birichino/a naughty
birra (f) beer
biscotto (m) biscuit
bisogno: avere bisogno di to need
bloccarsi: è bloccato it's stuck
bloccato/a blocked
bloc-notes (m) notepad
blu blue
blu marino navy blue
bocca (f) mouth
boccaglio (m) snorkel
boiler (m) immersion heater
bollire to boil
bollitore (m) kettle
bomba (f) bomb
bombola (f) del gas gas bottle/cylinder
bordo (m) border *(edge)*

borsa (f) bag
borsellino (m) purse
borsetta (f) handbag
botteghino (m) box office, booking
    office *(theatre)*
bottiglia (f) bottle
bottone (m) button
braccialetto (m) bracelet
braccio (f) arm
braccioli (m/pl) armbands *(swimming)*
bretelle (f/pl) braces
brillante bright *(light)*
brina (f) frost
britannico/a British
brocca (f) jug
bronchite (f) bronchitis
bronzo (m) bronze
bruciato/a burnt *(food)*
brutto/a ugly
buca (f) delle lettere letterbox
bucato (m) washing
buco (m) hole
buffet (m) buffet
buffo/a funny *(amusing)*
buio (m) dark
buon: a buon mercato cheap
buonanotte good night
buonasera good evening
buongiorno good day, good morning
buono/a good
burro (m) butter
bussare to knock
busta (f) envelope
bustina (f) da tè teabag

C

cabina (f) cabin
cabina (f) telefonica telephone kiosk
caccia (f) hunting
cadere to fall *(down/over)*
caffè (m) coffee
calcio (m) football
calcolatrice (f) calculator
caldo/a hot

calmo/a calm
calore (m) heat
calorifero (m) radiator
calvo/a bald
calza (f) sock
calze (f/pl) stockings
calzolaio shoe repairer's
calzoncini (m/pl) shorts
calzoncini (m/pl) da bagno swimming trunks
cambiare to change *(money, trains)*
cambiarsi to change *(clothes)*
camera (f) da letto bedroom
cameriera (f) waitress
cameriere (m) waiter
camicetta (f) blouse
camicia (f) shirt
camicia (f) da notte nightdress
camino (m) chimney *(exterior)*
camion (m) lorry
camminare to walk
cammino (m) walk
campagna (f) country(side)
campana (f) bell
campeggiare to camp
campeggio (m) camping, campsite
campo (m) field, court *(tennis etc)*
cancellare to cancel
cancello (m) gate
cancro (m) cancer
candela (f) candle
cane (m) dog
canna (f) da pesca fishing rod
cannuccia (f) straw *(drinking)*
canoa (f) canoe
cantare to sing
cantina (f) cellar
canto (m) song
capanna (f) hut
capelli (m/pl) hair
capire to understand
capitale (f) capital *(city)*
capitano (m) captain *(boat)*
capodanno (m) New Year's Day

capolinea (m) terminus
cappella (f) chapel
capra (f) goat
caraffa (f) carafe
caramelle (f/pl) sweets
carburante (m) fuel
cardigan (m) cardigan
carne (f) meat
carnet (m) di biglietti booklet *(bus tickets)*
caro/a darling, dear *(loved)*; dear, expensive
carriera (f) career
carro (m) attrezzi breakdown truck
carrozza (f) carriage *(rail)*
carrozza (f) letto sleeper/sleeping-car
carrozzina (f) pram
carta (f) paper
carta (f) di credito credit card
cartella (f) briefcase
cartina (f) map
cartoleria (f) stationer's
cartolina (f) postcard
casa: a casa (f) house, home: at home
cascata (f) waterfall
casco (m) helmet *(motorbike)*
casetta (f) delle lettere postbox
caso (m): in caso in case
cassa (f) cash desk
cassaforte (f) safe *(strongbox)*
cassetta (f) cassette, tape
cassetta (f) di pronto soccorso first aid kit
cassetto (m) drawer
cassiere (m) –a (f) cashier
castello (m) castle *(palace)*
catalogo (m) catalogue
catena (f) chain
catene (f/pl) da neve snow chains
cattivo/a bad
cattolico/a Catholic
cautela (f) caution
cavalcare to ride *(horse)*
cavallo (m) horse
cavarsela to manage *(cope)*
cavatappi (m) corkscrew
cavi (m/pl) di avviamento jump leads

caviglia (f) ankle
cavo (m) USB USB lead
c'è/ci sono there is/are
c'è? is there?
celibe single *(unmarried: man)*
cellulare (m) mobile *(phone)*
cena (f) dinner, supper
centimetro (m) centimetre
centrale central
centro (m) centre
centro (m) città town centre
centro (m) commerciale shopping centre
cera (f) wax
ceramica (f) pottery
cercare to look for
cerchio (m) circle
cerotto (m) plaster *(sticking)*
certamente certainly
certificato (m) certificate
certo certain, of course
cervello (m) brain
cervo (m) deer
cespuglio (m) bush
cesto (m) basket
chalet (m) chalet
champagne (m) champagne
chi? who?
chiamare to call
chiamarsi to be called
chiamata a carico del destinatario
    reverse-charge call
chiaro/a clear, light *(coloured)*
chiave (f) key
chiave (f) inglese spanner
chiedere to ask
chiesa (f) church
chilo(grammo) (m) kilo(gram)
chilometro (m) kilometre
chitarra (f) guitar
chiudere to close, shut
chiudere a chiave to lock
chiudere to turn off *(tap)*
chiuso/a closed, shut; blocked *(road)*
ciao goodbye *(casual)*

cibo (m) food
cicca (f) chewing gum
ciclismo (m) cycling
ciclomotore (m) moped
cielo (m) sky
ciglia (f/pl) eyelashes
cima (f) top *(mountain)*
cima: in cima a on top of
cimitero (m) cemetery
cin cin! cheers!
cinghia (f) strap
cintura (f) belt
cintura (f) di sicurezza seatbelt
cioccolato (m) chocolate
ciotola (f) bowl
circa about, approximately
cistite (f) cystitis
città (f) city, town
ciuccio (m) dummy *(baby's)*
classe (f) class
clima (m) climate
clinica (f) clinic
coda (f) queue
codice (m) di avviamento postale
    postcode
cognata (f) sister-in-law
cognato (m) brother-in-law
cognome (m) surname
colazione (f) breakfast
colla (f) glue
collana (f) necklace
collant (m) tights
collare (m) collar
collega (m/f) colleague
collezionare to collect
collina (f) hill
colloquio interview *(work)*
colore (m) colour
colpevole guilty
colpire to hit
colpo (m) di sole sunstroke
coltello (m) knife
comandare to order
combattere to fight

come like *(similar to)*, as
come? what?
cominciare to begin, to start
commedia (f) comedy, play *(theatre)*
commerciale commercial
commestibile edible
commissariato (m) police station
commozione (f) cerebrale concussion
comodo/a comfortable *(to wear)*, convenient *(to reach)*
compleanno (m) birthday
completo (m) suit
completo/a complete *(finished)*; full up *(booked up)*
complicato/a complicated
comporre to dial
comprare to buy
computer (m) computer
comune: in comune common *(usual)*
con with
concerto (m) concert
condimento (m) dressing *(salad)*
condizione (f) condition *(state)*
confermare to confirm
congelare to freeze
congelatore (m) freezer
congiuntivite (f) conjunctivitis
congresso (m) conference
coniglio (m) rabbit
connessione (f) connection
conoscere to know *(someone)*
consegna (f) delivery
consegnare to deliver
conservare to keep *(to put by)*
conservazione (f) conservation
consolato (m) consulate
contagioso/a infectious
contanti (m/pl) cash
contare to count
contatore (m) meter
contento/a pleased
continente (m) continent
continuare to carry on *(walking/driving)*
conto (m) account *(bank)*

conto (m) bill
contraccettivo (m) contraceptive
contratto (m) contract
contro against
controllare to check
controllo (m) control
controllo (m) dei passaporti passport control
coperchio (m) lid, cover
coperta (f) blanket
coperto/a overcast, dull *(weather)*
copiare to copy
coppia (f) couple *(pair)*
coraggioso/a brave
corona (f) crown
corpo (m) body
correre to run
corretta properly
corretto/a correct
corridoio (m) corridor
corriere (m) mail
corse (f/pl) automobilistiche motor racing
corse (f/pl) ippiche horse racing
corsia (f) d'emergenza hard shoulder
corso (m) course *(lessons)*
cortese polite
corto/a short
cosa (f) thing
cosa c'è? what's the matter?
cosciente conscious
costa (f) coast
costare to cost
costruire to build
costume (m) da bagno bathing costume, swimsuit
cotone (m) cotton
cotone (m) idrofilo cotton wool
cottage (m) cottage
cotto/a cooked
cravatta (f) tie
credere to believe, to think
crema (f) cream
crema (f) per il viso face cream
crema (f) per le mani hand cream

crema/schiuma (f) da barba shaving cream/foam
cristiano/a Christian
croce (f) cross
crociera (f) cruise
crudo/a raw
cuccetta (f) couchette, berth *(on ship)*
cucchiaino (m) teaspoon
cucchiaio (m) spoon
cucina (f) kitchen
cucinare to cook
cuffia (f) headphones
cugino/a cousin
cuoco (m) –a (f) cook
cuore (m) heart
cupola (f) dome
cura (f) cure *(remedy)*; treatment
curva (f) bend, curve
cuscino (m) cushion, pillow

D

danneggiare to damage
danno (m) damage
dare to give
data (m) date *(day)*
dati (m/pl) data
davanti a in front of
davvero indeed
dazio (m) duty *(tax)*
debito (m) debt
decaffeinato decaffeinated
decidere to decide
decollare to take off *(plane)*
dedito/a addicted
definitivamente definitely
delizioso/a delicious
deluso/a disappointed
dente (f) tooth
dentiera (f) denture
dentifricio (m) toothpaste
dentista (m/f) dentist
dentro indoors, inside
deodorante (m) deodorant
deposito (m) deposit

deposito (m) bagagli left luggage *(office)*
descrivere to describe
descrizione (f) description
desiderare to want
destinazione (f) destination
destro/a right, right-hand
detersivo (m) detergent, washing powder
detersivo (m) per i piatti washing-up liquid
dettaglio (m) detail
deviazione (f) diversion
di of; from; by *(author etc.)*; than
diabete (m) diabetes
diabetico/a diabetic
diarrea (f) diarrhoea
dichiarare to declare
diesel diesel
dietro behind
difatti in fact
difetto (m) fault, defect, flaw
difettoso/a defective, faulty
difficile difficult, hard
digitale digital
dimenticare to forget
dimostrazione (f) demonstration *(example)*
dipingere to paint *(picture)*
dire a to tell, say
diretto direct *(train)*
direzione (f) direction
diritto/a straight
disabile disabled
discoteca (f) disco
discussione (f) argument
disegnare to draw; to design *(dress)*
disegnatore (m), –trice (f) designer
disegno (m) drawing, design *(dress)*
disinfettante (m) disinfectant
dislessia (f) dyslexia
dispari odd *(not even)*
dispiace: mi dispiace I'm sorry
dispiace: non mi dispiace I don't mind
distanza (f) distance
disturbi (m/pl) di stomaco stomach upset
dito (m) finger

diversamente differently
diverso/a different
divertimento (m) entertainment
divertirsi to enjoy oneself
divertirsi to have fun
divorziato/a divorced
dizionario (m) dictionary
doccia (f) shower
documento (m) document
dogana (f) customs
dolce gentle, soft, sweet
dolce (f) dessert
dolcificante (m) sweetener
dollaro (m) dollar
dolore (m) ache, pain
dolori (m/pl) mestruali period pains
doloroso/a sore
domanda (f) question
domani tomorrow
donna (f) woman
dopo after, afterwards; later
dopobarba (m) aftershave
dopodomani day after tomorrow
doppia (f) double
doppiato/a dubbed
dormire to sleep
dove where
dovere must, to owe, to have to
droga (f) drug
drogheria (f) grocer's, drugstore
dunque so, therefore
duomo (m) cathedral
durante during
durare to last
duro/a hard, tough *(meat)*

E

e and
è is
ebreo/a Jewish
eccedenza (f) di bagaglio excess baggage
eccellente excellent
economico/a economical
edicola (f) newspaper kiosk
edificio (m) building

elenco (m) list
elenco (m) telefonico telephone directory
elettricità (f) electricity
elettrico/a electric
elezione (f) election
elicottero (m) helicopter
emergenza (f) emergency
emicrania (f) migraine
energia (f) energy
enoteca (f) wine merchant/shop
entrambi both
entrare to come in, to enter, to go in
entrata (f) entrance, admission charge
erba (f) grass
errore (m) mistake
esame (m) examination
esatto exact(ly)
esaurito/a sold out
esempio: per esempio for example
esente da dazio duty-free
esercito (m) army
esercizio (m) exercise
esperienza (f) experience
esperimento (m) experiment
esportazione (f) export
essenziale essential
essere in grado di to be able
essere to be
esso/a it
est (m) east
estate (f) summer
esterno/a external
estero: all'estero abroad
estintore (m) fire extinguisher
estrarre to remove *(tooth)*
età (f) age
etichetta (f) label
euro(s) euro(s) (m)
evidente obvious
evitare to avoid

F

fa *(adv.)* ago; *(verb)* (he/she) does
faccia (f) face
facile easy

fagioli (m/pl) beans
fallimento (m) failure
falsificare to fake
falso/a false
fame: aver fame to be hungry
famiglia (f) family
familiare familiar
fantastico/a fantastic
far male to hurt
fare to do, to make
farfalla (f) butterfly
farina (f) flour
farinoso/a powdery
fasce (f/pl) dressing *(medical)*
fascia (f) dell'ozono ozone layer
fatto (m) fact
fatto a mano hand made
fattoria (f) farm
favore: per favore please
fazzoletti (m/pl) di carta tissues
fazzoletto (m) handkerchief, headscarf
febbre (f) fever
febbre: avere la febbre (f) to have a
    temperature
fede (f) faith
federa (f) pillowcase
fegato (m) liver
felpa (f) sweatshirt
femminile female, feminine
ferire to injure
ferita (f) injury
fermare to stop
fermata (f) d'autobus bus stop
fermo! stop!
ferro (m) da stiro iron *(for clothes)*
ferrovia (f) railway
festa (f) festival
festa (f) party
festa nazionale (f) public holiday
fetta (f) slice
fiammifero (m) match
fidanzato/a engaged *(to be married)*
figlia (f) daughter
figliastri (m/pl) step-children
figlio (m) son

fila (f) row *(theatre etc.)*
filiale (f) branch *(bank etc.)*
film (m) film
filo (m) thread
filosofia (f) philosophy
filtro (m) filter
finanziare to finance
fine (f) end
fine (f) settimana weekend
finestra (f) window
finire to end, to finish
finito/a over, finished
fino a till, until
fiore (m) flower
firma (f) signature
firmare to sign
firmare: firmare il registro to sign the
    register, to check in
fiume (m) river
fluido (m) fluid
focolare (m) chimney *(hearth)*
foglio (m) leaf
folla (f) crowd
fondo (m) bottom
fondo (m) tinta foundation *(make-up)*
fondo: in fondo at the back
fontana (f) fountain
foratura (f) puncture
forbici (m/pl) scissors
forchetta (f) fork
foresta (f) forest
forma: in forma fit *(healthy)*
formaggio (m) cheese
fornello (m) cooker
forno (m) a microonde microwave oven
forse perhaps
forte loud *(volume)*
forte (f) strong
fortezza (f) castle, fortress
fortunato: essere fortunato/a to
    be lucky
forza (f) power *(physical strength)*
foto (f) photo
fotocamera (f) camera
fotografo (m) –a (f) photographer

fragile fragile
francobollo (m) stamp *(postage)*
frasario (m) phrase book
frase (m) sentence
fratellastro (m) step-brother
fratello (m) brother
frattura (f) fracture
freddo/a cold
frequente frequent
fresco/a cool, fresh
fretta: aver fretta to be in a hurry
friggere to fry
frigo (m) portatile cool box
frigorifero (m) refrigerator, fridge
fritto/a fried
fronte (f) front
frontiera (f) border, frontier
frutta (f) fruit
frutti (m/pl) di mare seafood
fruttivendolo (m) greengrocer
fulmine (m) lightning
fumare to smoke
fumatori: per non fumatori non-smoking
fumo (m) smoke
funivia (f) cable car
funzionare to work *(function)*
fuoco (m) fire
fuoco (m) d'artificio firework
fuori out (of)
furgone (m) van
fusibile (m) fuse

G

gabinetti (m/pl) toilets
galleria (f) d'arte art gallery
Galles (m) Wales
gallese Welsh
gamba (f) leg
garanzia (f) guarantee
gas (m) gas
gassato/a sparkling, fizzy
gatto (m) cat
gay gay *(homosexual)*
gelatina (f) di frutta jelly *(pudding)*

gemelli (m/pl) –e (f/pl) twins
generale general
genere (m) kind, sort
genere: in genere in general
genero (m) son-in-law
generoso/a generous
genitori (m/pl) parents
gente (f) people
gentile kind *(generous)*
gentiluomo (m) gentleman
genuino/a genuine
Germania (f) Germany
gettare to throw
gettata (f) jetty
ghiacciato/a frozen
ghiacciato/a icy
ghiaccio (m) ice
già already
giacca (f) jacket
giallo/a yellow
giardino (m) garden
ginocchio (m) knee
giocare to play
giocattolo (m) toy
gioco (m) d'azzardo gambling
gioielleria (f) jeweller's
giornale (m) newspaper
giorno (m) day
giorno (m) lavorativo weekday
giovane (m) youth
giovane young
girare to turn
giro (m) tour
giro (m) turistico sightseeing
gita (f) trip
giù down *(movement)*
giubbotto (m) di salvataggio lifejacket
giusto right *(correct)*
giusto/a fair
gol goal *(football)*
golf (m) jumper, sweater
gomma (f) rubber, gum
gomma (f) da masticare chewing gum
gomma (f) di scorta spare tyre

gonfiare to pump up
gonfiato/a swollen
gonna (f) skirt
governo (m) government
grado (m) degree *(temperature)*
graffio (m) scratch
grammatica (f) grammar
grammo (m) gramme
granchio (m) crab
grande big, large
grande magazzino (m) department store
grasso (m) fat *(adj/noun)*
gratuito/a free
grave serious *(grave)*
grazie (molto) thank you (very much)
grazioso/a pretty
grido (m) scream
grigio/a grey
griglia: alla griglia grilled
grotta (f) cave
gruppo (f) group
guadagnare to earn
guancia (f) cheek
guanti (m/pl) gloves
guardare to look (at), watch
guardare la TV to watch TV
guardaroba (m) cloakroom
guerra (f) war
guida (m/f) guide
guida (f) guidebook, travel guide
guidare to drive
guscio (m) shell *(egg, nut)*
gusto (m) taste

I

idea (f) idea
idratante (m) moisturiser
ieri yesterday
ieri: l'altro ieri day before yesterday
il the
imbarazzante embarrassing
imbarcare to embark *(boat)*
imbarcarsi to board
imbucare to post

immaginare to imagine
immediatamente immediately
immersione (f) diving
immondizia (f) rubbish
imparare to learn
impaziente impatient
impermeabile (m) raincoat
importante important
importare: non importa
   it doesn't matter, I don't care
importo (m) amount *(money)*
impossibile impossible
imposta (f) tax
impressionante impressive
improvvisamente suddenly
in in, into; to *(country)*
in precedenza in the past
in treno by train
incassare to cash
incidente (m) accident
incinta pregnant
incluso/a included
incrocio (m) crossroads, junction
indietro: all'indietro backwards
indigestione (f) indigestion
indipendente independent
indirizzo (m) address
indisposto/a unwell
indossare to put on *(clothes)*
infarto (m) cardiaco heart attack
infelice unhappy
infermiere (m) -a (f) nurse
infetto/a infected
infezione (f) infection
infiammato/a inflamed
infiammazione (f) inflammation
influenza (f) influenza, flu
informale informal
informazione (f) information
Inghilterra (f) England
inglese English
ingorgo (m) traffic jam
iniezione (f) injection
inizio (m) beginning, start

innocente innocent
inoltre besides
inquinamento (m) pollution
insalata (f) salad
insetticida (m) fly spray
insettifugo (m) insect repellent
insetto (m) insect
insistere to insist
insolito/a unusual
insulina (f) insulin
insultare to insult
intanto meanwhile
intelligente clever, intelligent
interessante interesting
interessato/a interested
intero/a complete, whole
interprete (m/f) interpreter
interruttore (m) switch
interruzione (f) di corrente power cut
intervallo (m) interval (theatre etc.)
intervento (m) chirurgico operation
intervista (f) interview
intorno a around
intossicazione (f) alimentare food poisoning
inutile useless
invece di instead of
inverno (m) winter
inviare to send
invitare to invite
invito (m) invitation
io I
iodio (m) iodine
Irlanda (f) Ireland
irlandese Irish
islam (m) Islam
islamico/a Islamic
isola (f) island
istruttore (m) instructor
IVA VAT

L

la the
là/lì there
labbra (f/pl) lips

lacrima (f) tear (cry)
ladro (m) thief
lago (m) lake
lamentarsi to complain
lametta (f) razor blade
lampada (f) lamp
lampadina (f) light bulb
lampione (m) lamp post
lampo (f) zip
lana (f) wool
largo/a broad, wide
lasciare to leave
lassativo (m) laxative
lato (m) side
lato: dall'altro lato di across (opposite)
latta (f) di benzina petrol can
latte (m) milk
latte (m) detergente cleansing lotion
lattina (f) can, tin
lattuga (f) lettuce
lavabile washable
lavabo (m) basin
lavanderia (f) laundry
lavanderia (f) a gettoni launderette
lavandino (m) sink
lavare to wash
lavare i piatti to do the washing-up
lavastoviglie (f) dishwasher
lavatrice (f) washing machine
lavorare to work
lavori (m/pl) stradali roadworks
lavoro (m) job, work
leggere to read
leggero/a light (weight)
legno (m) wood
lei her; she; you (formal)
lentamente slowly
lente (f) lens
lenti (f/pl) a contatto contact lenses
lento/a slow
lenzuolo (m) sheet
leone (m) lion
lesbica (f) lesbian
lettera (f) letter; letter (of alphabet)

letti (m/pl) gemelli twin beds
lettiga (f) stretcher
lettino (m) cot
letto (m) bed
letto (m) da campo camp bed
letto (m) matrimoniale double bed
lettura (f) reading
leucemia (f) leukemia
levata (f) collection *(postal)*
lezione (f) lesson
libero/a free, vacant
libertà (f) freedom
libreria (f) bookshop
libretto (m) di circolazione registration
    document *(car)*
libro (m) book
limite (m) di velocità speed limit
limonata (f) lemonade
limone (m) lemon
linea (f) line
linea (f) aerea airline
lingua (f) language; tongue
liquido/a liquid
liquore (m) liqueur
liquori (m/pl) spirits
liscio/a smooth
litro (m) litre
livello (m) level *(height, standard)*
livido (m) bruise
locale local
locale (m) notturno nightclub
Londra (f) London
lontano/a far *(away)*
loro they; their; theirs
lotteria (f) lottery
lozione (f) lotion
lozione (f) abbronzante suntan lotion
lucchetto (m) padlock
luce (f) light
lucente shiny
lucido (m) polish
lui he; him
luna (f) moon
luna park (m) funfair

lunghezza length
lungo along
lungo/a long
luogo (m) place
luogo d'interesse sight *(tourist)*

M

ma but
macchina (f) car
    in macchina by car
macchina (f) fotografica camera
macchinista (m) machinist
macelleria (f) butcher's
madre (f) mother
maglia (f) vest
maglietta (f) T-shirt
magnifico! great!
magro/a thin
mai never
maiale (m) pig; pork
mal (m) d'auto travel sickness
mal (m) di denti toothache
mal (m) di mare seasickness
mal (m) di stomaco stomach ache
mal (m) di testa headache
mal (m) d'orecchi earache
malato/a ill, sick
malattia (f) illness
male: fa male it hurts
mancare to miss
mancia (f) tip *(in restaurant etc.)*
mandare to send
mangiare to eat
manifestazione (f) demonstration *(protest)*
maniglia (f) handle
mano (f) hand
mantello (m) coat
manzo (m) beef
marca (f) brand
marcia: fare marcia indietro to reverse *(car)*
marciapiede (m) pavement
mare (m) sea
marea (f) tide *(high/low)*
margarina (f) margarine

marina (f) militare navy
marinaio (m) sailor
marito (m) husband
marmellata (f) jam
marmo (m) marble
marrone brown
martello (m) hammer
mascella (f) jaw
maschile masculine
maschio (m) male
materasso (m) mattress
materiale (m) material
matita (f) pencil
matrigna (f) step-mother
mattina (f) morning
maturo mature (cheese)
maturo/a ripe
mazze (f/pl) da golf golf clubs
me me
meccanico (m) mechanic
media medium (size)
medicina (f) medicine (subject, drug)
medico/a medical
medievale medieval
medusa (f) jellyfish
meglio better
mela (f) apple
memoria (f) memory
meno less
meno: a meno che unless
mensile monthly
mento (m) chin
mentre while
menu menu
menu (m) a scelta à la carte menu
menu (m) fisso set menu
meraviglioso/a wonderful
mercato (m) market
mercato (m) delle pulci flea market
merce (f) goods
mese (m) month
messa (f) mass (church)
messaggio (m) message; text
    message

mestruazioni (f/pl) period (menstrual)
metà (f) half
metallo (m) metal
metro (m) metre
metropolitana (f) underground (tube)
metterci to take (time)
mezza: (le due) e mezza half past (two)
mezza pensione (f) half board
mezzanotte (f) midnight
mezzo (m) middle
mezzo/a half (adj)
mezzogiorno (m) middle
mezz'ora (f) half an hour
migliore: il/la migliore the best
minestra (f) soup
minibus (m) minibus
minuto (m) minute
mio/a my; mine (of me)
miscela (f) mixture
mistero (m) mystery
misto/a mixed
misura (f) measurement, size
    (clothes, shoes)
misurare to measure
mite mild
mobili (m/pl) furniture
moda (f) fashion
modello (m) model
modem (m) modem
moderno/a modern
modo: in ogni modo anyway
modo: in qualche modo somehow
moglie (f) wife
molti many
molto much
molto very
molto/a a lot (of)
monastero (m) monastery
mondiale world (adj.)
mondo (m) world
moneta (f) coin
monouso/a disposable
montagna (f) mountain
monumento (m) monument

morbido/a soft
morbillo (m) measles
mordere to bite
morire to die
mortale fatal
morto/a dead
mosca (f) fly
moschea (f) mosque
mostra (f) exhibition
mostrare to show
motocicletta (f) motorbike
motore (m) motor, engine
motoscafo (m) motorboat
mucca (f) cow
mulino (m) a vento windmill
mulino (m) mill
multa (f) fine *(penalty)*
municipio (m) town hall
muovere to move
muro (m) wall *(outside)*
museo (m) museum
musica (f) music
musicale musical
musicista (m/f) musician
musulmano/a Muslim
muta (f) wetsuit
mutande (f/pl) knickers, underpants
muto/a dumb
mutuo (m) mortgage

N

naso (m) nose
nastro (m) adesivo tape *(sticky)*
Natale (m) Christmas
naturale natural; still *(non-fizzy)*
naturalmente naturally
nave (f) ship
navigare to sail
navigazione (f) sailing
nazionale national
nazionalità (f) nationality
né... né... neither... nor...
ne any
nebbia (f) fog, mist
necessario/a necessary

negozio (m) shop
negozio (m) di calzature shoe shop
negozio di ferramenta hardware shop
nel passato in the past
neonato/a (m/f) baby
nero/a black
nero: in bianco e nero black & white
    (film)
nessuno/a nobody; none
neve (f) snow
nevica it's snowing
nevicare to snow
nient'altro nothing else
niente nothing
nipote (f) granddaughter; niece
nipote (m) grandson; nephew
nipoti (m/f/pl) grandchildren
no no
noce (f) nut
noi us; we
noioso/a boring
noleggiare to hire
nome (m) Christian name
non not
non vale la pena it's not worth it
nonna (f) grandmother
nonni (m/pl) grandparents
nonno (m) grandfather
nord (m) north
normalmente normally
nostro our; ours
notizie (f/pl) news
notte (f) night
nozze (f/pl) wedding
nubile single *(unmarried woman)*
nudo/a naked
numero (m) number
numero (m) di targa
    registration number
nuora (f) daughter-in-law
nuotare to swim
nuoto (m) swimming
nuovo/a new
nutrire to feed *(inc. baby)*
nuvola (f) cloud

O

o or

obbligatorio/a compulsory

occhiali (m/pl) glasses, spectacles

occhiali (m/pl) da sci goggles *(ski)*

occhiali (m/pl) da sole sunglasses

occhialini (m/pl) goggles *(swimming)*

occhio (m) eye

occidentale western

occupato/a busy, engaged *(occupied)*

odiare to hate

odore (m) smell

offerta: in offerta (f) special offer

oggetti (m/pl) di valore valuables

oggetto (m) object *(thing)*

oggi today

ogni every

ogni tanto occasionally

ogni volta che whenever

okay OK

olio (m) oil

olio (m) abbronzante suntan oil

oliva (f) olive

oltre beyond

ombra (f) shade *(not sunny)*

ombra (f) shadow

ombrello (m) umbrella

ombretto (m) eyeshadow

ometto (m) coathanger

omosessuale homosexual

onda (f) wave

onesto/a honest

onorario (m) fee

opinione (f) opinion

opposto/a opposite

opuscolo (m) brochure

ora (f) hour; time *(on clock)*

ora (f) di punta rush hour

orario (m) timetable *(train)*

ordinario/a ordinary

ordine (m) order

ordine: in ordine tidy

orecchino (m) earring

orecchio (m) ear

organizzare to arrange, to organise

orientale eastern

originalmente originally

ormeggio (m) berth

oro (m) gold

orologio (m) clock

orologio (m) da polso watch *(clock)*

orribile horrible

ospedale (m) hospital

ospite (m/f) guest; host

osso (m) bone

ostello (m) (youth) hostel

ottenere to get

ottico (m) optician

ottimo/a fine, excellent

otturazione (f) filling *(dental)*

ovest (m) west

ovunque everywhere

ozono: che rispetta l'ozono ozone-friendly

P

pacchetto (m) packet

pacco (m) parcel

pace (f) peace

padella (f) frying pan

padre (m) father

paesaggio (m) scenery

paese (m) country; village

pagaia (f) paddle *(canoeing)*

pagare to pay

pagare in contanti to pay cash

pagina (f) page

paio (m) pair

palazzo (m) palace

palco (m) box *(theatre)*

palla (f) ball

pallacanestro (f) basketball

pallavolo (f) volleyball

pallido/a pale

pallino (m) spot

palo (m) pole

pancetta (f) bacon

panciotto (m) waistcoat

pane (m) bread

panetteria (f) baker's
panino (m) bread roll
panna (f) cream
panne: essere in panne to break down
pannolini usa e getta disposable nappies
pannolino (m) nappy
pantaloni (m/pl) trousers
Papa (m) Pope
paradiso (m) heaven
paralizzato/a paralysed
parasole (m) sunshade
paraurti (m) bumper *(car)*
parcheggiare to park
parcheggio (m) car park, parking
parchimetro (m) parking meter
parco (m) park
parco (m) dei divertimenti amusement park
parecchi several
parecchio/a plenty (of)
parente (m/f) relation
parere: a mio parere in my opinion
parete (f) wall *(inside)*
pari even *(not odd)*
parlamento (m) parliament
parlare to speak, talk
parola (f) word
parrucchiere (m) –a (f) hairdresser
parte (f) part
parte: a parte apart (from); except
» da nessuna parte nowhere
» da qualche parte anywhere
» la maggior parte most (of)
partenza (f) departure *(bus, train, plane)*
particolare: in particolare in particular
partire to depart, to leave *(bus, plane, train etc.)*
partita (f) game, match
partito (m) party *(political)*
Pasqua (f) Easter
passaggio (m) aisle
passaggio (m) a livello level crossing
passaporto (m) passport
passare to pass *(on road, salt etc.)*; to cross *(border)*; to spend *(time)*

passatempo (m) hobby
passato (m) past
passeggero (m) passenger
passeggino (m) push-chair
passione (f) passion
passo (m) step *(footstep)*
pasta (f) pasta; pastry
pasticceria (f) cake shop
pastiglia (f) throat lozenge/pastille
patata (f) potato
patatine (f/pl) potato crisps
patatine (f/pl) fritte chips
patente (f) licence *(driving)*
patrigno (m) step-father
pattinare to skate
pattumiera (f) dustbin
pavimento (m) floor
paziente (m/f) patient *(hospital)*
pazzo/a crazy, mad
pecora (f) sheep
pedaggio (m) toll
pedale (m) pedal
pedalò (m) pedal-boat
pedone (m) pedestrian
peggio/a worse
pelle (f) leather; skin
pelliccia (f) fur
pellicola (f) per diapositive slide film
penicillina (f) penicillin
penna (f) pen; feather
penna (f) a sfera ballpoint pen
pensare to think
pensione (f) pension; guest house; full board
pensione: in pensione retired
pentola (f) pot
pepe (m) pepper
per for, per
perché because
perché? why?
perdere to lose; to miss *(bus etc)*
perdonare to forgive
perfetto/a perfect
pericolo (m) danger

permesso (m) licence, permit *(fishing etc)*

permesso/a allowed

permettere to allow, let, permit

persiana (f) blind

personale personal

pesante heavy

pesare to weigh

pescare to fish/go fishing

pesce (m) fish

pescivendolo/a fishmonger's

peso (m) weight

pettine (m) comb

pezzo (m) bit, piece

pezzo (m) di antiquariato antique

piacere: mi piace I like *(food, people)*

piacevole pleasant

piangere to cry

piano/a flat, level

piano (m) plan; storey

piano (m) interrato basement

piano: al piano (m) inferiore downstairs

piano: al primo piano (m) on the first floor

pianoforte (m) piano

pianta (m) plant

pianterreno (m) ground floor

piatti (m/pl) sporchi washing-up

piattino (m) saucer

piatto (m) dish, plate

piazza (f) square

piccante hot, spicy

picchetto (m) peg

piccolo/a small

picnic (m) picnic

piede: a piedi (m) on foot

piegato/a bent

pieghevole folding *(e.g. chair)*

pieno/a full

pieno/a di sole sunny

pietra (f) stone

pigro/a lazy

pila (f) battery

pillola (f) pill, the pill

pilota (m) pilot

pinacoteca (f) art gallery

pinne (f/pl) flippers

pioggia (f) rain

piombo (m) lead

» senza piombo lead-free

piove it's raining

piscina (f) swimming pool

pista (f) track

pista (f) da sci ski-run/slope

pista (f) per principianti nursery slope

pista (f) di pattinaggio (f) ice rink

pittore (m) painter

pittura (f) painting

pittura (f) picture

più: di più more

più grande bigger

più lontano further on

più vicino nearest

piumone (m) duvet

piuttosto rather *(quite)*

plastica (f) plastic

po': un po' a little

pochi not many, (a) few

poco/a (a) little

politico/a political

polizia (f) police

polizza (f) d'assicurazione insurance policy

pollice (m) thumb

pollo (m) chicken

polmonite (f) pneumonia

poltrone (f/pl) stalls *(theatre)*

polvere (f) dust, powder

pomeriggio (m) afternoon

pomodoro (m) tomato

ponte (m) bridge; deck *(ship)*

pontile (m) pier

popolare popular

porta (f) door

porta (f) principale front door

portacenere (m) ashtray

portafoglio (m) wallet

portare to bring; to carry

portatile portable

portiere (m) porter
porto (m) harbour, port
porzione (f) portion
posate (f/pl) cutlery
possibilmente possibly
posta (f) post *(mail)*
posteggio (m) dei taxi taxi rank
posto (m) place *(seat)*, room *(space)*
potere (m) power
potere to be able, can
pranzo (m) meal, lunch
preferire to prefer
preferito/a favourite
prefisso (m) dialling code
prego don't mention it, you're welcome
prego? pardon?
premio (m) prize
prendere to take; to catch *(train/bus)*
prenotare to book, to reserve
prenotazione (f) booking, *(hotel etc)*
preoccupato/a anxious, worried
preparare to prepare
presa (f) di corrente socket
prescrizione (f) prescription
presentare to introduce
preservativo (m) condom
prestare to lend
presto early; quick(ly); soon
prete (m) priest
previsioni (f/pl) del tempo weather forecast
prezioso/a valuable
prezzo (m) price
prezzo: a metà prezzo half price
prigione (f) prison
prima earlier
primavera (f) spring *(season)*
primo/a first
principale main
principiante (m/f) beginner
probabilmente probably
problema (m) problem
profondo/a deep
profumo (m) perfume, scent
progetto (m) design *(plan)*

programma (m) programme
proibito (m) prohibited
promettere to promise
pronto ready
pronto soccorso (m) first aid
proprietà (f) property
proprietario (m) –a (f) owner
prossimo/a next
protuberanza (f) lump *(swelling)*
provare to try; to try on
provocare to cause
prua (f) bow *(ship)*
prurito (m) itch
pubblico (m) public
pulire to clean
pulito/a clean
puntino: a puntino medium *(steak)*
puntura (f) sting
puntura d'insetto insect bite
puro/a pure
purtroppo unfortunately
puzzare to smell

Q

quadrato (m) square *(shape)*
qualche parte somewhere
qualche volta sometimes
qualcosa something, anything
qualcos'altro/a anything else
qualcuno someone, anyone
quale which
qualità (f) quality
quando when
quanti/e? how many?
quanto/a how much?
quanto lontano? how far?
quanto spesso? how often?
quanto tempo? how long?
quartiere (m) district
quarto (m) quarter
quasi nearly
quelli/e those
quello/a that (one)
questi/e these

questo/a this (one)
questura (f) police station
qui here
qui vicino nearby
quotidiano/a daily

R

rabbia (f) rabies
rabbino (m) rabbi
racchetta (f) racket *(tennis)*
racchette (f/pl) da sci ski sticks
raccolta (f) collection *(rubbish)*
raccomandare to recommend
raffreddore cold *(to have a cold)*
raffreddore (f) da fieno hayfever
ragazza (f) girl; girlfriend
ragazzo (m) boy; boyfriend
raggi X (m/pl) X-rays
raggiungere to reach
ragione (f) reason
ragione: avere ragione to be right
ragione: hai ragione you're right
rana (f) frog
raro/a rare
rasare to shave
rasoio (m) razor
re (m) king
reale royal
reclamo (m) complaint
reddito (m) income
regalo (m) gift, present
reggiseno (m) bra
regina (f) queen
regione (f) region
registrare to record
religione (f) religion
remo (m) oar
rene (m) kidney
reparto (m) department
respirare to breathe
rete (f) goal *(football)*
rete (f) net
retro (m) rear
ribes (m) nero blackcurrant

ricambio (m) del gas gas refill
ricambio: pezzi di ricambio spare parts
ricciuto/a curly
ricco/a rich
ricetta (f) prescription *(medicine)*;
  recipe *(food)*
ricevitore (m) receiver *(telephone)*
ricevuta (f) receipt
ricezione (f) reception
riconoscere to recognise
ricordare to remember
ricordo (m) souvenir
ridere to laugh
riduttore (m) adaptor
riduzione (f) reduction
riempire to fill; to refill
rifiuti (m/pl) litter
righello (m) ruler *(for measuring)*
rimanere to stay
rimborso (m) refund
rimorchio (m) trailer
riparare to mend, to fix, to repair
riparo (m) shelter
riposare to rest
riposo (m) rest
riscaldamento (m) heating
riservato/a reserved
riso (m) rice
risparmiare to save *(money)*
rispondere to answer, to reply
risposta (f) answer, reply
ristorante (m) restaurant
risultato (m) result
ritardo (m) delay
ritmo (m) rate *(speed)*
ritorno (m) return
ritratto (m) portrait
riuscire to succeed
riunione (f) meeting
rivista (f) magazine
rompere to break *(inc. limb)*
rosa pink
rosa (f) rose
rosso/a red

rotatoria (f) roundabout
rotondo/a round
rotto/a broken
roulotte (f) caravan
rovescio (m) back *(reverse side)*
rovine (f/pl) ruins
rubare to rob, to steal
rubato/a stolen
rubinetto (m) tap
rumoroso/a noisy
ruota (f) wheel
ruscello (m) stream
ruvido/a coarse, rough *(surface)*

S

sabbia (f) sand
sacco (m) a pelo sleeping bag
sala (f) d'attesa waiting room
sala (f) dei concerti concert hall
sala (f) di prova fitting room
sala delle partenze departure lounge
salato/a salty
saldi (m/pl) sales
sale (m) salt
salire to get on *(bus)*
salmone (m) salmon
saltare to jump
salumi (m/pl) cold meats
salute (f) health
salute! (f) cheers!
salvagente (m) lifebelt
salvare to rescue
salve hello
salvietta (f) detergente baby wipes
sandali (m/pl) sandals
sangue (f) blood
sangue: al sangue rare *(steak)*
sanguinare to bleed
sano/a healthy
santo (m) –a (f) saint
santo/a holy
sapere to know *(something)*
sapere: non lo so I don't know
sapone (m) soap
sbagliato/a wrong

sbronza (f) hangover
scaffale (m) shelf
scala (f) mobile escalator
scalare to climb
scaldabagno (m) boiler, water heater
scalinata (f) stairs
scaricare to download
scarpa (f) –e (f/pl) shoe(s)
scarpone (f) boot *(shoe)*
scarponi (f/pl) da sci ski boots
scatola (f) box, tin
scattare to take *(photo)*
scegliere to choose, to pick
scendere to go down; to get off *(bus)*
scheda (f) form
scheda (f) telefonica telephone card
sci (m) ski, skiing
sciare to ski
sciarpa (f) scarf
sciopero (m) strike
sciopero: in sciopero on strike
sciovia (f) ski-lift
scippare to mug *(someone)*
scomodo/a uncomfortable
scompartimento (m) compartment
sconosciuto/a (m/f) stranger
sconti (m/pl) sales *(bargains)*
sconto (m) discount
scooter (m) scooter
scopo (m) goal
scottatura (f) sunburn
Scozia (f) Scotland
scozzese Scottish
scrivere to write
scultura (f) sculpture
scuola (f) school
scusi excuse me
sdraiarsi to lie down
se if
secco/a dry *(wine)*
secolo (m) century
secondo/a second *(adj.)*
sedersi to sit *(down)*
sedia (f) chair
sedia (f) a rotelle wheelchair

sedia (f) a sdraio deckchair
sedile (m) seat
seggiolone (m) high chair
seggiovia (f) chair lift
segnale (m) di libero dialling tone
segreto (m) secret
seguire to follow
selvatico/a wild
semaforo (m) traffic lights
sembrare to seem
semisecco medium (wine)
semplice plain, simple
sempre always; still (yet)
sempre dritto straight on
seno (m) breast
sentiero (m) path
sentiero (m) per pedoni footpath
sentire to hear; to feel
sentirsi to feel (ill/well)
senza without
sera (f) evening
serio/a serious
serratura (f) lock
servirsi di to use
servizi (m/pl) facilities
servizio (m) service (charge)
sesso (m) sex (gender/intercourse)
sete: ho sete I'm thirsty
settimana (f) week
settimana: due settimane (f) fortnight
settimanale weekly
sfogo (m) rash (spots)
sgarbato/a rude
sgradevole unpleasant
sgrassato/a low-fat
si yes
sia... che... either... or...
sicuro/a positive, sure; safe
sigaretta (f) cigarette
sigaro (m) cigar
significare: che significa? what does
   this mean?
Signor Mr
signora (f) lady
signora madam

Signora Mrs
signore (f/pl) ladies
signore (m) sir
signori (m/pl) men (gents)
Signorina Miss
silenzioso/a silent
simile similar
simpatico/a nice
sinagoga (f) synagogue
singolo/a single (room)
sinistro/a left
sintomo (m) symptom
sistema (m) system
slogato/a dislocated, twisted (ankle)
snello/a slim
società (f) company
sodo/a firm
soffitto (m) ceiling
soldi (m/pl) money
sole (m) sun
sole: prendere il sole to sunbathe
solido/a solid
solitario (m) lonely
solito: di solito usually
solo/a alone
soltanto only, just
sopra above
sopra: di sopra upstairs
sopracciglia (f/pl) eyebrows
soprattutto especially
sordo/a deaf
sorella (f) sister
sorellastra (f) step-sister
sorpassare to overtake
sorpresa (f) surprise
sorriso (m) mile
sotto below
sottopassaggio (m) underpass
sottotitoli (m/pl) subtitles
spago (m) string
spaventato/a frightened
spazio (m) space
spazzola (f) brush
spazzolino (m) toothbrush
specchio (m) mirror

speciale special
specialità (f) speciality
spegnere to switch off
spendere to spend *(money)*
spento/a off *(TV, light)*
sperare to hope
spero di sì I hope so
spesa (f) shopping
spesso often
spesso/a thick
spettacolo (m) performance, show
spezie (f/pl) spices
spiacente sorry
spiaggia (f) beach
spiccioli (m/pl) change *(small coins)*
spiegare to explain
spina (f) plug *(electrical)*
spingere to push
spogliarsi to undress *(oneself)*
spogliatoio (m) changing room
sport (m) sport
sporco/a dirty
sposarsi to get married
spugna (f) sponge *(bath)*
squadra (f) team
stadio (m) stadium
stagione (f) season
stampa (f) press *(newspapers)*
stampare to print
stanco/a tired
stanza (f) room
stanza (f) da bagno bathroom
stare to be
stasera tonight
statua (f) statue
stazione (f) station
stazione (f) di rifornimento petrol station
stazione (f) di servizio garage *(for petrol)*
stazione (f) ferroviaria railway station
stella (f) star
sterlina (f) pound *(sterling)*
stesso/a same
stile (m) style
stitichezza (f) constipation
stoffa (f) fabric

stomaco (m) stomach
stordito/a dizzy
storia (f) history, story
storto/a sprained
strada (f) street, road
straniero (m) –a (f) foreigner
straniero/a foreign
strano/a odd, funny *(peculiar)*, strange
stretto/a tight *(clothes)*
studente (m) –essa (f) student
studio (m) studio *(radio/TV)*
stufetta (f) heater
stupido/a stupid
su about *(relating to)*; on; up
subacqueo/a underwater
succedere to happen
successo (m) success, outcome
succhiotto (m) dummy *(baby's)*
sud (m) south
sugo (m) juice; sauce
suo/a his; her; hers
suono (m) sound
supermercato (m) supermarket
supplemento (m) supplement
supporre: suppongo di sì
    I suppose so
supposta (f) suppository
sveglia (f) alarm clock
sviluppare to develop
svuotare to empty

T

tabaccheria (f) tobacconist's shop
tacco (m) heel *(shoe)*
taciturno/a quiet
tagliarsi to cut oneself
tale such
tallone (m) heel
tappeto (m) carpet
tappo (m) plug *(bath)*
tariffa (f) fare
tasca (f) pocket
tasso (m) di cambio exchange rate
tavoletta (f) tablet
tavolo (m) tavola (f) table

tazza (f) cup
tè (m) tea
teatro (m) theatre
tedesco (m) –a (f) German
tegame (m) saucepan
teiera (f) teapot
telefonare to telephone
telefonata (f) call *(phone)*
telefonata (f) interurbana
   long-distance call
telefonino (m) mobile (phone)
telefono (m) telephone
televisione (f) television
temperatura (f) temperature
tempo (m) time; weather
temporaneo/a temporary
tenda (f) curtain; tent
tenere to hold, to keep
tensione (f) voltage *(electricity)*
terminal (m) terminal *(airport)*
termometro (m) thermometer
terra (f) earth, ground
terrazzo (m) terrace
terremoto (m) earthquake
terreno (m) land
terzo/a third
testa (f) head
tettarella (f) teat *(for baby's bottle)*
tetto (m) roof
tiepido/a warm
tinello (m) living-room
tintoria (f) dry-cleaner's
tipico/a typical
tipo (m) type *(sort)*
tirare to pull
tisana (f) herbal tea
toccare to touch
toccare: tocca a me it's my turn
togliere to remove, to take off *(clothes)*
tonno (m) tuna
torcia (f) torch
tornare to come back, to return
toro (m) bull
torre (f) tower
torta (f) cake

tosse (f) cough
tossire to cough
totale total
totalmente totally
tovagliolo (m) napkin
tra among, between
tradizionale traditional
traduzione (f) translation
traffico (m) traffic
traghetto (m) ferry
trainare to tow
tram (m) tram
trama (f) pattern
tramezzino (m) sandwich
trascurato/a careless
traslocare to move house
traveller's cheques traveller's cheques
traversata (f) crossing *(sea)*
treno (m) train
tribunale (m) court *(law)*
triste sad
troppo/a too; too much
trota (f) trout
trovare to find
tu you *(informal singular)*
tubo (m) pipe, tube
tuffarsi to dive
tuo/vostro/suo your
tuo/vostro/suo yours
tuono (m) thunder
turista (m/f) tourist
tutti/e all, everyone
tutto everything
tutto/a all, every

U

ubriaco/a drunk
uccello (m) bird
uccidere to kill
ufficiale official
ufficio (m) office
ufficio (m) oggetti smarriti lost
   property office
ufficio (m) postale post office
ufficio (m) turistico tourist office
uguale equal

u

ulcera (f) ulcer
ultimo/a last
umano/a human
un (m) una (f) a, an
unghia (f) nail
uniforme (f) uniform
università (f) university
uno dei due either
uomini (m/pl) men
uomo (m) man
uovo (m) sodo boiled egg
urina (f) urine
uscire to go out
uscita (f) exit; gate *(airport)*
ustione (f) burn *(on skin)*
utile useful

V

va bene all right, OK
vacanza (f) holiday
valanga (f) avalanche
valere to be worth
valido/a valid
valigia (f) suitcase
valle (f) valley
vaniglia (f) vanilla
vapore (m) steam
vasino (m) potty *(child's)*
vecchio/a old
vedere to see
vegano (m) vegana (f) vegan
vegetariano/a vegetarian *(adj.)*
veicolo (m) vehicle
vela (f) sail
velenoso/a poisonous
veloce fast
velocità (f) speed
vendere to sell
venire to come
ventoso/a windy
veramente really
verde green
verdura (f) vegetables
verniciare to paint
vero/a true

vero: è vero that's true
verso towards
vescica (f) blister
vestirsi to dress, get dressed
vestiti (m/pl) clothes
vetro (m) glass *(pane)*
via (f) way *(path)*
via aerea (by) air mail
viaggiare to travel
viaggio (m) journey
viaggio (m) di nozze honeymoon
viaggio (m) organizzato package tour
vicino (m) –a (f) neighbour
vicino/a close *(by)*, near
vigili (m/pl) del fuoco fire brigade
vigneto (m) vineyard
vincere to win
vino (m) wine
viola purple
visita (f) visit
visita (f) guidata guided tour
vista (f) sight *(vision)*; view
visto (m) visa
vita (f) life; waist
vivere to live
vivo/a alive
vivo/a bright *(colour)*
voce (f) voice
voi you *(formal/informal plural)*
volare to fly
volo (m) flight
volo (m) charter charter flight
volpe (f) fox
volta: due volte twice
volta: una volta once
vuoto/a empty

Z

zaino (m) rucksack
zanzara (f) mosquito
zanzariera (f) mosquito net
zia (f) aunt
zio (m) uncle
zolletta (f) di zucchero sugar lump
zucchero (m) sugar
zuppa (f) soup

index

index

222

index

Now you're talking!

If you're keen to progress to a higher level, BBC Active offers a wide range of innovative products, from short courses and grammars to build up your vocabulary and confidence, to more in-depth courses for beginners or intermediates. Designed by language-teaching experts, our courses make the best use of today's technology, with book and audio, audio-only and multi-media products on offer. Many of these courses are accompanied by free online activities and television series, which are regularly repeated on the BBC TWO Learning Zone.

Short independent study course
128pp course book; 2 x 60-min
CDs/cassettes; free online activities;
6-part television series

Complete independent course
288pp course book; 4 x 75-min
CDs/cassettes; free online activities;
20-part television series

Short audio course
2 x 70-min
CDs/cassettes